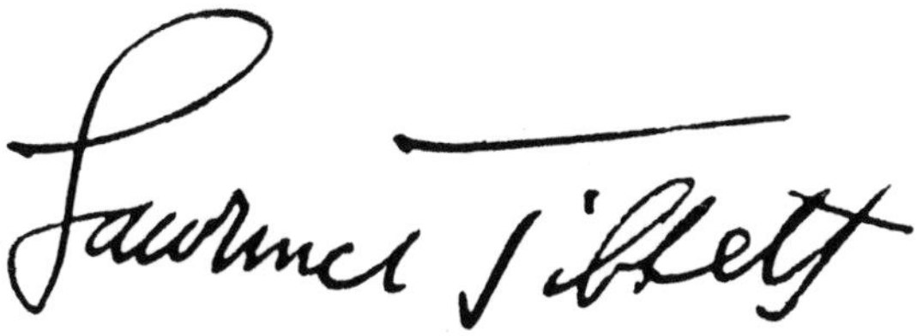

Lawrence Tibbett

OPERA BIOGRAPHY SERIES, NO. 6

Series Editors
Andrew Farkas
William R. Moran

Dear Rogue

A Biography of the American Baritone Lawrence Tibbett

by

Hertzel Weinstat

and

Bert Wechsler

AMADEUS PRESS
Reinhard G. Pauly, General Editor
Portland, Oregon

ISBN 1-57467-008-5

Printed in Singapore

Amadeus Press
The Haseltine Building
133 S.W. Second Avenue, Suite 450
Portland, Oregon 97204, U.S.A.

Library of Congress Cataloging-in-Publication Data

Weinstat, Hertzel.
Dear rogue : a biography of the American baritone Lawrence Tibbett
by Hertzel Weinstat and Bert Wechsler.
p. cm.
Discography: p.
Includes bibliographical references (p.) and index.
ISBN 1-57467-008-5
1. Tibbett, Lawrence, 1896–1960. 2. Baritones (Singers)—United States—
Biography. I. Wechsler, Bert. II. Title.
ML420.T52W45 1996
782.1′092—dc20
(B) 95-20937
CIP
MN

To Richard M. Tibbett,
whose continuous help, advice, support,
encouragement, warmth, and acceptance of this book
the biographers gratefully salute.

CONTENTS

FOREWORD

Few if any singers in the history of American opera have elicited such homage, floods of letters, and paeans of praise. At all times during his operatic career of more than 25 years, his thousands of concert, radio, and television hours, and his six motion pictures, Lawrence Tibbett gave every activity his full measure.

Whatever his pursuit, his handsome appearance and athletic six-foot-two-inch frame—together with a winsome smile—commanded attention. His acting, combined with the beauty and virtuosity of his voice, made him the most famous baritone of his era. I too idolized this man, my father, as one worships a hero.

From earliest memory, the infrequent "son and dad times" were forever etched in my mind. I recall listening with awe and adoration to his vocal exercises, which reached me through the cork-lined walls of his studio at our Beverly Hills home. The one and only fishing trip to Convict Lake in the Sierras. The thrill of being an extra on the set of *The Rogue Song*, with the actors, director, and extras all spellbound by his singing and applauding his acting. A product of boarding schools and camps with little if any family contact, I could not express or feel the love that a youngster normally grows into adulthood with, and I could only wonder at the teasing and curiosity many children and adults expressed toward me.

After his second marriage I saw little of my father, who by then was a household name in the days before television. Radio, concerts, opera, and motion pictures were the original sources of his audience; with the advent of improved recordings, his audience grew. I had a few brief visits with Dad and his second family in New York City and at the farm in Connecticut. We went "out on the town" several times, hunted oysters on Fire Island, fished off Montauk, and even worked the quarry on his farm. As a young man, during my four-year service in World War II, I saw my father three or four times, in Dayton, Ohio, or New York City.

Throughout his life, Dad loved touring cars and roadsters. Nothing was more pleasing to him than to drive the countryside wherever he was—America or Europe. Another pleasure was to stride down Broadway, Madison Avenue, or Fifth Avenue bareheaded, enjoying the gawking and calls of "Hello, Larry" from the passers-by. First to last he was always in his heart one of them.

The open lifestyles of the "Roaring 20s," Prohibition, and my father's propensity for alcohol affected the quality of his performances. Beginning in the late 30s and certainly by 1940, his vocal efforts suffered. He became falsely buoyed by rounds of vocal coaches and well-wishers, and he refused to seek less demanding, alternative avenues of endeavor. At the last he became immersed in self-pity and despair. In a sober moment, at our last meeting in 1959, he told me, "I only want to buy a small ranch, and rock on the front porch." In a sense, how prophetic.

At his funeral service (the second one) at Forest Lawn, Glendale, California, this "dear rogue" was eulogized by his own rendition of the haunting refrain "Goin' Home." No further truism was necessary.

My admiration and grateful thanks to biographers Hertzel Weinstat and Bert Wechsler, who have magically woven the life of Lawrence Tibbett into this book. His travails and mystical highs are eloquently stated with a sense of urgency and energy that pulsates from beginning to end. The detail is true, and the prodigiousness of his life is finely recalled. Even when recounting his final years, the pages rush on with candor and painful truth.

Please read this biography realizing Lawrence Tibbett saw and did it all. From the expanses of the West to the environs of Manhattan, from poverty to wealth, from obscurity to fame, from the country lane to the ethereal reaches of "De Glory Road."

With indelible memories and with love to him . . .
His son,
Richard M. Tibbett
Bishop, California

INTRODUCTION

Early impressions can be powerful and enduring. It was as a fledgling operagoer in Europe in the 1930s that I first discovered Lawrence Tibbett, in the movies. True, he did not project the romantic aura of Clark Gable or Gary Cooper—my heroes then—but his singing in such films as *Metropolitan* and *Cuban Love Song* added an immeasurable dimension to the total image.

I began collecting his records and listened to some of them on Hungarian Radio, among them selections from a strange, exotic-sounding opera called *Porgy and Bess*. Finally, in 1937, the man himself came to Budapest, one of the stations in his first concert tour of continental Europe.

A regular operagoer by then, opinionated enough but certainly not a "critic," I knew how to listen and compare. The baritones of the Hungarian Opera of my youth were a respectable lot, several of them of considerable European repute. I had also heard two of the best Italian baritones of the period, Basiola and Tagliabue, quite regularly on weekly radio broadcasts from Rome or Milan. Not one of them produced the resonant golden sound of Tibbett's Rigoletto, filling the accommodating acoustics of the auditorium.

A budding violinist with little tolerance for unfocused singing, I rejoiced in Tibbett's pure tone formation. It was an unforgettable operagoing experience for a youngster, already captivated by opera and on his way toward establishing golden singing standards in the mind, the basis for future critical assessments.

As a newcomer to the United States, I attended my first Metropolitan Opera performance on a Saturday afternoon, 29 November 1941. It was *La Traviata* with Jarmila Novotná, Jan Peerce (his house debut), and Lawrence Tibbett, Ettore Panizza conducting. My disappointment in Tibbett's Germont was almost painful. He looked handsome and acted with dignity, but his voice no longer had the richness and effortless ease remembered from the cherished 1937 encounter. It sounded worn, and as I was soon to learn, it was not a matter of passing indisposition. Though Tibbett had turned 45 only days before—an artist in the prime of life—vocal decline was already settling in.

My record collecting continued (it had never really stopped) and, as an American, I discovered an element in Tibbett's art that earlier I could not have appreciated: his expressive, flavorful, at times mesmerizing way with the English language in song. Now I could enjoy that rich and mellow sound in operetta excerpts by Romberg, in haunting interpretations of anglicized Tchaikovsky, and in his hair-raising dramatization of Loewe's Scottish ballad "Edward." All these, of course, were recorded in earlier years, preserving the unmistakable sound that triumphantly rang out in those movies of my youth.

In the postwar years I observed signs of Tibbett's further vocal decline, his ever-lessening appearances and eventual departure from the Met, and his transformation into a "radio singer." The questionable prominence of that new status saddened me, particularly in the context of various rumors circulating about the artist's alcoholism. His untimely death heightened the tragedy.

With Tibbett's disappearance from the scene it seemed to me that—aside from the ever-loyal but restricted circle of record collectors—his memory had likewise faded from America's collective consciousness. As the recording industry expanded into a vastness unimaginable to people of an earlier generation, baritones nowhere near Tibbett's greatness accumulated discographies far outstripping that of this onetime paragon.

How could this happen to an artist who was a true multimedia superstar 50 years earlier, before such terms were coined? Lawrence Tibbett was a leading baritone of the Metropolitan, Chicago, and San Francisco operas, an acclaimed concert recitalist, an internationally celebrated recording artist, and a Hollywood celebrity. If such a man could be forgotten, what then is immortality?

There is an important lesson as well as tragic story in this artist's meteoric rise, his relatively brief "glory road," and his pathetic decline. It is to be found in this book, and I am glad that, with the special insights provided by Lawrence Tibbett's sons, two of my friends and colleagues undertook to write it.

George Jellinek

PREFACE

Most of us, when our course is run, deserve the anonymity of the grave. Not so Lawrence Tibbett, one of the truly great stars of grand opera and the concert stage of the early 20th century. The opulence of his vocal art and the warmth of his personality earned for him many legions of admirers and friends.

Tibbett's career was equaled in America only by those of Caruso before him and Luciano Pavarotti and Plácido Domingo afterward—all three tenors, historically the most popular voice category of opera singers (and unlike Tibbett or Caruso, the celebrity of Pavarotti and Domingo is to a great extent due to their modern opportunity of exploiting the ultimate medium for vast exposure, television). Yet, a few years after his tragically early death in 1960, Tibbett became the forgotten troubadour of the opera world.

His sold-out concert at Chicago's Grant Park on 22 August 1939 was wildly successful and trumpeted in the newspapers, yet as late as June 1994, his name was overlooked when the magazine of the American Symphony Orchestra League published a list of famous opera singers who had appeared there; a research library in New York City lost track of Tibbett's donated memorabilia; and our preliminary contacts with publishing executives and their staffs revealed that they had never heard of Tibbett. Fortunately, our publisher remembered.

In the first two decades following Larry's death, Dr. Thomas R. Bullard's monograph, which originally appeared in England and which is quoted, with permission, throughout this biography, was the only critical work published. But slowly, Larry's accomplishments are once again being honored. *Lawrence Tibbett: Singing Actor*, published by Amadeus Press in 1989, is a wonderful backward look at the singer that includes a reprint of Bullard's monograph, Larry's articles for *American Magazine*, and other articles. Its contents would normally constitute the appendices of a biography, and we and its editor Andrew Farkas have come to regard it as such. Indeed, it was the absence of a full-length biography that prompted Farkas, in his own words, "to pay tribute to this magnificent artist with an anthology." In addition to William R. Moran's invaluable introduction and comprehensive discography through the LP era, the anthology contains a wealth of photographs. Although most of them have a direct topical relevance to the present text, Bert Wechsler and I, as biographers, chose not to duplicate any of those 96 illustrations. We hope that this volume will play a like role in reviving the name of Lawrence Tibbett.

I was a teenager when I first saw Larry's hit movie *The Rogue Song* and heard his warm, vibrant baritone sing "The White Dove"; ever since, Lawrence Tibbett's life and ultimate fate has piqued my interest and concern, hence this, his first complete biography. I trust it will return this great singer's image and voice to the memories of the living where he belongs—and perhaps explain why he became a missing star in the galaxy of grand opera.

I recall with appreciation the many good people who assisted me in my research for this biography, but first a loving remembrance of Pearl, my late wife, whose concern for my intellectual and physical well-being during our interviews throughout the United States sustained me along our "glory roads."

And a special thank-you to my present wife, Rebecca, whose loving care and patience since my recent accident have helped me enormously to return to a full life.

To the members of the Tibbett families in California and in Florida, without whose help this book could not have gotten off the ground; on the West Coast, the singer's sons Richard and Larry Jr., and also Larry Jr.'s daughter Lori. They welcomed me into their homes and gave me many hours of their time, as did Michael Tibbett, the singer's third son, who lived with his family at Vero Beach, Florida.

Next, I wish to thank the following colleagues of Lawrence Tibbett who sang with him at the Metropolitan and elsewhere, and whose memories of him filled me with admiration and a certain sadness:

George Cehanovsky, Frank Guarrera, Jarmila Novotná, Emile Renan, Jerome Hines, Matthew Ferruggio of the San Francisco Opera, and Floyd Worthington. Along with them, I'd like to thank both DeLloyd Tibbs and Hy Faine, former officials of the American Guild of Musical Artists who, along with Henry Jaffe, furnished me with much information concerning Tibbett's work during AGMA's swaddling days.

For much assistance and information concerning Bakersfield, California, the singer's birthplace, I am indebted to Christopher D. Brewer. For considerable insight into the life and times of Jane Tibbett, the singer's second wife, I sincerely thank Mrs. Elizabeth F. Cooper of San Francisco, and for a great deal of information on Tibbett's school days at Manual Arts High School in Los Angeles, I must thank General James H. Doolittle, Tibbett's classmate and longtime friend.

Mrs. Vera Gebbert of Washington, D.C., was exceedingly helpful on Tibbett's Hollywood years, as was Miles Kruger in California, and Joan L. Cohen of the Los Angeles County Museum of Art; also thanks to Mrs. Charles Gleaves for insight into Tibbett's first years at the Met.

My thanks, also, to the following close friends of the singer whose love and respect for him as an artist and as a man were in clear evidence during our interviews: Rupert Pole, Beatrice Wood, and Jacob Zeitlin, all of California.

A note of appreciation to Helen Moss, who was the singer's first accompanist before he joined the Met; to Fred Schang, Kurt Weinhold, Milton Goldman, and Harvey E. Fisk for their insights into the talent agency and public relations aspects of the entertainment industry in Tibbett's day; to Dr. Thomas R. Bullard, who granted permission for the valued use of his monograph on Tibbett's life, and to William R. Moran, for his work on Tibbett's involvement in the recording industry; to Joseph E. Doctor for his permission to include certain relevant portions of his book *Shotguns on Sunday*; and also to Doris Wyckoff, whose long friendship with Tibbett has been noted.

Finally, I thank Mrs. Ruth Chamlee, Walter Slezak, Francis Robinson, and George Jellinek, who introduced my valued collaborator Bert Wechsler to me.

Hertzel Weinstat
Forest Hills, New York

My thanks go first to George Jellinek, who had the happy prescience of bringing Hertzel and me together on this project, which I joined with joy. I had seen Lawrence Tibbett perform in his later years and knew his recordings intimately. As a student baritone, many times I had listened to his *Tosca* Te Deum, learning the timing and working toward my own interpretation. Other recordings of his, especially "Standin' in the need of prayer" from *Emperor Jones*, served as my guide.

Once launched into this story of Lawrence Tibbett, I benefited mightily from the unending patience and honesty of Richard Tibbett. Others who deserve my thanks are, of course, Hertzel; Karen Kirtley and Frances Farrell, whose search for excellence engendered amazing feats of resiliency in all of us; Andrew Farkas and William R. Moran, for their tireless efforts on behalf of this book; Mickey Wechsler (especially); Sallie Wilson; Stefan Zucker; Cantor Don Goldberg; Richard Klumper; Eugene Moon; my two computer gurus, Ken Sandler and Mannie Stonewood; Bill Zakariasen; Richard Boehm; Bill Murray; Dr. Vincent T. DeVita Jr.; Robert Merrill; Risë Stevens; Bidú Sayão; Jan Meyerowitz; Patrice Munsel; Helen Jepson; Rose Bampton; Reri Grist; Licia Albanese; Jerome Hines; Jarmila Novotná; Marta Eggerth; Jane Knox and Marjan Kiepura; Jens Henrik Stemland in Oslo; Hanna Hedman in Stockholm; Kori Lockhart in San Francisco; Danny Newman in Chicago; Nicholas L. King; James A. Drake; Ed Rosen; Richard Roffman; and the old "Ginger Man" regulars not already thanked.

Finally, many years after their gifts, my belated thanks to Gabriel A. Wechsler, who often talked to me about the Tibbett legend as I was growing up and gave me the opportunity to meet the man, and Irwin Hassel, who never succeeded in teaching me to play the piano efficiently, but who did teach me music.

Bert Wechsler
New York City

Part One 1896–1922

Chapter 1

THE LEAVENING

He started with nothing, gained the world, and then lost everything. During his career he sang for American presidents, European royalty, and music lovers on four continents, yet his "glory road" would take him through spectacular zeniths of fame and the nadir of personal hell. He was Lawrence Mervil Tibbet (original spelling), born on 16 November 1896, to Deputy Sheriff William Edward Tibbet and his wife, Frances Ellen McKenzie Tibbet.

His birthplace, Bakersfield, California, was originally a swamp, home only to wild animals and the Tejon tribe of Indians who had roamed its bogs and quagmires for centuries. With the arrival of the railroad in 1874, the town became an agricultural center, and its hay ranches prospered. The massive transport industry hauled cargoes of silver ore south from mining camps in the Inyo Mountains on the Nevada border to San Pedro, the port of Los Angeles; on the back haul the trains would bring supplies for the town. In 1899, when Larry was three years old, oil was discovered at the Kern River just northeast of the town, and Bakersfield soon boasted 700 producing wells. By 1903, a number of new oil fields had been found in the Joaquin Valley to the southwest, and Bakersfield became a booming crude oil and railroad town.[1]

Larry would recall the home of his earliest memories as a raw, tough place in the center of a farming community. George Wear, a local historian, provided a more detailed portrayal:

> Bakersfield had a number of saloons, a brewery, several places that, through courtesy, might be termed as hotels, a drugstore, several mercantile establishments, and yet more saloons. As in all Western towns in those days, there was a rough, floating population and killings were frequent, but the killers as well as the victims were of the usual irresponsible floating classes.
>
> Then there were the red-light districts, wherein several dance halls flourished, from which the sound of music, the stomping of the dancers, and unrestrained revels punctuated the night air.[2]

Murder, violence, easy sex, heavy drinking: these were everyday occurrences in the little town of Lawrence's early childhood. Fortunately, the Tibbet family lived on its outskirts, in a frame cottage at 716 K Street, and two older brothers, Jesse and Ernest, and Betty Lee, an older sister, provided young Lawrence with a feeling of stability and security.[3] But it was his mother who filled his small being with music.

His father, Will Tibbet, came from English stock. A Henry Tibbetts of London arrived in America on 13 July 1635 at the age of 39 on the *James* and settled in Dover Neck, New Hampshire. His son, Jeremiah, also born in England, married and had eight sons and four daughters. All later Tibbetts in this line, no matter how the name is spelled, descended from one or another of Jeremiah's sons.[4]

His mother, Frances Ellen McKenzie Tibbet, was of Irish descent, and she shared the lyricism that dominates Irish speech and folk songs. She was born in 1864 in Lebec, California, at Fort Tejon, when it was still a military installation, and her music and her children enabled Frances Ellen to withstand the drudgery of living in a semi-civilized town in California. She had a fine contralto voice and sang through the day in her small clapboard house and, on Sundays, in the Methodist church.[5] She firmly believed that if her children were constantly exposed to her singing and the singing in the church, they could also develop fine singing voices. Ernest and his little brother Larry did.

Almost from the beginning, Baby Lawrence seemed special. At 12 weeks he began to create sounds that seemed to his mother to be not unlike singing. At nine months a baby can produce sounds ranging between 207 and 2361 vibrations per second, and in addition—as many parents have learned to their dismay—can possess a flawless vocal technique, with absolutely uncanny projection.[6] By the age of four, Lawrence's voice had lost its infantile wail and had begun to assume a more personal sound, which his mother proudly noted. She also discovered in him an element essential to the making of any professional singer: innate musicality.

Lawrence made his first solo appearance in the Bakersfield Methodist church as a six-year-old boy soprano, singing "Jesus Wants Me for a Sunbeam." The baritone wrote the following reminiscence of this important occasion in his 1933 book *The Glory Road*,[7] a series of autobiographical sketches that are charming and full of self-deprecating humor:

> I was to sing without accompaniment, for in those days when I sang I just went ahead and sang, disregarding pitch and tempo. . . . I faced the vast audience of 35 or 40 people and instantly forgot the words and music.
>
> My mother was sitting in the front row, only a few feet away. She leaned over and whispered a cue, but I was too frightened to understand. She tried again. I shook my head helplessly and tears came to my eyes. The audience began to snicker.
>
> A bit angry and disgusted with her stupid son my mother leaned forward and said, hopelessly, "Well, try *The Star-Spangled Banner*."
>
> With new lift I burst out with "Oh-oh say, can you see-ee!" The audience rose, joined in the singing, and, when we all finished, applauded with the gusto that people seem to believe should reward even the worst singer of a patriotic song. My début was a great success, thanks to my mother and the Grand Old Flag.[8]

But bearded Will Tibbet, full-time deputy sheriff of Bakersfield, would have none of this. Give him and his pal Jeff Packard, newly elected city marshal, weekends of bear-hunting in the mountains. That was the good life! A dead shot, Will was a powerfully built man with a tall, muscular frame, eyes of blue steel, and a quick temper. For him, music, and in particular singing, belonged strictly to the womenfolk. This was Lawrence's father, whose adamant stance ended only when he and Jeff Packard died together in a shootout with criminals on 19 April 1903.[9]

Reliving the events of that long-ago Sunday through the eyes and memory of a six-year-old—and not always hewing exactly to the truth—Larry wrote in *The Glory Road*:

> One day, when I was seven years old, our gang was playing in the back yard, camping out—roasting potatoes and getting ready for a battle.

> I saw a man drive up in a buggy. He entered the house, and a moment later hurried out with my mother and they drove rapidly toward town. I gave it little thought for I had important work to do—there were "rustlers" hiding back of the barn and "Sheriff" Lawrence Tibbett had to shine up his wooden gun.
>
> Suddenly an older boy came running up the dusty road, leaped the fence, and yelled at me, "Hey, Larry, Jim McKinney just killed your father!"
>
> At first I thought it was a joke, part of a game. "Honest!" the boy insisted, all out of breath. "Cross my heart and hope to die! In the Chinese joss house! Your father went after Jim, and Jim got him! They carried him to Baer's drug store. I seen him!"[10]

It was no joke to Colonel Packard, Jeff Packard's father, who had come to Frances Ellen's door with the grim announcement that Will had been shot and was dying. If they hurried, she might still find her husband alive. As the wife of Bakersfield's deputy sheriff, Frances Ellen had long since made her peace with the idea of death.

Will had been taken to Baer's drug store, where he lay in agony on the hard floor. A third of his face had been shot away and what remained was laced with buckshot. Bakersfield in 1903 had no hospital. Will was removed to the Southern Hotel in town for surgery, but by the time his wife reached his side, he was dead. Also killed in the gunfight at the joss house were Will's buddy Jeff Packard and the murderous outlaw Jim McKinney.[11]

According to *The Californian* of 22 April 1903, the two peace officers received funerals the likes of which had never before been seen in the town. After the church service for Will Tibbet, the coffin was interred in the local Union Cemetery. Members of his fraternal orders served as pallbearers.[12] A squad of deputies, their rifles at the ready, fired three rounds into the air, followed by the sound of a bugler playing taps. It was a moving memorial.[13]

For Frances Ellen and her four children, it would be farewell not only to the husband and father of the family but, eventually, to his way of life. She had received Will's insurance money, and Bert Tibbet (Will's brother) signed over to her the reward he had received for killing McKinney. She vowed to leave the town where she felt she had never belonged, to pursue a new existence among people who were refined, who respected the arts, and who, above all, loved beautiful singing. Years later, in Los Angeles, her dream would become a reality.

In 1910, the city of Los Angeles covered an area of 85.1 square miles; its population had tripled over the last 10 years and now topped 300,000. Los Angeles was like an adolescent: sprawling, excitable, uncontrolled, uncertain as to its own nature. This was also true of many who had come to live there, about 20 percent of whom were foreign-born. "Who am I?" was a common inquiry among the thousands of German, English, Mexican, Irish, and Welsh immigrants. It was a difficult question to answer. And the Tibbets, recent arrivals from Bakersfield, had no deeper a sense of roots than the others.

For 14-year-old Larry, moving to Los Angeles was like entering another world. Unlike the central California town where he had grown up, Los Angeles boasted a large auditorium, a library with a collection of 110,000 volumes, and handsome federal and state buildings. Several museums with collections of Mexican and Spanish relics had been established. Twenty-one public parks were abundant with eucalyptus and palm trees, fragrant during the year with roses, great geraniums, saber-leafed yuccas, and heavenly scented orange groves.

Since leaving Bakersfield two years before, the widowed Mrs. Tibbet had not had an easy time. With her husband's insurance money she had purchased a small hotel in Long Beach. Having no experience in that business, she failed to make a go of it and decided that a rooming house would be less complicated. She found a promising building at Twelfth and Figueroa Streets in the center of Los Angeles. With the city's exploding population, the need for any kind of housing was urgent, yet Frances Ellen's plan barely succeeded. Her two older sons had left to marry, but with daughter Betty Lee's help, she was able to augment the family income by working as a practical nurse.

Los Angeles took pride in its various colleges and the celebrated University of Southern California, and the recently opened Manual Arts High School, which had already acquired an excellent reputation, was only three blocks from the Tibbet home. It was here that Frances Ellen enrolled her spindle-legged son Larry, with his long neck and ears that stuck out like doorknobs. Although nominally a vocational school, to a surprising degree Manual Arts was responsible for developing Larry's talent for the musical and theatrical arts. It became his second home.

Larry was so skinny and underweight at the time he enrolled in Manual Arts in the autumn of 1911 that his mother feared he might be tubercular. The school's physical examiner found that worry groundless, but the scare led to an important change in Larry's life. He began an elaborate routine of calisthenics: push-ups and sit-ups first thing in the morning, bicycling, running, swimming (which he loved most of all), and mountain climbing once or twice a month. It was a regimen he would augment during his years at the Metropolitan Opera, when he added his famous rowing machine to his daily workout. He even took the rowing machine with him on his tours. It was no accident that Larry became the lithest, most attractive singer of his time, with a resonant, almost brawny voice to match his physique.

The principal of Manual Arts High School was an iron-handed autocrat, German-born Dr. Albert C. Wilson, who bore a saber scar along the length of his cheek, the proud souvenir of the obligatory duel for university students in Germany. Over the years many of the school's alumni became known throughout the country: baseball star Stan Musial, California governor Goodwin Knight, movie director Frank Capra, novelists Irving Stone and Eugene Burdick, artist Jackson Pollock, and aviation pioneer General James H. Doolittle.

During Larry's first year at Manual Arts, he was shy and sensitive because of his still undeveloped physique, so it was perhaps natural for him to pick Jimmy Doolittle as his friend and hero. Jimmy, unlike Larry, was a true athlete. He grew up in Alaska, where he had become street-smart and learned how to use his fists. Jimmy seemed to embody all that Larry wished to be. For his part, Jimmy was impressed by his buddy's acting and singing.

After assiduously following his exercise regime, Larry felt he had built himself up enough to try out for the school's wrestling team, coached by Rob Wagner. What followed is described in *The Glory Road*:

> Jimmy was standing at one side of the gymnasium. "Hello, crow," I said. "Hi, nightingale," he sniffed. "See what Larry can do, Jimmy," said Wagner. There was a swish, and I was flat on my back on the mat and Jimmy was walking away brushing his palms. He turned and looked at my sprawling body. "For gosh sake, sing," he said.[14]

Later Larry would recall with wry humor the pain of feeling physically inferior during his adolescence. The ignominy remained for a long time, together with the humiliation of being too poor to join a fraternity or to date any of the girls. To make matters worse, his poverty was exploited in the school paper:

Bassett: Tibbet has a suit of clothes for every day in the week.
Finch: I have only seen him in one.
Bassett: Well, that's it.[15]

The cruelty of his peers affected Larry deeply. Although he later denied it, there is little doubt that his entire psyche began to crystallize into a single driving force: to rise above his poverty, to become rich one day. But how could young Larry prove himself? As a joke, Jimmy Doolittle had supplied the answer. "Sing."

By age 15, Larry had begun to take piano lessons on the family upright, and his high, boyish voice was changing. Still, he was able to sing with only a few tremulous breaks the favorites of the day: "I Love You Truly," "Just a-Wearying for You," "Sing Me to Sleep," and "The Rosary."

As a teenager, Larry had never been mettlesome or aggressive. Nonetheless, it was he who banded together a group of Manual Arts students to protest the rule that required boys to wear neckties to school even on the hottest days. He and other students appeared one morning with shirts open nearly to their waists. Dr. Wilson promptly sent them home and ordered them not to return until they were fully dressed. Most of the students obeyed and returned in proper attire, but Larry, in his first "union" experience, remained at home for two days. Dr. Wilson tried a bit of psychology when he finally sent for him, greeting him thus: "With your scrawny neck, Tibbet, and your funny face, you look like a giraffe. Why don't you cover up that Adam's apple and try to look halfway like a human being?"[16]

Scorn had its effect. Larry went home and wrapped the offending cloth around his neck. The principal's rankling words, "scrawny neck . . . like a giraffe," might have given Larry some reassurance, as he wondered when and where his changing voice was finally going to settle, that he did in fact have a chance to be a singer: a long-necked baritone rather than a short, chunky tenor. Tenors might be known to make more money (and win the soprano onstage), but Larry would ultimately prove that a good-looking baritone could earn just as much as a tenor—and gain for himself a soprano or two offstage.

The faculty at Manual Arts was justly well known for its work in the theatrical arts. Dance was taught by Marian Morgan, who formed the Marian Morgan Dance Troupe and took some of her students on tour. Rob Wagner taught wrestling but also taught history and art, and later became a publisher, editor, and scenarist. Maude Howell, a dramatics teacher just out of Stanford University, gave Larry his first lessons in stage acting. How well she succeeded can be noted from the following item in the school paper:

> In *Romeo and Juliet*, Larry Tibbet is delighting his fellow actors by his wonderful playing in the part of Mercutio. He is sure to win the hearts of his audience as his characterization is a very interesting one. He is finally killed in a duel and does his dying beautifully.[17]

The raw country boy from the frontier town of Bakersfield playing in Shakespeare at 18 and pleasing his peers! Who would have thought it possible? That he had a particular affinity for Shakespeare would be shown by some of his notable roles on the operatic stage, Iago and Falstaff, as well as by his first explosive Metropolitan success as Ford. He also sang Mercutio in Gounod's *Roméo et Juliette*, and his recording of the Queen Mab Ballad from it makes that fleeting aria, often sung only as a throwaway, a tellingly dramatic scene.[18]

During his years at Manual Arts, although Larry insisted that singing was his true love, his interest in acting never lagged. By 1914 little movie houses were sprouting all over Los Angeles, and Larry more than once auditioned for Hollywood's teenage acting roles. The school's dramatic society, in which the players designed their own costumes and painted the sets, added fire to Larry's enthusiasm for the stage. He became absorbed in the art of theatrical makeup, and the little group of student actors spent long hours learning to shade character lines on each other's faces. They produced operettas such as *The Chimes of Normandy* and *The Fairy Princess*, which gave Larry stage experience in both acting and singing. During his high school years, the gawky boy developed into a tall, slender young man with handsome features and, as his giraffe-like neck had prophesied, quite a promising baritone.

When Maude Howell decided to stage a little-known operetta called *The Courtship of Miles Standish*, Larry jumped at the chance to sing the lead. This inspired him to begin voice lessons with Joseph Dupuy, the father of a classmate and a noted California tenor. A charming, energetic individual, Dupuy evidently believed in the sincerity and innate talent of the young Tibbet, as he provided Larry with free lessons and $5 a week for singing in his church's choir.

During his senior year at Manual Arts, Larry worked at developing his speaking voice. He pored over the dictionary in his room, memorizing definitions and the pronunciation of new words. Every day, Frances Ellen would hear the most awful moans and groans emanating from her son's room. When she would ask what was going on, he would answer that he was only doing his homework.

Clearly Larry was heading toward the performing arts, but which would he choose, singing or acting? To this question was soon added another, natural for his age and stage of development: with whom would he fall in love? An adolescent often reaches out to his first love with an intensity that he will never know again. In the case of Lawrence Tibbet, his first love was, curiously, named Love.

Theater-oriented and intellectual, young Ynez Love won Larry's romantic, perhaps over-theatricalized heart during his last year in high school. We know little of Miss Love,[19] but we do know that she was high-strung and had to withdraw from school because of a nervous breakdown.

For solace, the young man turned elsewhere. Destiny presented him with a strong-jawed, ambitious young woman named Grace Mackay Smith, who saw in this handsome, talented youth everything that she craved. What Larry saw in her is just one of the many riddles in his life story.

Young Lawrence Tibbet was a typical wandering Californian, but his background was stable compared to that of Grace Mackay Smith.[20] She was born in Chicago on 20 September 1892[21] to a devoutly religious mother and a father, Corydon Dickinson Smith, who was an organist in a Christian Science church there. Even before Grace Smith was born, her parents' marriage was coming unglued. It held together through the birth of a second daughter, Katherine, but when Grace was only two, a final dissolution took place, and she thus had no conscious memory of a father's love, much as Larry, the young man for whom she felt such a strong attraction, could recall only a blurry image of the father lost to him during his seventh year.

Several years after Mr. Smith's defection, Grace developed pneumonia. Her mother moved her and her younger sister to the higher altitude of Colorado Springs, and thence to Salt Lake City. In that city founded by the Mormons, Mrs. Smith abandoned the liberal precepts of Scottish Presbyterianism in favor of the doctrine of the Latter-day Saints, with their particularly repressive attitudes toward women. From Salt Lake, the restless trio moved on to Portland, Oregon, then south to Los Angeles in a never-ending search for Mrs. Smith's Promised Land.

Throughout this rootless childhood, the domination of religion forced Grace to retreat into herself. Poetry and fiction provided an outlet for her fantasies, and she decided she wanted to be a writer. By the time she met Larry in high school, she had turned into a big-boned, well-shaped young woman, five foot nine, with rather plain features. Her hair was russet brown, with a reddish tint, and her eyes were greenish blue. She was articulate but brusque at times; her voice was frequently strident and grew in volume over the years, as though in an ever-increasing demand for attention. "She was a loud talker. When mother talked, people could hear her," Larry Jr. remembered.[22] She lacked the social graces, but she had a down-to-earth frankness of manner that either attracted or repelled. In Larry's case, it did both.

After the nervous collapse and exit of Ynez Love, a friendship developed between Larry and her unlovely successor. The mothers of the young couple became friends as well, but Mrs. Smith soon judged that Los Angeles did not offer the life that she was seeking and decided to return to Portland. Grace balked at this plan. Manual Arts had given her an opportunity to grow artistically, and now there was the fascinating Larry Tibbet.

Surprisingly for such a prudish woman, Mrs. Smith allowed Grace to stay on alone in Los Angeles, boarding first with a family called Bricker and then, when they moved away, with the Tibbet family itself. This arrangement was a financial boon to Frances Ellen, but it undoubtedly fanned the emotions of the displaced young boarder, thrown together every day with the son of the house. Young Larry was the sun around which the worlds of his mother and older sister revolved. To this universe another satellite was added. It was easy enough for Larry to accept adulation but difficult for him to return affection.

What Grace never realized is that a performing career, whether successful or not, exacts a heavy price of selfishness on the part of the artist. Above all, a performing artist is wedded to his career and to himself. He must not only give himself fully to his art but keep zealous watch over his health, his eating habits, even his sex life. When he does not, guilt often consumes him. Anyone emotionally involved with a singer, actor, dancer, or instrumentalist can make only a partial connection with that person as a human being; the rest of the artist is withheld for himself and for his service to his art.[23]

Here then were the two young people who came to live under the same roof long before they were married: the girl, not attractive but artistic, from a background completely lacking in a steady masculine influence; and the young man, fine looking, highly talented, also highly ambitious, who also did not remember a father's love but only the adoration of women.

In June 1915, Larry Tibbet graduated from Manual Arts High School and faced a world in which he was not sufficiently prepared to earn a living. He had acquired good academic training: he could read enough French and German to get along, he had a beginning actor's grasp of a number of Shakespeare's plays, he could be discerning when it came to some classical music, and he was able to sight-read the easier classical songs. In addition, he had been an able student in mathematics and English literature. This record prepared him well enough to enter college but not to be a wage-earner. But Larry had no yearning for the academic life. (He would later try to steer his twins, Richard and Larry Jr., away from higher education.)

The young man's future direction was further confused by his inability to choose between singing or acting as a career. For him, the theater was the more magical world, but he knew its pitfalls: acting jobs were hard to come by, and it was likely he would be out of work more often than not. Besides, he felt that being just another actor in a full cast would not offer many opportunities for individual expression and personal advancement. He had already acted with the Civic Repertory Theatre of California, and he had performed small roles in a Shakespearean troupe led by Tyrone Power Sr., but he had yet to commit to an actor's life.

Singing, on the other hand, lifted him into a world that was uniquely his own. For him, even singing a simple ballad was an exhilarating experience, and he believed he could make more money singing than acting.

Dupuy, Larry's singing teacher, suggested that Larry join the Orpheus Club in Los Angeles, a group of 60 men who met once a week for rehearsals and gave up to four formal concerts a year. With this group Larry made his first solo appearance as a baritone, singing "The Song of Hiawatha" at the San Francisco World's Fair in June 1915. His solo, along with the club's full presentation, won a $3000 prize. Dupuy was pleased and proud, and Larry began to pursue his voice lessons with renewed vigor.

He was fortunate to have Dupuy as his first singing teacher. Not only was Dupuy a fine tenor who sang all over Southern California, but as Larry's mentor, he was both sensitive and zealous. Larry was lucky not to have fallen in with a charlatan to whom novices were fair game; for then, as now, since no license was required (and who is competent to issue one?), anyone could hang out a shingle and profess to be a singing teacher.

Larry managed to pick up occasional jobs at Kiwanis Club functions and earned about $20 a week singing at weddings and funerals. Membership in local musical and theatrical groups gave him performance opportunities in operettas by Gilbert and Sullivan, Victor Herbert, and Rudolph Friml. By the end of 1917, he had begun to earn a small reputation as a serious and versatile baritone. Fate seemed to be deciding his future for him.

By now the young singer had grown to six feet, two inches, and had well-proportioned shoulders, a slim waistline, and finely molded legs which, when clad in tights and lit by footlights, would send legions of feminine admirers into paroxysms of ecstasy. His hair was a thick, luxuriant brown, and his eyes an intriguing blue. His speaking voice, enhanced by carefully wrought diction, was perfection itself. His smile was unforgettable.[24]

Every summer throughout this post–high school period, Larry would travel to Fort Tejon, south of Bakersfield, to work as a hand on a ranch owned by his mother's family. The outdoor life of a cowboy left him deeply tanned and as limber as a young sapling. As he worked, he sang the favorite songs of the day: "I'm a Lone Cowhand" and "Home on the Range." He was everyman's Curly of *Oklahoma!*, the Marlboro Man as a heroic baritone. Later, when he succeeded Frank Sinatra on radio's *Your Hit Parade*, he sang Cole Porter's "Don't Fence Me In" week after week. Here, he lived it and knew more about the feeling than Porter did. Larry was an American cowboy, and European opera was still a long way off.

In November 1916, Woodrow Wilson—who had run for re-election on the campaign slogan "He kept us out of the war"—was narrowly returned to the White House over Californian Charles Evans Hughes. California was almost as psychologically removed from the European battlefields of World War I as it was geographically distant. By the time of Wilson's re-election, however, a strong wave of public opinion had built up, albeit mostly on the East Coast, in favor of the United States' entering the war. The sinking of the Lusitania, 7 May 1915, a growing paranoia over spies and saboteurs, and virulent propaganda combined to create a widespread feeling of belligerence.

On 30 July 1916, the Black Tom Island disaster shook New York, New Jersey, and states as far away as Connecticut and Maryland. Thirty-four railroad cars loaded with explosives and waiting at the port for shipment to America's European allies had blown up. Flying fragments of metal gouged holes in the Statue of Liberty, nearly every windowpane in Jersey City was blown out, and the pavements of New York City were strewn with shattered glass from the Battery to the front door of the Metropolitan Opera House on Thirty-ninth Street. Everyone was sure it was German sabotage, though it was years before reasonable evidence seemed to prove this. But that was the East Coast. California did not concern itself too much about the incident.

The summer of Black Tom, Larry was contentedly living the bucolic life, working in the fruit orchards outside Los Angeles. He considered himself extra lucky when he was asked to sing in a rural church service and was rewarded with a night's sleep between clean white sheets in a comfortable bed. As a source of extra income he performed in the bars and inns that flanked the public roads, where patrons enjoyed quaffing beakers of brew while a tall young man sang movingly of home and mother.

At night Larry would write Grace a summary of the day's events along with his usual homilies:

> My little friend, just remember and abide by some of the little advices I have given you, but most important see to it that you give yourself advice and carry it out according to your power. But I must be on my way. I will drop you a note from some stopping place not far ahead.[25]

Very few of the notes and letters that passed between Larry and Grace during this phase of their relationship have survived, only those that Grace, for her own reasons, squirreled away. Even the few that remain reveal a strangeness in their intimacy. Larry, with his condescending references to Grace as "my little friend," appears to have adopted toward her the stance of a big brother rather than that of a lover. One can only wonder how Grace was able to swallow his patronizing strictures. Invariably his letters were brief and devoid of warmth except for an occasional more friendly closing line, while by contrast, her letters to him were lengthy, personal, and loving.

During March 1917, Larry and Grace took long bicycle trips together. They were thrilled by California's glorious sunrises and sunsets, especially at their favorite stopping place, Angelus Mesa near Los Angeles. These moments of companionship were cut short when Grace was called to Portland, where her mother had become ill.[26]

California was rocked at this time by the "Zimmermann Telegram," whether it was true or faked, and the war was no longer an exclusively East Coast concern. In essence, the German government offered to join with Mexico against the United States and aid Mexico in reconquering its lost territories of Texas, New Mexico, California, and Arizona. This was too much for West Coast Americans. The rest of the country reacted to the German U-boat sinkings of American ships, and Congress declared war on Germany on 6 April 1917.

Larry meanwhile continued his appearances with the Orpheus Club, including a recital in Santa Barbara where he sang the Prologue to *Pagliacci*, Oley Speaks's "On the Road to Mandalay," and Ben Jonson's "Drink to Me Only with Thine Eyes," selections that would become specialties of his during his career. On 8 March 1918, Larry sang his final concert with the Orpheus Club, at the Trinity Auditorium in Los Angeles. He was not liable for conscription until November, but by July he had signed up with the merchant marines.

Before Larry boarded ship, the U.S.S. *Iris*, Grace and he spent a day together in San Francisco. The weather was beautiful. They took the ferry to Berkeley and, with few words, strolled through the university campus. Finding an expansive tree, they sat beneath it until dusk. Larry told Grace that if he returned alive, he wanted to fulfill the need he felt to be a singer. The two made no plans for the future. The following day Grace found a job as a stenographer in Los Angeles.

Larry's letters to Grace during his time aboard the *Iris* reveal discrepancies with his autobiographical sketches. In *The Glory Road*, he asserts that the *Iris* was used merely as a training ship and was berthed in San Francisco Bay throughout the war. Most of his duties, he wrote, consisted of teaching seamanship to fledgling mariners. Yet in his letters to Grace, he described in minute detail the picturesque voyage of the *Iris* to South America.

In fact, he saw service aboard a number of ships during the war and after. Although Larry wrote very little about it, his last and most important voyage took place aboard the S.S. *Caderetta*, a leaky old steamer that sailed to Vladivostok, Russia, after the 1918 Armistice. The *Caderetta* bore a cargo of supplies and munitions for American soldiers and a locomotive for the short-lived post-czar Kerensky government.

His letters, which began "Dear Grace" and were signed simply "Lawrence," usually ended with "May the Fates deal well with you," but at least once he closed with "I long to see you." The letters included original poems that seem influenced by the popular songs of the time: "When the strong West-wind blows in from the sea / Keep eyes a-wide and ears awake / For there will be thoughts of me." At least one poem, he boldly intimated, was written for someone other than Grace.

Larry was now a big man physically and on occasion, like his father, hot-tempered. Yet in a quarrel he rarely resorted to using his fists. He had practiced peacetime body-building, and now the demanding labor of maritime life helped to build his muscles, contributing to the commanding physique that would become such an important asset to his career.

While Larry was *en route* to Russia, Grace and her grandmother Helen Barbara (Mackay) Gilmour had discovered and rented a small whitewashed cottage in the valley town of La Crescenta, on a hillside entirely surrounded by mountains. The cottage, just 17 miles from Los Angeles, had been built 40 years previously. Its front veranda overlooked a valley of peach and apricot orchards and vast vineyards. On one side of the cottage and growing over the roof was a honeysuckle vine. On a hill in the back stood four pine trees, standing proud. In this quiet and shady retreat, the hopelessly romantic young woman could dream in peace. As Grace Mackay Smith, brimming with anticipation, wrote in her diary:

> At last I have found a resting place—and beauty everywhere. Oh, the woods full of young things; the sky of young clouds; the trees of young leaves; the nests with young birds; the mountains with young breezes; and me with young hopes—scarcely alive—hopes for Him when again we roam the open together; talk over the dear intimacies and feel our pulses quicken with young springs of new joy.[27]

With Larry's homecoming, the relationship between Grace and the future singing artist, an enigmatic one to its very end, appeared to become warmer. Debarking in San Francisco after a year's absence, he telegraphed Grace:

> My dearest. I am home this day from far-away Japan. I am heading south on the first train. Tell no one. Let's have the joy of our own surprise. Lovingly, Lawrence[28]

His return was unexpected, and his mother had gone to Texas to visit relatives. Thus it was expected that he would stay with Grace.

From her journal we know that Grace Smith had not told Larry about La Crescenta, hoping only that he would react with enthusiasm to the cottage and its lovely setting. We know also that as she drove to meet Larry at the Los Angeles railway station, this moonstruck yet forthright young woman could not even remember what her "beau" looked like. Characteristically, during his overseas months, Larry had sent her a photograph of his ship, but none of himself.

According to Grace's memoir (written many years later and no doubt full of the distortions that time and her longings for romantic love created), her attempt to surprise the handsome young man was entirely successful.

> Larry's joy on beholding the cottage at La Crescenta knew no bounds. "My dear, how did you ever find anything so near to heaven as this?" he asked. His delight was every bit what I had hoped for, as he explored every corner. He reveled in the view. He strutted through the rooms, peeking into closets and banging doors, and he examined the wood-burning stove as I skipped after him like a happy child.
>
> We had our reunion, and my dear grandmother was kindness herself in making his homecoming a happy one. What a celebration we had—fried chicken with all the trimmings and blueberry pie. We had made a fire in the old-fashioned fireplace in our sitting room, using eucalyptus branches for firewood, and after dinner, we sat out in the garden. We were so happy.[29]

But Grace was soon deeply chagrined by the sleeping arrangements in the cottage she and Larry shared. Grandmother slept on a cot by the wood-burning stove; Grace had another cot in the living room; and Larry, the *grand seigneur*, slept on a comfortable queen-sized bed in the cottage's only bedroom.

On one of those nights, Grace could stand it no longer. Moonlight streamed through the windows, and the man she desired so urgently slept peacefully on the other side of a door closed to her. Naked, she rose and went to the door. It was locked. Angrily, she thumped at the door.

As Grace stood there feeling rejected and abashed, the door opened. Larry, his muscular body also unclad, pointed with a chuckle to the bed. "What took you so long?" he asked.[30]

Chapter 2

TO NEW YORK

It is safe to say that no marriage is easy. Perhaps it starts well and at least that is something. Consider, however, the case of the newly wed Mr. and Mrs. Lawrence Tibbet: he, with his primary awareness and drive directed toward his singing, not toward Grace; and she, passionately in love but frustrated and jealous of a mate who possessed far greater talents than she. The very notion of a mutually loving husband and wife was in jeopardy from the outset.

They were married on 19 May 1919 in the County of Los Angeles; Larry was 22 and Grace was 26. Hugh J. Crawford was the justice of the peace. Grace's grandmother and a friend of Larry's, Arthur Millier, acted as witnesses, and Lizabel Jimenez (a friend of Grace's grandmother) and Reginald Pole stood by. A week later the Hall of Records sent the couple the usual 14-by-25-inch certificate of marriage, which appears seldom to have been removed from its envelope.[1]

Typically, two accounts of the wedding ceremony exist, at total variance. From the day of the nuptials, it seems the difficulties were mapped out.

"We drove into town on a mad shopping spree," wrote Grace Tibbett in her memoirs, "getting our marriage license and making arrangements for the wedding." She remembers exhilaration. Millier remembered the ceremony quite differently:

> On May 19, on a hot afternoon, Tibbett, Grace, Arthur Millier and another friend—Reginald Pole—stood in the stuffy parlor of

> a Los Angeles justice of the peace. Grace wore white and a new straw hat heavily festooned with red cherries; she was lively and eager for the ceremony to begin. Tibbett, on the other hand, was aloof and withdrawn. He knew Grace loved him, romantically and devotedly. Did he love her like that? He thought he loved her for the dear, genuine person who loved him.[2]

Both Millier, an artist, and Pole, an actor and Shakespeare scholar, watched the ceremony with misgivings. Millier joked as he signed the marriage license, but Larry stood unsmiling. Grace and he had quarreled bitterly that morning, and Larry had stalked out of the cottage to stride for two hours in the hills. When he returned, Grace came running to meet him, her face radiant. "Oh, Joe!"—this was her nickname for him—"You fool, I do love you."[3]

It is interesting to speculate as to why Lawrence Tibbett married Grace. A passage in his autobiography shows that he certainly admired her:

> Although our marriage did not last forever it was an adventure and an important event in my life. When I was married I was a dreamer and wanted to sit under a palm tree and philosophize. . . .
>
> Grace had courage, dash, ambition. She was temperamental—much more so than I. She had an unerring sense of comedy, real acting ability. She was witty and would have made a great comédienne had she been given the opportunity. Her real ambition, however, was to write, and no less an authority than Rupert Hughes said she had marked ability as a poetess.
>
> We had some very, very good times together—and some awfully rotten ones. We were both mercurial in our dispositions. I had my singing; she had her poetry.[4]

Five days into their marriage, Grace wrote this poem:

> Dark shadows spread
> their wings
> Ghosts of forbidding ills stalk down the long
> aisles of my dreams
> At the end
> A small door
> Forever closed
> It is your heart.[5]

Perhaps the real clue to Larry's marriage was that Grace gave him the same unswerving devotion he had known all his life from his mother, and to a lesser extent, from his older sister Betty Lee. He was accustomed to devoted support, for many an artist an absolute necessity in the attempts to build a career. Larry surely recognized that a woman like Grace would fight for him and believe in him through all the trials of the difficult and frustrating life he had chosen to embrace. He also realized, but refused to face, that she would continue to fight, often contentiously, for a love he could not give her.

From the beginning the Tibbets quarreled incessantly, each trying to dominate. Larry had begun to experience nagging doubts about his future as a singer while Grace, though bubbly and cheerful most of the time, could exhibit a strong stubborn streak when it suited her.

Disharmony reigned in the Tibbet household by the time the fraternal twins, Richard Mackay and Lawrence Ivan, arrived on 9 February 1920 at French Hospital in Los Angeles. They were premature and weighed only four pounds each at birth. Grace nearly died.

On the night of the dual birth Larry opened in Palm Springs as Iago in Shakespeare's *Othello*, the first of two performances. He had been coached by his friend Reginald Pole, an experience that must have been invaluable when Larry later sang Verdi's setting of the role on the world's operatic stages. The designer of this production was Lloyd Wright, the son of the eminent architect whose name he bore, but whom he despised. He and Larry became close friends.

Grace recovered; she and the twins came home from the hospital, and additional strains now weighed on the marriage as Larry struggled to meet the financial demands of a growing family. Although he did not mind standing over a steaming tub to wash diapers, he refused to get up in the night when the babies cried. He needed his sleep and strength for his singing. Slowly, he had expanded his singing engagements, and he was now attached to the First Presbyterian Church in Los Angeles, where he sang solos and joined in duets and quartets from the sacred music repertoire.

Larry received his first real break in the early spring of 1921 when he was hired to sing at Sid Grauman's Million Dollar Theater in Los Angeles. Grauman considered Larry a close theatrical look-alike to Charles Ray, a popular movie star of the period. Shortly after he went to work for Grauman, Larry contracted to sing in *The Firefly* and *The Mikado* with the California Opera Company at $100 a week.

He managed to hold his job at Grauman's for about 15 weeks, until

Grauman booked the film *The Golem*, which featured the lament "Eli, Eli." Larry knew absolutely nothing about the vocal embellishments of the Jewish cantorial tradition, so he sang the song straight, as written. He lost his job with Grauman.

Larry now decided to make a drastic change: he would leave the cottage at La Crescenta which was, after all, more a fantasy of his wife's than his reality, and he would go to New York to further his career. His decision was strengthened by three men, each of whom, in unique ways, would help to transform his life.

The first was Basil Ruysdael, born Basil Millspaugh, a former bass with the Metropolitan Opera Company. After graduating from the School of Engineering at Cornell, he changed his name and his direction when he turned to the operatic stage. A huge, hulking man, he had a deep, dark bass and sang the roles of Hunding and Fafner in Wagner's *Ring*.

During World War I, the Metropolitan did not produce operas in the German repertoire, and Ruysdael was one of the singers who suffered. He continued with such roles as Varlaam in *Boris Godunov* and the King in *Aida*, but he left the company in 1918 and moved to California. There he appeared in light opera, made a respectable film career, and taught voice. He later returned to the East and would serve as the announcer on some of Larry's radio programs.

At auditions for a production of *The Mikado* in which the towering bass was to play the title role, Larry met the man who would become his teacher and who gave a great stimulus to his career. As Larry wrote in his memoirs, "Basil Ruysdael, huge, hearty, blunt, with a torrid vocabulary, changed my entire point of view toward music."[6]

Larry had been sure of himself as a high-toned singer. When he sang, he would throw back his head with his eyes half shut and over-concentrated on the music in an attempt to appear cultured. He was determined to show Ruysdael just how cultivated he was, as he wrote amusingly in his memoirs:

> For my tryout I sang a love song, in my most elegant manner. It was about the wafting of the south wind, the frisking lambs, and God's own out-of-doors. I expected that it would knock Ruysdael over, but when I finished and turned to look at him he was still in a perpendicular position. He stepped up to me, put his fists on his hips, fixed a cold eye upon me, and said, "Listen, fellow, what is this south 'wined' that seems to be blowing out here in California?"

> "Why, why—" I was flabbergasted. "Wined? Why, you know—wind."
>
> "Uh, huh. What kind of language is this you're talking? What's this 'ahn-da' and 'lahm' and 'lo-va' and 'kees' and 'Gawd'?"
>
> "Well, er," I tried to explain. "You know how it is—when you sing you pronounce a little differently."
>
> "Why?" he demanded bluntly.
>
> "Well, if you don't know, Mr. Ruysdael," I said hopelessly, "a big Metropolitan star like you—if you don't know, I can't explain. It's just that in high-class singing you say 'ahn-da' instead of 'and,' and 'lahm' instead of 'lamb.' I never heard a singer say 'win-d.' It's always 'wined.'". . .
>
> Ruysdael . . . almost crushed my shoulder in his huge hand.
>
> "Look here, fellow," he said. "Singing is just speaking words to music. Try that song again. Sing it as you would tell me about it if we were sitting together at lunch—just speak the words on the tune."
>
> It was the best singing advice I ever had. It had never occurred to me that the best singing is the most natural singing.[7]

During his career, Larry would be indebted to many teachers, conductors, and vocal coaches, but Ruysdael's help, partly because it was the most timely, was the most important. Larry's superb diction was always a highly admired facet of his art.

The so-called methods of singing teachers can be, to say the least, bizarre. Piano pedagogy, especially in "teaching" strike and release, can also be arcane and obtuse, but at least it deals with muscles and body parts one can see and feel. If a position looks or feels unnatural, it is almost immediately apparent to the thinking student. But how to teach voice?

Except with the aid of the mirror called the laryngyscope, the position of those two tiny folds in the larynx, the vocal cords, which vibrate against each other to produce sound, cannot be seen. They cannot be physically fixed into a "position," like a ring finger, even if a "correct" position were known. Everything has to be suggested: "Place the hands behind the back, and chase an imaginary dove around the room," says one teacher. "Think of stinking fish to produce the head voice," urges another. "Sing high notes with a black snore," advises a third. One has only to eavesdrop on conversations between voice teachers and/or their students to hear these and other like imperatives.

Svengali, in George du Maurier's novel *Trilby*, added a word to the language when he "hypnotized" a tone-deaf barmaid into becoming a great singer. Is the teaching of singing a mesmeric act that works for one and not for another? To some extent, it can be. But as Larry would later write about a hypothetical singing teacher: "If he makes singing a mysterious process, if he begins to deal in hocus-pocus, quit him."[8]

Ruysdael, with his credentials as a former bass of the Metropolitan Opera, normally charged his students $10 an hour, but, aware of Larry's financial constraints, he saw the young singer for nothing, utilizing various methods to help develop and free his voice. Ruysdael would sneak up behind him, cry "Loosen up!" and give him a knock on the back that would almost send him to his knees. Larry had to keep singing no matter what his teacher did to him. Ruysdael would clutch Larry's jaw and shake it from side to side. He would make him lie face down on the floor, roll over, get up, climb onto a chair, and jump down, all the while singing, while Ruysdael jabbed him with his fists and shouted "Relax! Relax!"[9]

Most teachers and students would be appalled at such violent methods of bringing forth a singing voice. But in this case, the rich, royal-sounding baritone of the man who would become Lawrence Tibbett began to emerge under Ruysdael's unconventional tutelage.

A second important person, the man who might be described as Larry's true mentor, now entered his life. This was Rupert Hughes. Born in Missouri, Hughes had lived in New York and London and served under Pershing in the United States–Mexican border war of 1916. He was a man of incredible versatility and creative energy, and a flood of fiction and nonfiction works flowed from his pen. His plays had toured in the United States and had been seen as far away as Australia. Despite his large literary output, Hughes also found time for another keen interest, music. He had composed a number of attractive songs and also lectured on musical subjects.[10]

When Larry met him, Rupert Hughes was in his late 40s and living in Los Angeles. Hughes was scheduled to speak to members of the Ebell Club, a women's organization in that city, and he needed a singer to illustrate his lecture. Several members of the club suggested to Tibbet that he do the singing, and he went to see Hughes, who was himself to play the accompaniment. When Larry finished his audition, Hughes leaned back thoughtfully, looked at him, and said, "You have one of the most beautiful voices I have ever heard."

The baritone was flustered and pleased by the famous man's praise, and indeed he was hired for the engagement, but he assumed that after this Hughes would forget him. He was astonished when later he and Grace received a dinner invitation from Hughes.

> At dinner [Hughes] asked, "What do you intend to do with your life?"
>
> I didn't exactly know. There didn't seem to be much money in singing, so I had thought I might become an orchestral conductor, a position which not only paid well but was highly honored and was a thrilling artistic expression. I had bought a book on conducting and had practiced for hours in front of a mirror, leading a phonograph like nobody's business.
>
> "You have a career in that voice," Hughes said. "You ought to go to New York."
>
> I had heard so many dreadful singers praised that I had learned to scoff at compliments. But I realized that Hughes was no flatterer and that he knew music.
>
> "Lord!" I said to myself. "What if he's right!"
>
> "New York?" I asked aloud. "In order to amount to anything I'd have to study in Europe, wouldn't I? And if Europe were as close as Catalina Island I wouldn't have enough money to get there."
>
> "New York," Hughes said firmly, "is the music center of the world. American singers will soon come into their own and a foreign reputation won't mean a thing. Borrow the money. Some day, with that voice, you'll be able to pay it back."[11]

Hughes never realized how hungrily Larry swallowed every word, every nuance of the conversation, especially the prophecy that American singers would come into their own without the necessity of foreign training.

Borrow the money, certainly—but from whom? It would have to be an enormous sum. The training of an opera singer involves not only costly hours of work with a teacher but also a coach for the interpretation of the huge repertoire the singer has to absorb. At least three languages would have to be learned well enough to sound idiomatic when sung, let alone understood—Italian, French, and German. And a suitable accompanist would be a continuing expense.

On top of that would come the costs of daily living: rent, food, a wardrobe, those vital incidentals.[12] Geraldine Farrar, a star of the less expensive era that preceded Tibbet's, wrote in her memoirs that it had cost her $30,000 to obtain the training that enabled her to prepare for her chance when it came. (She was able to borrow the money and later paid back every cent.)

How was this impoverished Californian ex-cowboy to obtain such a vast sum? At just the right time in this juncture of Tibbet's life, the third important figure appeared.

James G. Warren was a businessman and president of the Orpheus Club with which Larry had so often sung. In the summer of 1922, acting on his own initiative, Warren wrote to Frank La Forge, a highly respected vocal coach in New York City, recommending Tibbet as a young singer of great promise. (Warren's daughter Elinor was then studying piano with La Forge's partner, Ernesto Berúmen.) He concluded his letter: "There is no finer young man of my acquaintance, nor one I think more of than Lawrence."[13]

Warren then gave a promise of financial aid to Larry in the following way: he would pay the initial premium on a $25,000 insurance policy on the baritone's life. This would make it possible for Larry to borrow enough money on the policy's surrender value to go to New York and meet the expenses of his training plus living expenses. In addition, the loan would provide enough income for the support of Grace and the twins, who would remain for the time being in California.[14]

Now everything required for the beginning of Larry's long uphill struggle had fallen into place—with one exception: he had to tell Grace of his plan. Grace later described the occasion:

> One day in late August [1921] he came home in the afternoon and said to me, "Grace, I have some good news and perhaps some bad news for you. But whatever I tell you I hope you will try to be fair."
>
> I didn't need any great intelligence to know what was coming. Hadn't I known from my first day at La Crescenta that all good things had to end! And what of our dinner with Rupert Hughes? Larry was never the same after that. I forced myself to listen as Larry continued. "I saw Mr. Warren today and I had a long talk with him about my career. He said if you could manage without me for a year he would take out a life insurance policy and borrow enough money on it to provide for you and the twins. But how can I leave you to go three thousand miles away when the boys are so small?" The twins were then a year and a half old.[15]

On 17 April 1922, Grace, Larry's mother Frances Ellen and the babies went to see Larry off at the railway station, the same station where Grace fancied they had been so happily reunited after the war. Now her husband was even more distant, more aloof, and more preoccupied by anxious anticipation of his life in New York City.

Larry's friend Reginald Pole was now living in New York and would help this son of a murdered deputy sheriff, this would-be opera singer who had rarely heard an opera. Los Angeles was not the desert, but Larry knew that the eastbound train, heading for that great city by the Atlantic Ocean, would take him into an entirely different, high-powered world, at the hub of which—as far as he was concerned—stood the Metropolitan Opera House.

Which prospect made him happier: to leave Grace behind, or to rush toward the fine, unsure madness ahead of him?

Larry's five-day train odyssey took him across a country in the throes of radical change. It was the Roaring 20s, and morals and customs were in a state of disarray. Even the length of women's skirts had shifted dramatically. Some sociologists trace the changes to the Volstead Act: only two months after the signing of the 1918 Armistice ending World War I and over the unexpected veto of President Wilson, by act of Congress, Prohibition became law. Liquor was not to be "manufactured, nor sold, nor given away" and so of course was far more prized than when it was legal and easily obtainable.

It was now necessary to break the law in order to get a drink. But if you broke one law, which of the others would you choose to obey? Which customs and which restrictions would you respect? With this loosening of the bonds of a previous morality, women shook off their Victorian morals, bobbed their hair, showed their legs, and, as never before, ran openly with men.

Larry arrived in New York City on 22 April 1922. Waiting for him were his friend Reginald Pole and Pole's 19-year-old companion, Beatrice Wood. Wood, who was from San Francisco, had already trained in Paris at the Comédie Française. Seeing Larry through bemused, newly cosmopolitan eyes, she was rather put off by his hayseed appearance: his wrinkled topcoat and slouch hat, not to mention his round, chubby face atop a long neck.[16] He did seem to have a lively personality, however, and a nice sense of humor as he joked about the dapper English cut of his friend's clothing.

"Goin' to hell" as New York may have been, the arts flourished. Radio had become widespread in the city. Caruso had died the previous August, but the Metropolitan had already announced for their next season singers such as Fedor Chaliapin, Adamo Didur, Beniamino Gigli, Maria Jeritza, Giovanni Martinelli, Rosa Ponselle, Titta Ruffo, and

Antonio Scotti. Playing on Broadway were *Anna Christie* with Pauline Lord, Booth Tarkington's *Rose Briar* with Billie Burke, George Bernard Shaw's *Back to Methuselah* (in three parts because of its length), Pirandello's *Six Characters in Search of an Author*, and John Barrymore's electrifying *Hamlet*.

The Barrymore production had sparked a renewed interest in Shakespeare. Forthcoming productions of *Romeo and Juliet*, starring Ethel Barrymore, and *The Merchant of Venice*, with David Warfield, were in the works. Pole himself had plans to produce *King Lear* and was hoping that Larry would repeat his West Coast role of Edgar.

That year the hit musicals on Broadway included the *Ziegfeld Follies*, Irving Berlin's *Music Box Review*, and the Franz Schubert gloss *Blossom Time*. Audiences emerged from the theaters humming such songs as "What'll I Do?," "Say It with Music," and "Song of Love." Hollywood products in the Broadway movie-houses included *Orphans of the Storm* with Lillian Gish, *Blood and Sand* with Rudolph Valentino, and Robert Flaherty's trailblazing documentary, *Nanook of the North*.

Reginald and Beatrice took Larry to a large building just off Central Park West, at 14 West Sixty-eighth Street, the studios of Frank La Forge and the Mexican pianist Ernesto Berúmen. This pair of musicians were well known and highly regarded. Their students were of the highest caliber, and La Forge especially was strongly connected in the music business. If you could study with La Forge or Berúmen, your career had already taken a large step forward.

Besides being one of the top vocal coaches in New York, La Forge was a fine concert pianist, composer, and accompanist for such leading singers as Geraldine Farrar, Amelita Galli-Curci, Margarete Matzenauer, and Ernestine Schumann-Heink. He was also the vocal coach of the tempestuous New Zealand–born soprano Frances Alda, who later would be instrumental in getting Larry into the Metropolitan.[17]

It was agreed that the further training of the baritone would begin at once. La Forge's secretary found a studio apartment for Larry on Central Park West, a few blocks from La Forge's studio. Mrs. Bette Flynn, Larry's new landlady, was a good-natured Irishwoman who let him use her piano. The rent, including breakfast, was $9 a week. Larry paid only $10 a week to La Forge, but it was as hard for him to part with these sums then as it is for young singers today to afford the going rents and rates of New York City.

Dupuy and Ruysdael had taught Larry the basics of good singing. Now La Forge began to coach him in repertoire and interpretation.

Larry would have other vocal coaches after La Forge, but La Forge was the most important in his artistic development, pushing Larry far beyond his previous level of accomplishment. He taught Larry how to express emotion within the musical context, and how to convey the exact meaning of the words to an audience through posture, motion, and gesture. La Forge also guided Larry in learning many of his operatic roles.

Helen Moss, one of Berúmen's most talented students, helped Larry to learn a large repertoire of concert songs in several languages. Helen came from a wealthy, well-connected family. Her mother, Edith Johnson Moss, was a well-known Long Island concert singer, and her father, L. Howard Moss, was a physician. When Helen was three years old, she sat at her mother's piano, picking out melodies. At barely five, she was able to accompany her mother's practice sessions. To the Moss mansion on the precocious child's sixth birthday came President William Howard Taft, for whom she performed MacDowell's "To a Wild Rose." The rotund chief of state had lifted her up and kissed her on the cheek.

When Helen came to study with Ernesto Berúmen, he ordered her to memorize her music. She also had to learn French, German, and Italian in order to gain a truer conception of the meaning of the songs in her repertoire, to recognize good translations, to revise bad ones, and to assist singers with their diction. Berúmen was the first pianist in the United States to train accompanists to pay such close attention to these details of their unique craft.

Larry became a special project of Helen's. As described by Helen Moss herself, her work with him came about in the following manner:

> One day La Forge took me aside and said, "Miss Moss"—people were so dreadfully formal in those days—"would you be willing to accompany Lawrence Tibbet without any remuneration? I feel this man is destined to be a great artist at the Met, but he needs one year of solid work before I believe he will be ready for an audition. I would like you to work with him—if you are willing to do so."
>
> At the time I had my own studio at Carnegie Hall and was accompanying many singers. I was also giving piano lessons. How I managed all this and Larry, too, I have no idea. I was quite young then, and agreed to help Larry without my usual fee.[18]

Twice a week, invariably dressed in the same shabby slacks and sweater, Larry traveled to Orchard Street, Richmond Hill, Queens, where Helen lived with her parents and three brothers. She preferred to work with Larry at her home rather than at her studio, knowing he was more relaxed there.

Aware, too, that Larry lived in near-poverty, she made certain that he had a good meal at the Moss home when work stopped at six. The Mosses' Swedish cook could turn out a succulent leg of lamb, a fine cherry pie, and other epicurean delights. Larry always felt happily at ease with the Moss family. He also enjoyed occasional political arguments with Dr. Moss, who was an ardent Republican.

After supper the family gathered in the living room. It had become obvious to Helen that Larry was at his social best as a singer, and, like any entertainer, he relished being at center stage. Occasionally, as a change of pace, he would break into a dramatic soliloquy. Larry had a special flair for Shakespeare, which Helen discovered one evening when he held her brothers enthralled by one of Falstaff's monologues. Sometimes she wondered whether he preferred acting to singing, then she simply decided that he excelled at both.

Such an evening would end with Larry and Edith Moss singing a popular duet of the day. When he reluctantly left for home, Helen usually managed to sneak a bag of raisins into his jacket pocket. For the lonely young singer, the Moss family served as a much-needed stimulant, providing companionship and relaxation after the stiff formality of La Forge's studio.[19]

When Larry left La Crescenta and set out for New York in 1922, Grace rented a small house in the Laurel Canyon section of Los Angeles. She arranged for Frances Ellen, Larry's mother, to stay with her and take care of the twins, an arrangement both Larry Jr. and Richard thoroughly enjoyed. The boys were later able to walk from their new home to their kindergarten class at Madam Gordon's School, where their playmates included children of the stars. Grace left home every morning for her job in downtown Los Angeles; the monotony of her leisure time was broken by several musical events, including a song recital by Fedor Chaliapin and a symphony concert with violinist Fritz Kreisler as soloist. Grace's friends were kind, but they had lives of their own and could not provide her with the support and attention she desperately needed.

Larry wrote to her only intermittently, when events moved him. Insensitive to her feelings, he asked after everyone but Grace herself. His letters nevertheless provide graphic pictures of his early days in New York City. He confessed that his principal amusement was to stand on street corners to watch the girls go by, maintaining that these girls—mostly Jewish and Italian—were far more attractive than their sisters who performed in Broadway shows.

Of his progress, Larry wrote that La Forge seemed satisfied and had invited him to attend a musicale in which eight other singers from the studio were to participate. In his next letter he told Grace that the evening had been as boring as the devil. He fervently hoped La Forge would never again invite him to such an event.

Three weeks later he wrote and berated Grace for asking that he write more frequently. "For heaven's sake, stop fussing and nagging across these three thousand miles—it's irritating even at this distance." Apparently Grace was concerned about his spirits, for he continued, "You must not worry about me—I will let you know if I am thinking of making my demise."

His letters usually did contain several items of interest to Grace. In one letter, he lets her know that Mr. Patton, his agent for church singing jobs, had found him work at $10 per job and promised to keep him busy on Sundays. In another letter, reiterating that La Forge liked his singing, he suddenly burst out with an afterthought that Grace found highly disturbing. "I don't like La Forge very much. He is too effeminate—just as I feared! I can generally smell these rats a few thousand miles away." Then, realizing that such feelings were better left unsaid, he swore Grace to silence. "Please keep my impressions of La Forge et al quite *entre nous*—you understand, it would not do."[20]

To further the name of their best students, La Forge and Berúmen sponsored monthly noonday musicales at their studios, in a small private auditorium, and at Aeolian Hall in midtown Manhattan. These concerts attracted leading musical personalities; invitations were limited to critics, singers, and other musicians, and so appearing at the musicales could be quite influential in building a career. Larry made his first professional New York appearance in a concert at Aeolian Hall on 3 November 1922. Accompanied by Helen Moss, he sang the *Pagliacci* Prologue with such power and lyric beauty that the audience rose to its feet as one, applauding and shouting for more.

Larry followed with encore after encore, until he had sung every song in the portfolio he had brought with him. Still the audience clamored for more. Among his encores was Mussorgsky's "Song of the Flea." La Forge had a low opinion of this song, considering it merely a showpiece for the general audience, not for professionals. He had made Larry promise not to sing it at the concert, and Larry had reluctantly agreed. Now the audience was demanding still another song, and Helen, unable to hold back any longer, cried, "C'mon, Larry, let's do the 'Flea.'" Larry hesitated, then took Helen by the hand and headed for the piano. He sang the "Flea" so lustily that once more he brought down the house.[21]

Larry sent Grace an account of the concert:

> Everything went quite well at Aeolian Hall on Friday, except my high notes weren't particularly good. I was in splendid voice, though. The audiences liked me quite well—better than anyone else on the program. They recalled me about five times. And afterward Mr. La Forge said "I am convinced that there is a big place for you in New York." He also said I should busy myself immediately with the preparation for a debut recital for an early date, which means he thinks me very capable. He said he was certain that he could influence Warren to furnish the money for one or possibly two recitals, which would cost over a thousand dollars for that alone!
>
> The day before my Aeolian appearance, I went to sing for Mr. I. H. Duval, the agent. I sang the Prologue for him. Duval told me that I was the best taught; that I sang better than any American student he had ever heard. . . . He said my Italian diction was splendid—thought I spoke the language [and] that undoubtedly I had a great career before me; that I sang the Prologue as well as Zanelli. So much for Duval.

About this time, a teacher and entrepreneur, Felix Hughes (no relation to Rupert), appeared and offered to teach Larry at no charge. Though Hughes lacked the preeminence of La Forge, Larry accepted this tempting offer. Still an inexperienced, even foolish, young man, he also tried to keep on with La Forge, whom he had come to dislike.

This got him into a fine mess. As he reported to Grace:

> La Forge apparently will do little for me as long as I continue with Felix Hughes, and Hughes is just as jealous of La Forge—and I, the important person (to myself) in this mess, don't like any of them in particular, so there you have it. All I seem to be doing here is dancing a disgusting diplomatic jig.

In addition, a would-be backer had presented himself, a certain Mr. Catts. But how would this affect his arrangement with James Warren, who had made it possible for him to come to New York in the first place?

> I cannot throw Warren over if he continues to help me, which he says he will, even if Catts will back me. Here is the situation: La Forge advises two debut recitals; one here and one in Boston, very soon. Such a venture will cost nearly $2000. In speaking to Warren I experience the same difficulty in talking as before—nothing definite. He said I must get to making something soon. I then told him another man was interested in backing me and [Warren] hemmed and hawed a bit and said of course he too would see me further than the original $1000. And the conversation was left in that state.
>
> I spoke to La Forge about the matter, and he said unless Warren would be definite he would advise pursuing Catts. L. F. agreed that Warren was a difficult man to handle in such a situation and that Catts would probably give me more and with a free hand.

It was all very troubling. Meanwhile Christmas approached and he wrote home warmly.

> The lovely presents from all my beloved family greatly helped me to relieve the homesickness inevitable at this holiday season. The two splendid volumes of songs will be used immediately. I had neither of them. The walking stick from the twins was just what I wanted. In fact, I was going to buy myself one; for most all gentlemen carry them here. The fruits from Mother were splendid, and I still am munching them—thinking fondly of California the while. And what a beautiful silk shirt from my dear sister. What would you advise? I also received a pair of silk hose from my landlady and family, and some nice remembrances from some people around here—neckties (3). Reginald and Beatrice gave me a beautiful imported cravat; my organist at church also contributed.

He also reported that he had obtained two "splendid engagements," one at Vassar College and the other for a noonday musicale at the Brick Church on Fifth Avenue.[22]

In the meantime, Reginald Pole and Beatrice Wood had lost little time in establishing Larry socially in New York. They introduced him to their legions of friends, which led to singing engagements in private homes in Manhattan and Brooklyn. At first his appearance was hardly stylish, but when he opened his mouth to sing, very little else mattered.

"His personality was like the sun when he strode into the room,"

Beatrice recalled. "He was of the earth, a Westerner. He was an aspect of the vitality of the West and projected that vitality."[23]

In 1923, Pole produced Shakespeare's *King Lear*. True to his promise, he gave the role of Edgar to Larry, providing the baritone with his New York stage debut. Unfortunately, Pole had failed to provide enough rehearsal time for the production, and it was a dismal flop, running for only two performances and apparently never noticed by the *New York Times*.

That same year, however, Larry was to tread the boards of another stage, one of the largest in the world, framed by an immense proscenium that was gilded and decorated with plaques carved with the names of six great composers. This theater, on Broadway between Thirty-ninth and Fortieth Streets in Manhattan, was the Metropolitan Opera House.

Part Two 1923–1927

Chapter 3

CURTAIN CALL

Larry's dislike of La Forge notwithstanding, either his guardian angel or his subconscious intuition saved him from severing their connection entirely. La Forge was truly a dynamic force in New York's music world. The Aeolian Hall concerts, in which he presented his students more formally than in his studio, were only one example of his prestige and power. Of the 13 February 1923 concert, the critic from *Musical Digest* wrote:

> The Frank La Forge–Ernesto Berúmen Noonday Concerts in New York's Aeolian Hall are increasing in interest. They are held once a month, and the auditorium is always nearly filled. Not a program is without its excellence; not a concert which does not present to the audience young artists of prominence.
>
> We were particularly impressed last week by Tibbet, a baritone who will have only himself to blame if he doesn't make a career. You know the average American baritone: good voice, engaging style (sometimes) and a business-like demeanor. Mr. Tibbet has some of the latter, but so much more of tone and singing instinct that many a listener began to lean forward when a few phrases of "Eri tu" had been sung.
>
> A fine low and middle voice, we thought as this singer swung along, but doubtless tight top notes. What was our surprise when this young newcomer sailed upwards with confidence and vigor that imparted a bit of a thrill. Here is a voice that seems sure to "free out" nicely. Just a little less force up above, a steadier breath

> support during *messa di voce*, some additional experience and the public will hear from this young man. He disclosed a rhythmic sense, and he "went in time." There was a burst of real applause at the end, and Mr. Tibbet had to return half a dozen times to make his acknowledgements.[1]

Preparing for these concerts wracked the nerves of singer and accompanist alike. Helen Moss recalled that, experienced pianist as she was, she fumbled a chord during one of Larry's sessions with La Forge. She was dreadfully embarrassed and La Forge was furious. "Miss Moss," he snapped, "what happened to your concentration? Our accompanists do not make such dumb foul-ups."

Larry defended her, his deep voice as soothing as his manner. "Mr. La Forge, we performers rarely make mistakes but if we do, isn't it better to ignore them?" With a smile on his lips he turned to Helen. "Let's try this again, Miss Moss."

Helen Moss remembered that she had to restrain herself from jumping up from the piano and kissing Larry.[2]

The two worked extremely well together. She enjoyed accompanying him more than any other singer she worked with. Under the guidance of this extraordinarily gifted young woman, Larry mastered lieder by Mozart, Schubert, Schumann, Beethoven, and Brahms, as well as *chansons* of Fauré and Debussy. They also prepared many encore pieces, especially old English airs, which Larry often later featured in his regular concert programs.

Temperament dominates the artist's world, and temperament, regrettably, put an end to this rewarding collaboration. Frances Alda was planning a world concert tour and needed an accompanist. Since Alda was one of the Met's biggest stars *and* the wife of general manager Gatti-Casazza, La Forge assigned Helen the task of mastering Mme. Alda's concert repertoire. Moss soon discovered that the dark-eyed diva was very demanding and was absolutely convinced that no one on earth could accompany Alda to Alda's liking.

This was a far cry from Helen's relaxed cooperation with Larry. She told her fiancé, banker Philip Bliss, of the projected tour, which would keep her abroad for over a year. He immediately gave her an ultimatum: choose between the tour or marriage to him. Helen chose to give up the tour, using the ultimatum as an excuse to get out of the situation with Alda. When she told La Forge, he was shocked and angry and berated her so harshly that she never returned to his studio. Nor did Helen Moss and Larry ever work together again.[3]

Dictatorial as La Forge might have been, he was not only an exceptional vocal coach but also a skillful conniver. He helped his singers obtain auditions to the Metropolitan and sought opportunities for those who were inclined or more suited to concert careers. For even his best singers, however, it was not an easy task to gain entry to the Met. It was particularly difficult for those who, like Larry, lacked European operatic experience. Still, through hard work, patience, and politics, La Forge managed to funnel many of his students into the old brick building on Broadway. He kept his ear cocked for the slightest rumor that Gatti was open to hearing new voices, and at every chance he marched into the Met to arrange auditions.

La Forge was able to schedule an audition for Larry on 19 April 1923. It had been only a year since the Californian had come to New York, yet such were his vocal gifts that after a seven-month period of high-powered training with La Forge and Moss, the opportunity that he most desired came to him.

A singer's career is bedeviled by all sorts of uncomfortable moments: suffering the critique of a teacher or some other expert, making a debut, having to sing over a cold. But of all the unnerving aspects of the profession, auditions are probably the worst. The bare stage confronts him, open to the darkened auditorium. Somewhere out there sit the supreme judges; if they can be seen at all, they often look glazed and disdainful. The awful feeling that "it's now or never" is enough to make young aspirants wonder why they ever agreed to this particular form of torture.

With one or, for the fortunate, two arias, a hopeful singer soars high or is grounded. If the singer's voice at that particular moment fails to respond, a chilling "thank you" will echo from the auditorium, and that is it. Unless a sensitive judge happens to recognize the potential of a voice, the unsuccessful auditioner rarely receives a second chance at the Met.

And yet it is generally acknowledged throughout the profession that no one has devised a more satisfactory method for unknown singers to be heard by opera conductors, producers, and directors than by a direct audition. Even if, as is usually the case today, an audio tape, or even a video cassette, is supplied in advance, the singer is ultimately judged on the live appearance.

Here is Larry's own account of this fearful audition, with Frank La Forge himself accompanying, for the Metropolitan Opera Company:

> We walked out on the stage. Out of the dark auditorium came a voice: "What will he sing?"

La Forge, at the piano where he was to play my accompaniment, cleared his throat and said hopefully, "The prologue from *Pagliacci*."

"Didn't he bring anything else?" said the voice wearily.

We had lost our first battle. La Forge put the music for the prologue aside and opened "Eri tu."

In the beginning there is a high F sharp. My voice cracked on it. My knees were shaking as I struggled through the aria.

"Sing something else," the voice said.

I sang Valentin's aria from *Faust*.

"Thank you," came from the blackness of the auditorium.[4]

After such an audition at the Metropolitan, most supplicants would have been cast into the outer darkness. But in Larry's case, destiny played a role in the persons of La Forge and Alda, the willful wife of Gatti.

Three weeks passed after the audition with no word from the opera house. La Forge decided to act. He telephoned Alda and asked her to hear Larry sing. Wheels turned. (It must be said, incidentally, that Alda was ever susceptible to the attentions of an attractive man.) Larry was summoned to the Met for a second audition. On this occasion the baritone was not afflicted by nerves and was able to show his best. By now he knew how it felt to stand on that bare stage and thrust his voice out into the dark, vast cave. He sang Iago's Credo from Verdi's *Otello*. This time the reaction was no bodiless "thank you" from the darkness, but the offer of a contract.

All the ambitions of this brash, unpolished young singer from a frontier town in California, a singer who had never sung with any opera company anywhere, seemed to have been realized. His dangerous risk in borrowing the money to advance himself in "the music center of the world" had paid off—perhaps. After all, when the Credo was finished, Larry had been congratulated by none other than the famous baritone Antonio Scotti. He had not recognized the man, but La Forge identified his admirer for him.[5]

Giulio Gatti-Casazza was a large, magisterial figure who was known for his shrewd business sense. When he was quite young, Giuseppe Verdi, by then an old man, had advised him that the only successfully managed opera house was a full opera house. Gatti's financial astuteness included driving the hardest of deals with his artists. Even in the boom years of the mid-1920s, he had the foresight to build up a large reserve of funds for emergencies. This fiscal attitude proved extraordinarily prescient, for when the stock market crash of 1929 sent shock waves through America's economy and opera seemed an extravagance that few could still afford, the Met had some "savings" upon which it could draw.

Consequently, when Gatti offered Larry the long-dreamed-for contract, the contract that would solve all of Larry's financial problems, he named a salary of only $200 a month! Larry was shocked. Fifty dollars a week! How could he support a wife and two children in the most expensive city in America on such a small sum? Stunned, the singer drew back, saying that he would have to consider the matter.

Again, the wily La Forge asked Alda to intervene with her general manager–husband. Fifty dollars a week was a starvation wage. Could it not be raised to sixty? Reluctantly, Gatti agreed, and the contract was signed on 8 May 1923 by Larry and Gatti to run 23 weeks, from 5 November 1923 to 13 April 1924 "inclusive," but the artist must appear 14 days before the season's engagement for rehearsals at half salary.

From today's point of view, it is a strange document, now housed in the Archives of the Metropolitan Opera. The Company is bound to do little more than pay the agreed sum, supply costumes but not "gloves, feathers, wigs, tights, boots, shoes, and similar items," and notify the artist of the repertoire. The artist, however, is responsible for everything, including any claims resulting from an injury on stage. A series of deductions are taken for certain infractions, including reimbursing the Company for a replacement, even in the case of the artist's dying during a performance. In a codicil to the contract, signed separately, the 11 rules of the Metropolitan Opera Company are set forth, including number 8, "It is forbidden to attend rehearsals on the stage with canes, cloaks, or hats," and number 9, "Smoking is prohibited in the Opera House and no alcoholic drinks shall be brought into the Opera House."

Larry was to be responsible for 28 roles, most of them *comprimario* parts to be sure, but also the leading roles of Amonasro in *Aida*, Escamillo in *Carmen*, Valentin in *Faust*, the Herald in *Lohengrin*, and Silvio in *Pagliacci*. Additionally, the major bass role of King Dodon in Rimsky-Korsakov's *Coq d'or* was listed, as was the first-act bass role of the Marquis in *La forza del destino*. Failure to appear in these roles on demand would result in a substantial financial loss to the artist.

In August 1923, little more than a year after he left California, Lawrence Tibbet "of the Metropolitan Opera Company" headed west for concerts in the Hollywood Bowl and his operatic debut, as Amonasro in *Aida* on 20 September. Grace and the three-and-a-half-year-old twins would accompany him back to New York. Some suspected that he finally brought Grace and the twins to be with him in New York to forestall gossip about his behavior with women, but whatever the motivation, Grace was overjoyed. She spent hectic days packing bedding, blankets, and the family's clothing, as well as her books and her husband's record collection. She dispatched box after box to New York, never dreaming that years would pass before she could afford to redeem them from the warehouse. The cost of freight and storage nearly emptied their bank account. As Grace recalled years later:

> We went to New York with sentimental baggage and an armful of offspring. Since Larry was now experienced in New York matters, he spent most of the time on the train preparing us mentally and spiritually for what he knew I would have to go through in the greatest of cities.[6]

Yet how much could he prepare Grace when he himself was still a maverick, an inexperienced Westerner in "the greatest of cities"?

The first performance of Mussorgsky's *Boris Godunov* in the 1923–24 season was a matinée, 24 November. Boris was sung by Fedor Chaliapin, perhaps the greatest interpreter the role has ever known. Among the large cast were José Mardones as Pimen, Mario Chamlee as the False Dimitri, and Margarete Matzenauer as Marina. In the audience for Larry's debut were Grace, his mentor Frank La Forge, and his close friends Reginald Pole and Beatrice Wood. Not completely lost in the last-act Kromy Forest was the wandering Jesuit monk Lovitsky: Larry, his one scene sung only in Latin. He was not even on the stage at the same time as Chaliapin.[7]

His debut had presented him with a new name. "Tibbet" was misprinted as "Tibbett" in the program, and he decided to retain that spelling for himself and his family. Thereafter, "Lawrence Tibbett" was to appear in Metropolitan programs in New York and on tour for 27 seasons: 602 times in 49 roles. In spite of his eventual mega-star status worldwide, he was never an occasional guest on that stage, but remained a Metropolitan house artist for his entire career.

Four days after this inconspicuous first appearance, his career took an unexpected turn. For his first season at the Met, the baritone had expected to gain experience on the huge stage by performing the small *comprimario* roles traditionally given to green newcomers. This was the advice he had been given by many people, and it was good advice. With his usual brashness, however, and because he wanted to make himself seem more important and valuable to the management, he had listed the leading baritone role of Valentin in Gounod's *Faust* as part of his repertoire. Although he knew and had sung Valentin's opening aria, his claim to know the complete role was an outright falsehood that almost immediately caught him out.

On Wednesday, 28 November, the opera house called Larry to tell him that the Spanish baritone Vincente Ballester, the Valentin scheduled for *Faust* that coming Friday, had canceled because of illness, and Larry was expected to replace him.

In a panic, Larry rushed to Wilfred Pelletier, then an assistant conductor at the Met, and confessed his canard. Pelletier had perceived the promise in the baritone's voice and liked the lanky young man, but with only two days to go before the performance, he knew it would not be easy to teach him the role. Larry was not yet a "quick study," nor did he have a particularly retentive memory. Another problem was his inexperience in singing a complete role in French. And then there was his lack of practical operatic stage experience.[8]

For the next 48 hours, aided by endless pots of coffee, Pelletier drilled this reckless but appealing young singer. The role of Valentin, though not long, is an important one, and the character is very visible when he is onstage. He appears in only two scenes: in the first he has a short recitative and the aria "Avant de quitter ces lieux," and then he leads the Chorus of the Swords; in the second he has a trio with Faust and Mephistopheles, then a grand death scene ending with a chilling curse on his sister, Marguerite.

The aria was indeed under his belt, albeit in his and La Forge's way, not the Metropolitan conductor's, but to learn the ensembles without the other singers and with only piano accompaniment in the little time remaining was a real challenge. To make matters worse, Larry did not know the staging: where Valentin *should* be, where all the others, the principals and the chorus, *would* be, on that great stage. During the previous season, the Met had presented only two performances of *Faust*, and it is doubtful that Larry had attended either of them, although La Forge could have procured tickets for him. No dress rehearsal was scheduled for such a familiar work, which was lucky perhaps, for Larry would have had even less time to concentrate on his role.

On the evening of 30 November 1923, less than a week after Larry's debut, the curtain went up on a bizarre performance. In the cast of this *Faust* were three of the company's most celebrated stars: as Méphisto, Chaliapin; as Faust, the handsome tenor Giovanni Martinelli in the prime of his career; and as the demure Marguerite, Larry's operatic "godmother," Frances Alda.

As his first scene commenced, Larry stood in the wings terrified. Everything about his quickly supplied costume suffocated him: his dun-colored jacket, his pants, his boots. His hands, somewhere in wide-brimmed gloves, were soaked with perspiration. In his makeup of bobbed black wig, false mustache, and goatee, he did not seem to be himself. A long trick sword dangled at his side, and in one hand he clutched the "sainte medaille," the medal to which he first sings, given to Valentin by Marguerite to protect him in battle. Indeed, Larry felt embattled as the choristers—villagers, students, burghers young and old, matrons and maidens—gathered onstage to celebrate the Kermesse, the village fair.

In the pit, conductor Louis Hasselmans, who had been apprised of the situation by Pelletier, was ready for anything. The tall, manly looking Valentin strode onstage, followed by the smaller, less manly looking Siebel (mezzo-soprano Ellen Dalossy in the "trouser role"), who was in love with Marguerite. Hasselmans gave Larry his cue, and the introductory recitative began. The aria, Valentin's prayer for heaven to protect Marguerite while he is off to war, follows immediately. Requiring no stage movement, just beautiful singing, it went extremely well. From then on, however, all was peril.

Clad in vivid scarlet, Chaliapin sang his Calf of Gold aria (and repeated part of it[9]), cynically extolling the worship of Mammon. Larry was so fascinated by the Russian's theatrical magic that he nearly forgot his own problems.

Next, with a flourish, the Fiend struck the inn sign in the form of a large cask, and wine flowed to the feigned amazement of the villagers. "As soon as Chaliapin toasts Marguerite," hissed Siebel/Dalossy to Larry, "run toward him with your sword before you."

Mephistopheles sardonically raised his glass of wine in a salute to the maligned Marguerite, and Valentin obediently dashed forward with sword drawn to avenge the insult to his sister. Here Méphisto draws a magic circle about himself with his own sword, and with his weapon he breaks Valentin's sword in half. This leads into the choral scene, the first of Valentin's three ensembles. Chaliapin eyed Larry warily. Would the newcomer release the snap that separates Valentin's sword into two parts at the right time? Tibbett did, and the Russian was so relieved that this time he danced his triumphant jig around the baritone.

A chorister, perched in an artificial tree above Larry, hissed, "Make the cross, make the cross!" Tibbett quickly turned his broken sword around and extended the cruciform hilt toward the towering bass. The soldiers followed suit, and faced with the phalanx of dreaded crosses, Mephistopheles cowered, his evil powers thwarted. Larry's part of the act was safely over, and he exited the stage.

Valentin's other act was still to come, and Larry rushed to his dressing room to review the score. He felt more secure, realizing that his colleagues would continue to offer help on the stage, and with their aid he completed the performance with no major gaffes. The duel with Faust had to be improvised, which must have been interesting: an Italian tenor versus a young American who grew up seeing Hollywood films. Luckily for Larry, when a character finally dies, he is required only to lie still on the ground.

Francis Robinson, then director of the Met's press bureau and unofficial company historian, could not recall a performance in which the chorus had so actively helped a leading singer who was in dire trouble. The choristers had averted certain disaster for the 27-year-old Californian who had come into their midst only six days earlier. They had prompted him by throwing him lines from the treetops, from behind a canvas church, from any point from which they could do so inconspicuously. This generous help from the choristers, as well as from the official prompter seated forward under the center of the stage, was a tribute to the effect of Larry's personality on those around him, even those who had known him for only a short time.[10]

Due appreciation was shown Larry in the next day's *New York Times*; music critic Olin Downes had evidently not realized the baritone's handicaps that evening and credited the American artist—a "tall, spare figure of youth and modest demeanor"—with having two moments in the spotlight as Valentin. Larry's French was pronounced clear and the quality of his voice fine and fresh, although Downes hoped he would learn to better project it into the far reaches of the Metropolitan house.[11]

A week later Larry sang Valentin again. This time he was prepared. He had learned his lesson, and in later years not only was he always prepared, he proved the most helpful of colleagues to those who were unsure of *their* staging. Soprano Rose Bampton, among others, noted that Larry could anticipate that a fellow singer was going to feel insecure at a certain moment and would be there with help when needed.[12]

That first season the baritone learned many lessons as he performed the smaller roles of Marullo in *Rigoletto*, Fléville in *Andrea Chénier*, the Herald in Primo Riccitelli's *I Compagnacci*, and the Marquis d'Obigny in *La Traviata*. In further performances of *Boris* he graduated to the role of Tchelkalov (only slightly longer than his original Lovitsky, but at least he could now watch Chaliapin die). And he learned the important difference between performing in opera and performing in song recitals.

During those years, the Metropolitan presented popularly priced Sunday night concerts with its house artists and with instrumental greats such as violinist Efrem Zimbalist, cellist Pablo Casals, and pianist Vladimir de Pachmann, offering a wide range of selections. On one Sunday evening in December 1923, Larry sang Valentin's familiar aria, and on another Sunday a month later, he sang the role of the High Priest in Act One of Saint-Saëns's *Samson et Dalila*. The following month found him participating in a special performance to benefit Gatti's Metropolitan Emergency Fund, at which he sang Escamillo in the fourth act of *Carmen*. All these appearances were invaluable in honing the operatic and theatrical skills of the young baritone during his first year with an opera company.

In this period Larry also learned much about life backstage: the clash of artistic temperaments and the bitterness of professional rivalries. He saw how jealously baritones such as Scotti, de Luca, and Danise guarded their roles. He learned well. Years later he admitted that he had not allowed Leonard Warren to do to him in *Falstaff* what he had done to "old" Scotti in his own breakthrough appearance.[13]

By the end of his first season with the Met, Larry found that he loved performing in opera. Opera is drama, and he was an actor; opera is music, and it allowed him to express eloquent emotions as a singer. In short, singing at the Metropolitan became the focus of his theatrical career. No matter how often he sang throughout the world, no matter how many millions would hear his voice over the radio, on records, and in the movies, every autumn at the beginning of the opera season, as surely as the birds wing south, he returned to his beloved Met.

Meanwhile, Grace's exciting new life in New York City was in sharp contrast to her life at La Crescenta. Her days and evenings were now crammed with tea parties, theater parties, and dinner parties. The delights of the city went to her head. She set out on one shopping spree after another, though she could ill afford them on her husband's salary of $60 a week. She had quickly established her own circle of friends, including Helen Pole (Reginald Pole's first wife) and Elinor Warren (James Warren's talented daughter), women of high intellect with whom she met nearly every day.

They lunched at Schrafft's, the Stage Door Inn, and other restaurants in the theater district. Often they took in a show. Grace could not get enough of theater. At least three times a week, accompanied by one or two of her friends, she would go to the Met to hear Larry or take in a play or a musical, relatively expensive events.

On 12 February 1924, after debuting as Escamillo in *Carmen* at the Metropolitan, Larry came home feeling ill. Grace at first thought it was a simple case of the flu. Two days later Larry was so sick that he had to be taken to St. Luke's Hospital, where the physicians were unable to determine the exact nature of his illness. For several days Larry lay in bed, moaning and tossing with fever, while Grace could do little but wait and worry. Helen Pole remained close to Grace, lending her support. Telegrams arrived from Larry's mother and sister, and also from James Warren. On Sunday, 17 February, Larry's fever broke as suddenly as it had come, and he quickly recovered. The cause of the illness remained a mystery.

A week later, La Forge gave a party for a group of singers from the Met, and Grace, relieved by her husband's continuing recovery, accepted an invitation to attend. When she returned home, she found an envelope in her purse containing $200. Although the envelope was unmarked, Grace, in tears, guessed that the money was from La Forge. She was correct.[14] That sum, plus a loan of $300 from Rupert Hughes, enabled Larry to pay his hospital and medical bills and to set off by train for California for recuperation and rest in the sun.

Larry's financial problems were to plague him well into his career. Between Gatti's parsimonious treatment and Grace's extravagances, Larry became dependent on loans and handouts for many years. A letter from Larry to "Jimmy," dated 18 June 1927, included a repayment of $100 that had been due "some four or five years."[15]

His first contract with the Met had given the company an option to renew for three additional years at a salary of $100, $125, and $150 a week for each successive year. For his second year, the Met chose to exercise its option by offering him $75 a week. Larry protested vigorously, and the parties finally compromised on $90 a week. He had learned that the Metropolitan defined the term "option" as its inalienable right to do with him whatever it pleased, and there was as yet no singers' union to contest Gatti's sovereign decisions.

Given the financial responsibilities of supporting a family and maintaining a working career, which included constant coaching and learning of new repertoire as well as acquiring wigs, shoes, and other miscellaneous accoutrements at his own expense to complete the costumes of his various roles, the still unknown Tibbett could hardly have afforded to quit the Met, even if he considered it in anger.

In November 1924, his second season at the Metropolitan, Larry added the role of Schlemil in Offenbach's *The Tales of Hoffmann* to his repertoire. It is a small character part, but Larry was noticed in a cast that included the soprano Lucrezia Bori, the lyric tenor Miguel Fleta, and baritone Giuseppe de Luca. Larry also sang another Valentin and another Silvio, and he appeared in a Sunday evening concert at which he first sang Wolfram's Song to the Evening Star from *Tannhäuser*. Wolfram would become one of Larry's most beautifully realized portrayals.

The New Year turned, and on its second evening, 2 January 1925, Larry sang Ford in *Falstaff*.

At the old Metropolitan Opera House, late in autumn 1924, a problem arose during the preparation of the gala revival of Giuseppe Verdi's comic opera, *Falstaff*. Ballester, the same baritone whose illness had presented Larry with the opportunity to sing his first Valentin, was again ill. He had been cast for the important role of Ford but was forced to drop out.

Verdi's last opera is a complicated ensemble opera with as many as nine soloists singing at the same time; at one point, the men sing in one meter while the women scheme in another. Ballester's withdrawal dealt a serious blow to the rehearsals under renowned conductor Tullio Serafin and left a distinct gap in the cast—a gap, moreover, which appeared far from mended when Gatti-Casazza announced that the Ford in the Met's future would be Lawrence Tibbett, the obscure young baritone who had joined the company only the previous season.

Gatti had first consulted with his wife about Larry's ability to assume the role, possibly because she was also going to be in the cast. Larry was at the time on a tour with Alda, and she wired Gatti that Larry could definitely do it. She immediately started coaching him in the role.[16]

Serafin had been struck by the resonant beauty of the young singer's voice and the intuitively dramatic manner in which he moved about the stage. Nonetheless, Larry was inexperienced, especially when compared to the rest of the cast, which included some of the most celebrated operatic stars of the era: Antonio Scotti, the superb singing actor whose 25 years with the Metropolitan was being honored by this *Falstaff* revival; the honey-voiced superstar tenor Beniamino Gigli; the beloved soprano Lucrezia Bori; and the imposing Alda. Marion Telva was to appear in the mezzo character role of Dame Quickly. To sing with such luminaries, each supremely self-confident and each boasting legions of fans, was a nerve-wracking ordeal for a still insecure young artist afflicted with an unsure musical memory.

The rehearsals began. The stage directions were given in Italian then translated for the Westerner, who—an appalling fact to his European colleagues—had never set foot on Italian soil! Larry also required extra coaching from Serafin. Feeling inferior in such company and faced with a score of such complexity, he made numerous mistakes.

Work slowed, and tensions mounted. The stage director, William von Wymetal, by necessity gave a great deal of time and attention to Larry. Gigli and Scotti amused themselves by making snide remarks about the young baritone until Larry, correctly surmising what they were saying in Italian and beside himself with rage, threatened to sock Scotti. The grand old man then threw a tantrum and walked off the stage.[17]

A conference was hastily called with Gatti, the conductor, the director, and two assistant managers. Should Larry be allowed to continue? Had anyone else on the roster been available for the role, the answer would probably have been replacement, but since no one was available, and since Gatti was loath to bring in an expensive artist from outside the company, Larry stayed.

The afternoon before the premiere, Larry and Grace went out to lunch. Despite his musical mistakes and seeming ineptitude onstage during the rehearsal period, the baritone declared, "You know, Grace, I've worked Ford to the *death*. If I don't hit the bell this time, we might as well pack up and head back to California."[18]

Opening night was 2 January 1925. Scotti was gracious to the beginner that evening, visiting Larry in his dressing room before the curtain to help him adjust his forked crêpe-hair beard. As the two baritones stood together, they presented a study in contrasts. Larry was taller, with a round, almost cherubic face, while Scotti had a jutting chin and a proud Roman nose. The famous Italian baritone loved American cigarettes and smoked them constantly. Sensing Larry's nervousness, he sought to relax him with one off-color joke after another.

The lights in the opera house dimmed. Maestro Serafin, for whom *Falstaff* had also been revived, strode briskly into the orchestra pit, bowed to the welcoming applause, and raised his baton. The opera has no overture, not even a prelude, so the massive gold curtains flew swiftly apart on the skittering opening notes, revealing the Garter Inn, Falstaff's habitual watering hole.

Although the role of Ford is subordinate to that of Falstaff, Ford appears in all but one scene and has an extended, very exposed aria. Only in the first scene of Act Two does he figure prominently, when the bubbling comedy suddenly turns darkly serious as Ford launches into the monologue that begins "È sogno? O realtà?" (Is it a dream, or truth?).

What preceded Ford's outburst had been frothy and lighthearted. Now Ford, the husband of Alice, masquerading as Signor Fontana, has no idea that the Merry Wives are scheming to make a fool out of the absurdly vain Sir John Falstaff. In his own *amour-propre*, Ford is sure that Alice is out to betray *him*. Instantly, the comic gives way to the most primal of human emotions, jealousy, that same marital jealousy that Verdi summoned with such intensity and torment in his earlier *Otello*.

Provided that the Ford is a first-rate artist, the audience is now gripped by near-tragic passions, unique in an evening that is otherwise irresistibly upbeat, and that ends with the whole cast facing the footlights in a fugue that begins "Tutto nel mondo è burla" (Everything in the world is a joke).

The time came for Larry, and what occurred was one of those extraordinary moments that can take place only in an opera house. Falstaff exited to change into his elaborate wooing outfit. "È sogno?" Larry began, and in the words of veteran critic Oscar Thompson, he "took fire. He sang like a demon possessed. He hammered the table angrily and threw down a cup so hard that it smashed into a multitude of pieces. Unlike most singers, Tibbett did not look at the conductor or prompter for directions. Instead, his gestures and his singing had a freedom that only veterans acquire. His passionate voice startled the audience and held it spellbound."[19]

Larry later wrote: "In my aria in the second act I tore my heart out. . . . I went through the scene with terrific desperation, power, and abandon."[20]

"Authoritative. Magnetic," declared critic Lawrence Gilman in the next day's *New York Herald Tribune*. "[He] took the audience completely captive."[21]

After the brief comic exchange that finishes the scene, the curtains closed, and there began one of the most unprecedented and certainly unpremeditated ovations in the history of the Metropolitan Opera. Scotti, Telva, Giovanni Paltrinieri (the Bardolph), Adamo Didur (the Pistol), and Tibbett came before the curtain to acknowledge the applause. Since that evening's performance honored the much-loved Scotti singing the title role, the veteran then appeared alone before the curtain. As that is usually enough between scenes in an act, Serafin raised his baton to begin the next scene, but in the darkened house the beating of frenzied hands, the excited clamor, continued without letup.

Larry had gone upstairs to change his costume. Although he knew that he had done well, working out some pent-up aggressions in his aria, he assumed that the continuing ovation was entirely for Scotti. In his little second baritone's dressing room two flights above the stage, he could hear the stamping of feet from the auditorium, but not the cries of "Tibbett! Tibbett!"

Angelo Cassamassa, dresser for the male artists, came running up the stairs with a message that Gatti wanted to see Larry at once. Could Larry have done something wrong? Had he displeased the general manager? He hurried down the iron staircase and could now hear the roar of applause but still thought it was for Scotti. At the foot of the stairs stood Gatti, looking not at all pleased that the spotlight for the incomparable Italian had been stolen by the upstart American. There was nothing for it, however. He pointed to the stage and, in his usual broken English, told Larry to get out there—alone.

Momentarily taken aback, Larry quickly recovered and walked out before the house. Seeing him again, uncertain and modest, the huge audience rose to its feet with a roar, applauding even louder.

Writing in *The Glory Road*, Larry remembered:

> Alone I stepped out in front of that audience, the audience that had come to cheer Scotti. A thundering wave of applause and cheers smashed me in the face. I almost fainted. I still get goose flesh all over my body when I think of it. Thirty-five hundred persons had their eyes on me. They were cheering *me*! Not Scotti, nor Alda, nor Bori, nor Gigli, nor Kathleen Howard [the Meg Page], but ME! There's no thrill in the world like that![22]

Of that 16-and-a-half-minute show-stopping ovation, Oscar Thompson wrote in *The American Singer*:

> The demonstration at the close of the scene went into the Metropolitan annals as among the historic ones . . . much as the greater one for Jean de Reszke in the *Lohengrin* performance (Dec. 3, 1900) that marked his return to the Metropolitan after his reported breakdown. Tom Bull, the veteran doorkeeper who kept the time of both performances, told the writer that there was really no comparison between the two ovations, that accorded Jean de Reszke actually lengthening the first act of *Lohengrin* by a full half hour. But Jean de Reszke was the idol of opera. The slim young man, hiding his smooth face behind Ford's Elizabethan beard, was almost a stranger.[23]

This was the added ingredient that made the 3500 people in the audience rise excitedly to such a communal frenzy: they were present at the discovery of a remarkable artist and a great future star.

In 1978, in conversation with her biographer James A. Drake, Rosa Ponselle mused about that dramatic evening:

> That incident in *Falstaff* does Tibbett a disservice, in my opinion. There are two things that bother me about that story. For one thing, it makes it sound like Tibbett never had to work hard. You'd think he got the role of Ford by just walking in off the street and having it handed to him. No work, no study, just dumb luck. The other thing that bothers me is, it makes it sound like Tibbett also didn't have to work hard after *Falstaff*, either. You get the impression that the Metropolitan just handed him all these roles, one right after the other, and he sang them, and everybody lived happily ever after. But Tibbett worked very, very hard. I sang with him, so I know. You can't create characters and sing the way that Tibbett did without very, very hard work.
>
> To me, what the *Falstaff* story shows is that if Scotti was professional, he would have brought Tibbett out with him. No one in the audience would have made much of it, because their performances as Falstaff and Ford depended on one another. Bringing Tibbett out for a curtain call would have been the natural thing to do. Scotti made a big mistake that night. That performance was his undoing.[24]

After the performance Larry, Grace, and La Forge left the opera house and walked across Broadway to Child's Restaurant for dinner. They were too emotionally drained to say very much. Finally, with a wan smile, La Forge remarked, "I think you'll get some pretty good notices."

"I hope they do more than to say I was 'adequate.'"[25]

Larry and Grace stopped at a telegraph office to wire the good news to his mother in Los Angeles, and then they went home to bed.

The next day throughout the country the press coverage of Larry's triumph was ecstatic. The *New York Times* decided it was a front-page story and ran it with the headline "American Baritone Stirs Opera House."[26] Every review was exuberantly positive.

Before eight a.m. the next morning the doorbell rang at the Tibbett apartment. To her shock, Grace, answering in a robe and curlers, found a dozen photographers and reporters on the threshold. She ran to waken the new star of the Metropolitan Opera, who frantically stuffed himself into some clothes. Grace could find only a black velveteen dress with inappropriately long sleeves. The twins, puffy-eyed with sleep, were quickly made presentable.

At eight-thirty that morning, the Tibbett family met the press, interrupted by the continuous ringing of the telephone and the delivery of congratulatory telegrams. A crew from Fox Movietone News arrived later that day and took the family to Central Park, where the Tibbett twins threw snowballs and rode their sleds as cameras turned and clicked.

Larry sent Alda flowers and a thank-you note for her invaluable assistance. But she later heard from Adamo Didur that Larry refused to return to her tour as, with this publicity, he now could make $1000 a night rather than the $200 a week that she was paying him.[27] The board of the Metropolitan, led by Otto Kahn, sent Larry a letter of congratulations for his success.[28] In subsequent performances of *Falstaff*, Larry was given a solo curtain call after his aria at the scene break. The audience expected it.

Soprano Bidú Sayão's husband, the baritone and vocal teacher Giuseppe Danise, often spoke to her of Larry in later years. "He always told me about the Ford. He said that Tibbett had started his career in that moment."[29]

In the next month Larry received more than a thousand letters. His life story had been broadcast throughout the European operatic world, his success reported by newspapers in many languages. Managers appeared with immense offers, as much as $3000 a concert, which the Tibbetts regarded skeptically. Curiously, they paid more attention to a casual note that arrived a week after the baritone's triumph and made no reckless promises. It came from the management firm of Lawrence Evans and Jack Salter.

"My partner, Salter, and I enjoyed your performance of Ford immensely. If there is anything we can do for you, please let us know."[30]

Evans and Salter had started out as impresarios in Atlanta and had been taken up in 1918 by the diva Amelita Galli-Curci. Her previous manager, Charles L. Wagner, had been accused of embezzling thousands of dollars from her.[31] To replace Wagner, Galli-Curci offered the young men her complete management contract (100 concerts a year at $5000 an appearance) if they would move to New York, which they did. Evans and Salter always represented a small but highly select roster: under the simple rubric "Managers," their 1927 letterhead tastefully listed Galli-Curci, Schipa, Rethberg, Tibbett, and Lhévinne. Three years later, Lhévinne was off the list, and only Homer and Menuhin, then 14 years old, had been added.[32] In 1930 they joined four other concert management concerns to form Columbia Artists Management, which began business as a conglomerate on the first day of the next year.[33] In early 1939, Evans and Salter added soprano Dorothy Maynor to their list.[34]

Larry, aware that whomever he chose to manage him could make or break his career, decided to meet with Evans and Salter. When the two men faced Larry in his living room, they impressed him as being shrewd, sharp, and knowledgeable.

Evans asked in his boldly direct manner, "What do you think, Mr. Tibbett, that you are worth right now as a concert artist?"

Taken aback, the singer stammered that he had been offered $3000 for an appearance. Smiling tolerantly, Evans replied, "My partner and I tend to be conservative in such matters. We do not feel that at this time you are worth more than $750 a performance. It's our desire to take you under our management with the understanding that we'll build your career gradually."[35]

There was something both frank and confident about Evans's manner that impressed Larry. Grace, who had considerable influence with her husband, concurred. At the end of the meeting, the young baritone signed a long-term contract with Evans and Salter, a decision he never regretted. Evans became Larry's manager and business advisor for many years, as well as a close and valued friend.[36]

And so, on the strength of one short dramatic scene in an infrequently performed opera, a legendary career began, fashioned not solely in the opera house but on the concert stage, in film, over the airwaves, and in the recording studio. Still, financial success did not come easily for Larry. Despite all the publicity over his rocketing to recognition in *Falstaff*, he did not become a wealthy man overnight. Though he did gain important personal management, he was locked into his Metropolitan Opera contract for two more years. Chafe as he might, he had to finish out this season with a raise of $100 a week, plus a bonus for the four remaining Fords. The performances previously scheduled for him, even the tiny roles, remained.

Those performances included three more secondary but still important Silvios. But it was demeaning for a baritone heralded by all for greatness to still sing the few measures of Morales in *Carmen* or the few lines of the Marquis d'Obigny in *La Traviata*. Larry also appeared in six Sunday evening concerts. He sang "Eri tu" and the *Pagliacci* Prologue, and in one Sunday concert he was able to get the feel of the elder Germont in the gambling scene of *La Traviata*. At another, he performed "Song of the Flea." Gatti's approach to his young new star was conservative and in some respects Evans and Salter were equally so. They did not feel that Larry was ready for a full-out concert career.

But in April, Larry did sing a concert at Carnegie Hall, and included a song composed by Elinor Warren to a poem by Grace. The song was "My Parting Gift" (which was recorded by tenor Frederick Jagel for Victor in 1935). The *Salt Lake City Tribune* of 6 April 1925 told of Larry's singing Grace's song in an article headlined "Salt Lake Girl Attains Dream," adding that the concert was filled "to the back rows." The story also recapped Larry's recent success in *Falstaff*.[37]

That spring, Grace and the twins preceded Larry to Los Angeles. There she was featured with a front-page photograph and two-column interview about her husband's success in the 9 May 1925 *Los Angeles Morning Times* and was guest of honor at the Women's Lyric Club Ball. These were good times for Grace: reflected glory perhaps, but good nevertheless.

Chapter 4

THE BEGINNING OF FAME AND JANE

On 1 June 1925, following the end of the Metropolitan season, Larry returned to Bakersfield, a local boy who had made good. Even if the Met continued to treat him like a junior employee, his hometown welcomed him as a hero.

Driving from Hollywood with Grace, his mother, and his sons in a borrowed Buick touring car, he stopped to see an uncle and his maternal grandmother, then continued on to Lebec, California, his mother's birthplace. When they arrived in Bakersfield, he and the family visited the small house where he was born. His mother wept. He did not visit his father's grave.

All this was dutifully reported in the local press.[1] This was gratifying to "the star," which was how he was regarded in this territory. Like visiting royalty, he participated in a groundbreaking ceremony for the new Community Hotel, and he was guest of honor at a large luncheon, where he was introduced with some imagination as the "Abe Lincoln of Song."

At the banquet, Larry gave a speech in praise of the town where his father had been murdered and belittled the great metropolis where he would choose to live for the rest of his life:

> People talk a lot about New York, but it isn't America. It's American least of all. It's just a great big market place! Here people live—real people. It is places like this that Americans will have to

depend on for the foundations of their lives. . . . Many of the cities of the Northeast are too foreign.[2]

That evening he gave a recital at the local Hippodrome Theater, and his hometown audience went wild.

On this trip west Larry looked up some of his old chums, many of whom belonged to a Los Angeles men's social club called The Bohemians, the first of its kind in Southern California. The members included Lloyd Wright, son of the famous architect and himself an architect; Merle Armitage, manager of the Los Angeles Opera Company; and Richard Day, an art director for United Artists Films. The friends met at various hotels and restaurants. One evening Larry created a commotion when he and a crony turned continued unwanted attentions to some of the waitresses.

Larry always found it great to be among his pals, for they were, after all, men, who demanded—and returned—his loyalty and respect. Women, on the other hand, were fair game to Larry; his attitude, for the most part, was that they were there for his gratification. Since he was tall, handsome, and possessed of that passionate singing voice, yearning young ladies often boldly sought him out. He took his pleasures when and where they presented themselves.

His huge success at the Metropolitan had instantly projected him into the exclusive world of New York society and its women, who were unlike any he had known before. One of his new acquaintances was the youthful Vera Cravath, daughter of Paul D. Cravath, an eminent lawyer and member of the board of directors of the Met. (Later, as the wife of William Francis Gibbs, designer of the liner *United States*, she would serve on the Metropolitan board herself.) Vera Cravath conceived a teenlike crush on Larry, as did a number of her friends, and he found himself invited to parties in the city's loftiest social circles.

Even Vera Cravath's mother fell victim to the Lawrence Tibbett fad, never missing one of his performances and always collecting him backstage to take him to some soirée at which bootleg liquor flowed. Increasingly, Agnes Huntington Cravath and Larry attracted attention together. Neither showed any concern for their spouses, their children, or the consequences of their behavior, but then it was a time when few paid much attention to proprieties.

A liaison, if one is lucky, has practical advantages. In his memoir, Larry credits Mrs. Cravath, who had been on the stage, with teaching him the correct way to take curtain calls:

> "You're popping out and in," she said. "Stand still when you get out there. Let them see you! Look at each person in the opera house and make him think you're a good friend of his. And, after you step back, don't wait until they *demand* your presence. When the applause seems to be dying, take another bow!"[3]

But when Larry was finished with a personal companion, for whatever reason, it appears that he was finished forever. Testifying to this trait are the sharp recollections of Helen Moss, the pianist and coach with whom he had studied so intensely when he first came to New York:

> While I had found working with him a truly wonderful experience that I shall cherish as long as I live, and his voice—still—enthralls me as much as it did long ago, Lawrence was no paragon of virtue. I do believe he had serious flaws in his character. For example, while he was commendably ambitious, he did have a way of shutting the door to anyone—including myself—who helped him on the way up. He shamefully neglected his wife and children in California. I read his autobiography in *American Magazine* and discovered to my chagrin that he never once mentioned my name or my hard work for him at all!
>
> Another thing about Lawrence. He was constantly trying to become part of high society. I believe he was ambitious for the Met primarily for what it could bring him in the way of money and glamor. He constantly buddied up to the leading musical personalities of the day. I was told that after his success in *Falstaff*, he became the darling of New York society, and that he went completely feral after things opened up for him.
>
> When he became famous, his wit and talent made him much sought after. He would sing anywhere, anytime. A music critic whose name eludes me now once told me that it made him sad to see how Lawrence messed up his life: personally, he was brilliant, but entirely too avaricious for his own good.
>
> I'll never forget when he came to Hartford for a concert five years after I married. Even though we had not been in contact at all, I had a glimmering of hope that he would personally invite me to the concert. But never a word from him. I was so angry and disenchanted! Nevertheless, when he came to Bushnell Hall, I went backstage to see him. He was so stunning in his tails, wide wing collar, and waistcoat that he quite took my breath away.
>
> "How nice of you to come," he murmured formally, as though I was just another of his admirers.
>
> During all the time I worked for—and with—Lawrence, en-

> tirely without fee or remuneration from him, he never once, by word or deed, acknowledged his appreciation to me. He had earned some money singing in churches, certainly enough to have invited me out for an inexpensive meal once in a while, instead of always presuming on my family for meals. He could have invited me to a concert occasionally, instead of depending upon me to obtain tickets, or given me a token Christmas gift—just to show his awareness of all my efforts for him. But I cannot recall even a "Thank you, Helen!"
>
> Oh, yes! Lawrence did invite me out *once*, after a concert at Aeolian Hall, *for an ice cream soda*![4]

Larry's callow treatment of Helen Moss was not an isolated incident. He similarly rejected Beatrice Wood after he became famous, in spite of the many earlier efforts of Reginald Pole and Beatrice on his behalf. Larry once arranged for Pole to read Shakespeare to his wealthy New York friends, but his friend was so boring that Larry never again repeated the gesture (which is perhaps understandable). When Beatrice sought to talk over old times with Larry, he chatted amiably about his own concerns and showed absolutely no interest in hers.

Grace meanwhile was pursuing her own interests, and in 1925 she privately published *Word Etchings*, a thin volume of poems. The author's name is given only as Mrs. Lawrence Tibbett, the dedication is "to Lawrence, my husband," and its frontispiece is "a portrait of Mr. Tibbett by Arthur Millier." Despite this auspicious beginning and although it is possible that Grace didn't consciously intend it, Larry doesn't come out too well in the book. Obviously a product of Grace's intense inner life, its pages are filled with poems about nature, babies, and most revealingly, a superabundance of poems concerning unrequited love, many written to a lover who is somewhere else. "Love Is Gone" is the title of one poem; "You Do Not Care" is another, and in "Jealousy" Grace laments:

> In my mind I would
> Make you free
> To walk unhampered
> In this world
> Free to feast your gaze
> As long as desired
> On all feminine loveliness.
> In my heart
> I would banish them all

From the Universe
Nail them to crosses
Stand alone in your sight.
What a distance
Lies between
Heart and mind.
I would make you free.[5]

Also in 1925, it appears that New York's high society came to Larry's aid financially. A William M. Sullivan mailed him a list of nine people who had formed a committee and subscribed a total of $5250 to a fund for Larry's assistance. Sullivan suggested in the undated cover letter that Larry send individually written thank-you notes to each, a draft of which he enclosed. The list included a Harriman, Clarence Mackay, and a Crocker. Five of the nine were women.[6]

Financial ease continued to elude the young singer. His reputation was growing and he had many singing engagements, but it was expensive to live the kind of life that Larry lived.

The 1925–26 season at the Metropolitan found Larry singing Ford, the Herald in *Lohengrin*, and Silvio in *Pagliacci*, together with the small role of Fléville in *Andrea Chénier*. He was given the opportunity to enlarge the scope of his repertoire with Ramiro in the premiere of Ravel's small opera *L'Heure espagnole* and was called "a very prince of operatic comedy."[7] In a January Sunday concert he sang Iago's Credo publicly for the first time.

Four evenings after this concert, on 21 January 1926, Larry was offered an opportunity to demonstrate his remarkable vocal and dramatic powers, an opportunity he seized upon with all the ferocity of which he was capable. Earlier that year the Metropolitan had mounted a work by Umberto Giordano, the composer of *Andrea Chénier*, called *La cena delle beffe*, based on Sem Benelli's melodramatic play of the same name. In the cast were Gigli and Alda, but the biggest, most flamboyant role in the opera belonged to the baritone, in this case the great Titta Ruffo. Ruffo sang the first three performances and then left to fulfill engagements in South America. Lawrence Tibbett would now embody the brutal, jealous Neri Chiaramantesi.

To Mme. Alda's near terror, Larry played the part of the Renaissance lover enraged at the faithlessness of his mistress to the hilt. He slapped and pushed her so much more violently than the staging called for that, as she went flying through the door, the man in the wings who had been assigned to catch her, missed. The soprano went sprawling on the floor.

Out front, the audience was impressed by such overwhelming realism. Among the spectators was George Cehanovsky, a consummate artist whose career included 2386 performances with the Metropolitan, predominantly in *comprimario* roles. He recalled that evening of triumph for Larry:

> One day I went to the Met to hear *La cena delle beffe*: at that time it was Titta Ruffo's best opera. But for that performance Tibbett was assigned to replace Ruffo—which I resented. I had never heard of Tibbett before.
>
> When Larry appeared on the stage as Neri, he simply dominated everyone else. He absolutely made Gigli and Alda—who were famous artists in their own right—appear like children. Tibbett was at least six feet tall; Gigli was a short five foot eight, so Tibbett towered over everyone onstage. But that was not all! The way he sang Neri in Italian! It was impossible to believe that Larry had been singing at the Met for only three years!
>
> This, then, was my first experience in hearing Larry Tibbett. After this, I had another chance to hear the same opera with Titta Ruffo, who was not in his best voice. I remember thinking that I preferred Tibbett. At that time I was just a beginning singer at the Met, but even then I felt that Tibbett was going to go places.[8]

Larry, however, was not convinced that he was going forward. Though he sang the Giordano opera three more times, the rest of the season included only more Fords (not, after all, the title role), more Silvios, and another lowly Schlemil. On the spring tour of 1926, however, he was allowed his first full performances of Tonio in *Pagliacci*, Wolfram in *Tannhäuser*, and Mercutio in Gounod's *Roméo et Juliette*, all within nine days.

Others might think that his career had taken off, but Larry knew that he still lacked seniority among the more famous Italian baritones and that Gatti, especially in New York, would continue to favor his countrymen with the choice roles. He had decided that since he was presently prevented from reaching the top of the opera world, he would build his career by touring the country as a recitalist.

Larry's concert career began in earnest in 1925, with bookings arranged for the time periods when he did not have opera commitments. This would, of course, distance himself from Grace and the twins, but

Lawrence Evans, his manager, agreed that Larry was ready for this important change and began actively scheduling concerts for him.

As an art form, recital singing is entirely different from performing in opera. The lone artist on the concert platform enjoys none of the traditional dramatic aids: no costumes, scenery, surging orchestra; no other voices to lend variety to the evening in duets or soaring ensembles. A solitary, vulnerable figure, the vocal recitalist, stands almost motionless in the curve of the piano and, within the space of perhaps three minutes, must establish the mood of each song, create the emotion called for, and tell a complete story. He then moves on to another story, another mood, which he must create anew. He makes few gestures and must not move about unnecessarily. Even a tenor's heels should remain flat on the floor.

All his effects must be accomplished by nuances of the singing voice, exemplary diction, and to a certain extent, subtle facial expression. A successful recital is the result of the highest artistry and can be a profound experience.

The only other participant in a traditional vocal recital is the accompanist, with whom it is vital that the singer have the closest rapport. Evans not only handled Larry's bookings but obtained for him an accompanist who proved ideal. Stewart Wille was a quiet, reserved pianist. He and Larry worked together harmoniously for 20 years, until Wille's hearing began to fail. Larry signed him to an exclusive contract, and Wille also worked with Larry on the baritone's operatic roles.

Although the finest accompanist can often surreptitiously help the vocalist along, the solo artist is in control of the situation. The singer sets the tempo for the music; if there is a major mistake, the piece can even be started again. Singer and accompanist form a simple unit, led by the soloist, whereas opera involves highly complex teamwork by a veritable army of participants and the man gesticulating before the orchestra.

Since only one voice is heard throughout the entire concert, the experienced recitalist will arrange a program that offers a variety of tempos, moods, styles, and if possible, languages. Opera singers will often add an aria or two, since it is expected of them; but for most operatic fare, the piano is a weak substitute for full orchestral accompaniment.

When Larry turned to recital singing, he had to suppress his unique large-stage dramatic talents to some extent. To replace the external gestures of passion, he had to learn the internal ones. *Fortissimos* were not accompanied by arms held wide open, and *mezza voce* had to be almost personally moving to the listener. Larry handled both with astonishing ease. Kurt Weinhold, former president of Columbia Artists Management, described Larry's concert manner:

> Tibbett had an outgoing personality and a unique knack of greeting an audience when he came out—with great self-assurance, a friendly smile. He occasionally said a few words about his songs to ease an audience. He might say something special about an encore. Intimacy was not in Tibbett's nature. He was too exuberant, too dramatic in everything he did. Not only was he a dramatic baritone, but his was a dramatic personality. And he had that enormous knack for making friends with an audience.[9]

Evans and Salter sent ahead a press book to each town in which Larry would appear, to be filled in with the date and place of the concert and to help with newspaper publicity. It was enthusiastic, to say the least:

> LAWRENCE TIBBETT AND HIS AUDIENCES
>
> Holding an audience spellbound, whether it be in an opera aria or a simple song, is the notable achievement of Lawrence Tibbett, famous American baritone, who will be heard here. . . .
>
> There is no grabbing for hats or dragging on of wraps when a Tibbett recital is ended. The trouble is to get the mass of people to leave.
>
> Instead of hurrying from a hall that has rocked with the applause of a tremendous audience, after a program made doubly long by encores, Lawrence Tibbett remains backstage to meet in person as many of his listeners as he can.
>
> Tibbett is human.[10]

Larry quickly discovered that the life of a touring singer, although financially rewarding, had its drawbacks. As there were no commercial airline flights between cities, all travel was on trains without air-conditioning. The coaches were often unbearably hot in summer, cold in winter, and drafty always. Sloppy food and sleazy hotels were sometimes all that were available, as were beaten-up, untuned pianos.

Page one of the 4 November 1922 *Musical America* has a large feature article that reports heavy gouging of the artists on tour by railroads and hotels, which made touring even less romantic. It is reported that one Midwestern hotel charged an artist $16 for one night. All iniquities certainly had not been cleared up by the time Larry hit the road.

From 1925 through 1950 (as carefully documented by his secretaries Florence Foster and later by Doris Wittschen),[11] Larry averaged 12 concerts a month. To this must be added his appearances at the Metropolitan during the opera season and the many informal recitals and song fests in which his zestful nature involved him, along with his singing at parties, his singing in the shower (to which his neighbors objected!), and performances at the White House for Presidents Coolidge, Hoover, Roosevelt, and Truman.

In addition, during the summer months Larry sang at the Hollywood Bowl, the Bohemian Grove, Robin Hood Dell outside Philadelphia, and Lewisohn Stadium in upper Manhattan. He also sang at the Watergate concerts in Washington and summer festivals that seemed to spring up spontaneously. In time came films, radio, and recordings.

Such a schedule would kill anyone without the constitution of a horse. Larry, a true Californian and former puny youth, had developed an obsession with physical fitness. To promote good circulation, he would stand on his head before a performance. Arriving in a town on tour, he would riffle through a notebook filled with the names of local chiropractors and go for a treatment to loosen up his travel-tightened bones and muscles.

Larry became an enormously popular concert artist, selling out the house wherever he appeared. His programming was shrewd. As originally advised by Evans and Salter, he would usually begin with an aria by Handel, additionally beneficial to singers for warming up the voice, the serene "Where E'er You Walk" or the grave "Hear Me, Ye Wind and Waves." A group of lieder including his favorites by Schubert or Brahms might follow. The first half of the program would inevitably finish with a rousing aria, such as *Ballo*'s "Eri tu" or the tortured lament of Herod from Massenet's *Hérodiade*.

For the second half, Larry would change to English or Scottish folk songs, or contemporary American airs. He was a great believer in singing in English, even upon occasion operatic selections in translation. Next came the encore songs, which became absolute requisites whenever he sang: "Short'nin' Bread," "Song of the Flea," "Drink to Me Only with Thine Eyes," "On the Road to Mandalay," "Sylvia," and others that his loyal audiences demanded.

In addition to Larry's astute showmanship, his vocal control, which made it possible to shade down to the loveliest of *pianissimo*s, and the unique voice itself, yet another factor led to his huge success as a recitalist: he glamorized every concert in which he appeared. Women accounted for 75 percent of Larry's concert audiences,[12] and his way was such that each felt he was singing only to her. Many must have wished to be gathered into the arms of the dashing baritone in his splendid white tie and tails (he did the best he could).

Larry enjoyed his concert tours. In the early years they took him away from his increasingly unhappy marriage with Grace; later he came to savor them for their own sake. Whenever he had extra time, he would visit a factory or learn something about a shipyard, a coal mine, or the inner workings of a bank. He enjoyed becoming a part of the community in which he appeared.

Most of all he liked people and went out of his way to meet them. Soon they were calling him Larry and treating him like a longlost friend. He accepted invitations to receptions at the homes of the concert sponsors following evenings of concertizing. Unlike many artists, he enjoyed himself at these affairs, savoring the chance to relax and be fussed over for an hour or two as the tensions of the performance abated.

In 1928, on one of his early concert tours, Larry met a worshipful 12-year-old, Doris Wyckoff, at the reception following a recital in Charleston, West Virginia. The baritone agreed that she and her girlfriend could call the next morning at his hotel to pick up autographed photographs. Doris later recalled her experiences with the rising star.

> I was born in West Virginia and grew up in Charleston. I graduated from high school at 14, so although my first meeting with Lawrence Tibbett occurred when I was only 12 years old, I was pretty grown up for my age—a sophomore in high school. One of my best friends, a young lady named Dorothy Potter (her father Louis Potter was instrumental in bringing Mr. Tibbett to Charleston), and I went to all the community concerts, but this one was particularly exciting for me and for Dorothy because her parents were going to have a reception for Mr. Tibbett and his accompanist, Stewart Wille.
>
> After the concert we went to the Potter home; they had invited everyone who was involved in community concerts there. We were awe-struck girls, and although this was a large party, Tibbett and Wille went out of their way to be particularly nice to a couple of 12-year-olds. At the end of the affair, Tibbett invited us down to their hotel to pick up a signed photograph first thing in the morning.
>
> The next morning Dorothy and I went down to the Kanawha Hotel, where they were staying. They had a piano in the room, so we had an impromptu concert for about 15 minutes—just a little

> one, but it was their way of putting us at our ease. Then they autographed pictures for us. We had brought a little Brownie camera with us, so we asked them if they would mind coming outside and letting us take a picture of them. They thought this was very funny, but they obliged, and we took some pictures, which I still treasure.[13]
>
> After this they were on tour, and Dorothy and I both received postcards and letters from different places for about a year. At Christmastime that year I received a dozen red roses, and believe me, at 13 I was really thrilled.
>
> We kept in touch—with what frequency I don't remember, but three years later they were coming again to Charleston. By this time his reputation had really soared! I don't recall whether he was into his movies yet, but he was very well known by this time, whereas the first time he came to Charleston his main claim to fame was that he was the youngest singer at the Met. The last two Christmases I had received roses from him, so I was not surprised when I received a telegram from him asking me to dinner after the concert.
>
> Mother was so sweet. She took me to buy a new dress—a very pretty black dress with a white collar. When he came to town the day of the concert he called me and arranged to pick me up. I had a date for the concert which I broke, because when Tibbett called he had invited me to stay backstage. Well, that was much better than sitting out front with my boyfriend. After the concert we went to dinner. Believe me, I was the focus of all eyes because I was dining with a very famous singer.[14]

This unusual relationship was to continue sporadically throughout the rest of Larry's life. Toward Doris, Larry was always the soul of fatherly tenderness, even after she came of age.

In 1926, Larry joined the artists of RCA Victor's classical division, Red Seal, with his recording of the *Pagliacci* Prologue. It was immediately added to the Victor catalogue for Italy as well, and he later wrote that in the first year of release the recording earned him $10,000 in royalties. This must have given a tremendous boost to his ego as well as his finances. Even today, that reading of the Prologue is an individual and very human interpretation. It remains among the most exciting and definitive performances of the aria on record.[15]

The 1926–27 season at the Metropolitan offered Larry new challenges, which he accepted eagerly. On 20 November 1926, he appeared before the gold curtain in New York for the first time in a clown's costume with a white-powdered face and grotesquely arched eyebrows to sing Tonio in *Pagliacci*. He had finally graduated from the secondary baritone role of the ardent Silvio to the malevolent leading baritone in Leoncavallo's popular opera.[16]

In a strange turn of repertoire, Larry briefly presented two new characterizations to his New York audience. In November, he sang one of three Kothners in Wagner's *Meistersinger* in New York. (His first crack at the role had occurred in spring 1925, on tour.) December found him taking on, for the first time anywhere, the comic, bustling Fra Melitone in Verdi's *La forza del destino*, with Rosa Ponselle and Ezio Pinza in the cast.[17] In January he sang for the first time in New York a role he had debuted on tour the previous spring, Mercutio in *Roméo et Juliette*.[18] Ten days later came his debut as one of the three kings, Manfredo, in Italo Montemezzi's sweepingly melodramatic *L'amore dei tre re*.[19]

On 17 February 1927 Larry created the role of Eadgar in *The King's Henchman* by Deems Taylor and Edna St. Vincent Millay.[20] This was the first in a series of American operas he premiered over the years, one of Larry's (and Gatti-Casazza's) most important contributions to the history of American music.

In front-page coverage, music critic Olin Downes of the *New York Times* judged this new work to be the most effectively and artistically wrought American opera that had yet reached the stage.[21] (The Met had previously staged only such provincial American works as *Mona* and *Cleopatra's Night*.) He credited the young baritone's careful enunciation of some of Millay's best lines with materially heightening the opera's effect.[22] Over and over, the clarity and beauty of Larry's diction, whether in English or other languages, would be singled out for critical praise. He knew that words were vital if the listener were to be reached.

Finally, that 1926–27 season twice witnessed Larry's interpretation of yet another new role for him, that of the sinister Dapertutto, one of the four villains in Offenbach's *The Tales of Hoffmann*, with its high-lying aria. (He would add the other three to his repertoire in January 1937.) His earlier problems with learning and memorizing new roles, the problems that surfaced with Valentin and Ford, seem by now to have been conquered.[23]

But for Larry, the real triumph of the 1926–27 Metropolitan season was that he had not been given a single *comprimario* role. Unquestionably, he had become a leading baritone of the Met—but his original contract still had one more year to run. It continued to require him to perform whatever roles were assigned to him at what had become an absurdly low salary.

On the Met tour that spring Larry undertook three new roles in the space of nine days, Alfio in *Cavalleria rusticana*, Germont in *Traviata*, and Telramund in Wagner's *Lohengrin*, a role he would never sing in New York. Although one would think he would be towering in it, Regina Resnik suggested that Larry's voice was not big enough for the powerful role.[24]

The *Los Angeles Evening Express*, as the second item in Eileen Hennessey's society column of 5 April 1927, reported that "Mrs. Lawrence Tibbett and her twin sons Richard and Ivan [as Larry Jr. was often known] will arrive here from New York this evening and will temporarily make their home at the Ambassador Hotel until Mr. Tibbett arrives in a few weeks to spend the summer months with his family. Mr. Tibbett will appear here this Fall as one of the stellar lights of the coming Los Angeles Grand Opera Season."[25] Larry was just learning the art of publicity, but he was already adept at taking his wife off the scene.

Late in the summer of 1927, Larry met Mrs. Jane Burgard, the woman who would eventually change the course of his life. He later recalled his first meeting with Jane:

> Herbert Hoover . . . was the guest of honor at the home of George T. Cameron, owner of the *San Francisco Chronicle*. I was in San Francisco for a holiday at the Bohemian Grove, where, during my vacation, I sang *St. Francis of Assisi*.
>
> At the reception I was asked to sing, and I did, gladly. After a number of encores I felt I had given my voice all the use it should have that evening and decided that neither wild horses nor Herbert Hoover could make me sing again. Then a lovely lady approached me. She had read of my success as Ford in *Falstaff*, she said. She had followed my career through the newspapers. Wouldn't I please— And I found myself singing her favorite song, "Drink to Me Only with Thine Eyes."
>
> She was Mrs. Jennie [Jane] Marston Burgard, a New York girl, living in San Francisco, the daughter of Edgar L. Marston, a retired banker. She knew music, was fond of the opera, and we instantly became good friends.[26]

When Larry described Jane Burgard as a "lovely lady," he was not indulging in romantic rhetoric. She *was* lovely: a statuesque five feet, eleven inches tall and about 130 pounds, with eyes of extraordinary blue[27] set into a cameo face with startling white skin and crowned with a bob of coal-black hair. She was pregnant and wore a loosely flowing black gown with a low décolleté trimmed in white.

The two met again a week later at a tea party given by Mrs. Cameron. Ironically it was Jane's husband, John Clark Burgard, a San Francisco broker, who had arranged to have Larry sing for the 70 or so guests. As there were more people than chairs, some of the posh audience sat on the floor. But that afternoon Larry sang for only one person, Burgard's wife Jane, who took a front-row seat and kept her eyes fixed only on him. Thus began a searing love affair of which only Larry's closest friends were at first aware.

Jane exactly filled the specifications that Larry sought in the women he became involved with of late. She was beautiful, wealthy, and a well-born member of New York society. Her father owned the company that produced the famous Pond's Extract, which claimed to be useful for everything from healing cuts to alleviating stomach disorders. Burgard, her second husband, was the father of her two sons, Clark ("Sonny") and Marston. Their third son, to be called Peter, was on the way. All three had their mother's striking combination of dark hair and light eyes.

Jane was born in Burlingame, California, near San Francisco, on 13 September 1899 and attended an all-girls finishing school in Poughkeepsie, New York. A dull first marriage to Robert J. Adams, son of the Chiclet chewing-gum tycoon, lasted a year, and soon afterward she made a second, equally dull marriage to Burgard. Wherever she went, however, there was always plenty of money.

When Jane first saw Larry, and then heard him sing, she realized that to be with him could bring her the excitement she had always longed for and had yet to find. But she was carrying her husband's child and was not prepared to dissolve her marriage; moreover, she, unlike Grace, sensed that Larry's ascendant career would make it difficult to maintain a secure relationship with him. Whether she considered Grace an obstacle is unknown.

Peter was born, and Jane, who by that point had stopped seeing Larry, began to lose weight so dramatically that her doctor became alarmed. Jane told him about her recently broken-off affair, and he warned her that she would surely die of malnutrition if she did not see Larry again. Following this strange and not particularly medical prescription, the affair resumed, but the lovers remained separated more often than not.

On 27 September 1927, Larry first appeared with the San Francisco Opera, starting an association that would last until 1949. His debut was as Ford to Scotti's Falstaff, any supposed bad feelings buried by fees, fame, and acclaim. Larry also sang his role in *La cena delle beffe*, repeating his Metropolitan success, but it was in the following year, 1928, that he had his first real San Francisco success, when he replaced Giuseppe Danise as Amonasro in *Aida*. Of that impersonation, critic Redfern Mason of the *San Francisco Examiner* called Larry "virile," "heroic," "intense," and "impassioned"; Mason went on to suggest that the substitution was a put-up case to heighten excitement.[28]

In late September and October 1927, Larry sang 13 concerts booked by Evans and Salter: two in San Francisco, two in Los Angeles, and one each in Fresno, San José, Seattle, Tacoma, Spokane, Portland (Oregon), Salt Lake City, and Pueblo and Denver, Colorado.[29] One might say that Larry was working his way across the country, back to New York.

In the 1927–28 season, Larry first appeared before New York audiences in Wagner's *Tannhäuser* as the gentle, self-effacing Wolfram. Critics noted his lyric singing, and the role became one of his most highly praised portrayals. Of Larry's future in Wagner, Irving Kolodin would write:

> [Wolfram was] a role he often sang with suavity and expressiveness. . . . This pointed a way toward such other lyric baritone roles as Sachs [*Die Meistersinger*] and the Wanderer [*Siegfried*], which, regrettably, Tibbett chose to ignore in favor of the more strenuous Amonasro, Rigoletto, and Scarpia.[30]

His Escamillo of the same season did not enjoy the same reception. Downes, in a sour mood, complained that Tibbett wasn't notably well cast as the Toreador, but he was impressed with Larry's fine French diction and by his dramatics in the Toreador Song's second verse. He describes how Larry leapt onto a table and, "bestriding this improvised podium masterfully," proceeded to bring the bullfight narrative to life with the clear movements and gestures of a born actor.

Just how scathing an opera critic can be is shown by Downes's comments on the Carmen of that same evening, the adored Maria Jeritza. He accused her of dancing a version of the Hawaiian hula in the first act and of "conspicuous ineptitude" in the second. Her French, he believed, "would have been repudiated in the Franco-Prussian War." Summing up Jeritza in the role of Carmen, he reasoned she apparently lacked an appreciation of the opera's nature and declared her unfit for the lead in every imaginable way, including technical facility, style, and physical appearance.[31]

Many famed prima donnas have been excoriated for their Carmens, but put beside Downes's criticism of Jeritza, his reservations about Larry's Escamillo seem like great praise indeed. Larry could live with that.

Part Three 1928–1934

Chapter 5

THE SONG OF THE ROGUE

As America swung into the year 1928, the mood of the era soared. Skirts were never higher, morals never lower, and crime in the form of bootlegging and related mob violence was rampant.

The stock market climbed even higher than the skirts. On 12 March, a stock called Radio opened at 120½ and closed at 138½. The next day it jumped another 21½ points. This was madness! Blue chip companies followed the same frenzied upward path: General Motors up 9¼ in a single day, RCA up 12¾. Aviation stocks were particularly manic: Wright Aeronautical soared 34¾ points within a week. Curtis leapt 35½ in the same time. Where would it end? How could one maintain sound judgment in such times?

The answer is that few people did. Millions played the stock market, from the great financiers to the man on the street. They frantically bought shares on margin, meaning that they had to put up very little money but would have to pay out more if the prices dropped. But of course that would not, could not happen.

Broadway, meanwhile, seemed to have found a social conscience. The play *Porgy* was running, and so was *Showboat*. Both would have an eventual impact on Larry's repertoire. Talkies had arrived, and Al Jolson's *The Jazz Singer* was in the theaters.

The year 1928 also brought the first election when the question of the national ban on liquor came prominently into view. The Democratic candidate for president, New York governor Al Smith, a Catholic and a "wet," advocated the right of each state to decide the question of Prohibition for itself. The Republican, Herbert Hoover, who had come to public attention by organizing food relief for Belgium after the 1915 German invasion, was on record as saying that Prohibition was "a great social and economic experiment, noble in motive, far-reaching in purpose." He did not choose to call attention to the results of the "Great Experiment," however, and the electorate, choosing to ignore the omission, overwhelmingly voted Hoover into office.

> February 2, 1928
> Dear Mr. Tibbett:
> Your splendid performance on the General Motors program has brought us many compliments. You deserve our sincere expression of gratitude for the splendid co-operation you have given us, and we hope it may bring you satisfaction to know that your efforts are greatly appreciated.

This letter was signed by Gordon Kingsley of the General Motors Corporation.[1] Larry's radio career was up and running with the new year.

That spring, as part of celebrations at the University of Southern California during which he was awarded an honorary master of arts in music, Larry sang the title role in a performance of Mendelssohn's oratorio *Elijah* with Henry Perry conducting on 5 June 1928.[2] This is a part that could well have been perfectly suited to his voice and temperament.

Later that year, Larry learned that "you never can tell which way opera temperament is going to jump."[3] Maria Jeritza, the ever-scrappy darling of opera fans and royalty, if not always the critics, was singing *Tosca* in Cleveland with the Met, and Larry was the Scarpia, a role he had first undertaken only a short time before, on 19 September 1928 in San Francisco, also opposite Jeritza. (In San Francisco that season Larry also sang Tonio, Manfredo in Montemezzi's *L'amore dei tre re*, Neri in *La cena delle beffe*, and the Amonasro that caused such acclaim.) The much-performed Puccini opera ran its routine course until the end of the second act, when the villain attacks the diva and she falls to the floor. Jeritza liked to remain prone as she sang her big aria, "Vissi d'arte." This time, however, she wished to fall on the *far* side of the stage, where she would be alone in the spotlight.

As Larry, in character, held her threateningly, she hissed, "Let me go! Let me go!" He hung on at first, not comprehending. Before the act began she had said to him, "This is our last performance. Let's make it a good one. Let's go after each other!" Now, when she pounded him with her fists and pushed, he thought she was acting. When he realized what she really wanted, he stubbornly vowed there would be a "dead Tibbett" onstage before he would let her take over the scene for herself.

They fought like wildcats. Following the stage directions, he tried to kiss her shoulder. She lunged at him, and the sequins on her gown made deep cuts in his chin. He pulled her hair and she pulled his. Larry wore a heavy brass chain around his neck, and she yanked it and broke it, cutting the flesh as the links parted. Neither of them could sing now; they just muttered and gasped. Jeritza was determined that she would get to the other side of the stage, and Larry had made up his mind that she would sing at his feet. He finally managed to get a hold on her that was a mixture of hammerlock and half nelson, and threw her on the couch. She rolled to the floor—and sang.

When the act ended the two exhausted singers looked like a couple of stray cats. The applause was tremendous. They took their bows, and Larry prepared to weather a volley of invective from the fiery prima donna. The audience was still applauding when the two started for their dressing rooms. She looked at him, smoothed her hair, and smiled.

"Well," she said, "we gave them their money's worth."[4]

The 1928–29 New York season was heightened for Larry by his role as Jonny in *Jonny Spielt Auf*, written in 1926 by the Viennese composer Ernst Krenek. A popular scandal at the time (it featured a relationship between a black musician and a white woman), the opera combines American jazz and experimental tonalities with conventional composition. Marion Bauer, in her *Twentieth-Century Music*, wryly notes that, while it was not that good an opera, "*Jonny* filled Krenek's pockets with cash."[5]

The Metropolitan made Jonny a white man in blackface and deleted all allusions to race from the original.[6] Larry alternated as Jonny with Michael Bohnen. He played the band leader, the blasé cabaret entertainer, in a way that was sharp-witted and bouncy. Of Larry's first performance on 27 February 1929, Samuel Chotzinoff of the *New York World* insisted the next day that "if all God's children got voices like Mr. Tibbett's . . . and a happy genius for doing the black-bottom in the midst of travail . . . then Jonny would have been translated into Harlem English and exposed to the comradeship of his brothers on upper Seventh Avenue."

Also that season, three weeks before *Jonny*, Larry sang his first Marcello in *La Bohème*, a "bread-and-butter" role that he later seldom sang. Maria Müller, Martinelli, and Pinza shared the stage with him in this production. With his sixth Metropolitan season wrapped up, Larry responded enthusiastically to Hollywood's call and, despite the misgivings of his colleagues, embarked on a spectacular new venture that was to drastically alter his lumbering progress at the Met.

A press release about the new movie being shot on a Metro-Goldwyn-Mayer lot in Culver City in the spring of 1929 might have read something like this:

> *The Rogue Song*, based on Lehár's operetta *Gypsy Love*, music by Herbert Stothart. Starring Metropolitan Opera baritone Lawrence Tibbett with Catherine Dale Owen. Director: Lionel Barrymore. Cameraman: Charles Schoenbaum. Color.

Larry was not the first opera singer to go to Hollywood. Years before, the greatest of tenors, Enrico Caruso, a singer not particularly blessed with the good looks of a matinée idol, had appeared before the cameras, as had the luscious Mary Garden and Geraldine Farrar. But these opera stars had appeared in silent films, a sample of Hollywood's legendary logic. *The Rogue Song* would cut a new path. It was to be a full-length sound film. Audiences all over the world would not only see a handsome baritone of the Metropolitan but would hear his rich, vibrant singing voice. To that end, on Larry's first day on the set of *The Rogue Song*, the studio planned to run what was known as an "A" test on the sound stage. Larry was expected to participate in a full dress rehearsal with costumes and scenery at which a dozen important executives, including the "czar of Hollywood," Louis B. Mayer, would be present. It was not Mayer, however, who had had the idea of hiring a Metropolitan Opera star for a motion picture, but his close assistant Ida Koverman, an opera buff and the reputed "brains" of MGM. She had been the first to imagine the possibilities of the Tibbett voice and looks on the silver screen.

Lionel Barrymore, who could do just about anything creative—write, direct, produce, act, compose, and paint—had drawn the assignment to direct the film. Later he wrote about the experience:

> The film was a devil of a motion picture to make because in 1929 the "playback" had not yet been invented. The playback is the system of recording voices or orchestras on records in advance and at

> leisure, then playing back the music, which is perfect by this time, while the singers merely go through the illusion of performing. But with *The Rogue Song* they had to record sight and sound in one take, at the same time.[7]

In front of the scene, ready to shoot the first day's rehearsal was cameraman Charles Schoenbaum, who had an uncanny eye through his lens and also away from it. He was the man who, from a lineup of 30 cowboy extras he had filmed, picked out one in the rushes and said, "Look at that face! He's going to be a star!" It was the then-unknown Gary Cooper. Schoenbaum advised another Hollywood newcomer to go home, find a nice guy, and be a good wife and mother. That was Nancy Davis, who later married divorced actor Ronald Reagan, and who was heard from again.

When Larry strode onto the set in his swashbuckling Cossack uniform, the lights were focused, the microphones set. The movie executives strained forward, including the ruthless mogul Mayer, the man who had already discovered Greta Garbo and who would take credit for the discovery of Clark Gable, Judy Garland, Robert Taylor, and Lana Turner. Barrymore gave the signal to roll the cameras. The offstage orchestra began to play, and Larry's cue came. The opera star took a deep breath, burst into song—and blew out a light valve in the camera.

Silent shock on the sound stage was followed by nervous giggles, then a crescendo of laughter. Repairs had to be made before the scene could be resumed. This false start broke the ice and established a rapport between Larry and the film crew that lasted throughout the shooting. It also created an awed respect for the naked power of an operatic voice.

Everyone in the company had been cautioned in advance against annoying or otherwise bothering the famous singer—the world's highest paid baritone, or so they thought. His automobile was waiting for Larry whenever he left his dressing room or the set. He often left it parked and walked. A valet was assigned to him. Larry sent him back and waited on himself. He showed no pretensions.

Frances Marion, screenwriter for *The Rogue Song*, reminisced about Larry. She recalled how the studio executives were totally mistaken in their expectation that the opera star would be a stuffed shirt. As Marion saw it, Larry was in love with the whole human race and naturally expressed his feelings in song. He sang drinking songs to the extras on the set and love songs to the waitresses in the commissary; he sang on the way to the studio, on leaving the studio, and anywhere a party was in full swing. Many of his friends who understood the care that should be given to such a voice warned Larry to be careful.

"Why?" he would say, "I'm happiest when I sing. A voice doesn't last forever, and while I have it I intend to enjoy myself, and to give pleasure to others."[8]

Two days after he started *The Rogue Song*, advisors had already taken him to task:

> "See here," they warned, "this business of being a good fellow is all very well. But you must remember you are a big opera star and you shouldn't be so familiar with every Tom, Dick and Harry on the set. You should carry yourself in keeping with your position and have dignity and poise that command the respect to which you are entitled."

Larry's response was to rise to his full six feet, two inches and make an unmusical sound commonly known as the raspberry.[9]

A few days later he was interviewed by a magazine writer who asked him about his murdered father, Deputy Sheriff Will Tibbet of Kern County.

"Yes," replied Larry, "and my uncle Ed ran the best saloon in Bakersfield. The Buckhorn, they called it. It was run like a bank and any guy who started something . . ."

"You wouldn't want me to print that!" the interviewer interrupted.

Larry's eyes widened. "Certainly, why not? I'm not ashamed of it—in fact, I'm mighty proud of it. As I said before, it was the best saloon in town."[10]

Work in those days of the wondrous new talking picture was not easy. Lionel Barrymore recalled that to film one scene, he sat high on his camera boom overlooking a set that comprised the entire length of Stage 16: three separate rooms and a hallway. The script called for Larry to hold a high A-flat while he walked from one end of the set to the other, then to sit down and pour himself a tankard of stage beer. The take had to be repeated all afternoon. As if that were not enough, it was a steamy mid-August day, and Larry was required to wear a heavy woolen uniform. When the scene had finally been shot to Barrymore's satisfaction, Larry, without his uniform and with his chest bare, was seen gulping down tankards of real beer.[11]

On the set Larry played practical jokes on Barrymore and the cast. During a banquet scene he secretly emptied the flagons of cider and filled them with claret. How jolly the costumed courtiers suddenly became while the scene was being filmed! Larry enjoyed himself immensely and especially appreciated the antics of two young British comedians MGM had borrowed from the Hal Roach studio. Their names, not yet familiar to American audiences, were Stan Laurel and Oliver Hardy. They turned the tables on Larry by squirting a tube of shaving cream in his face and by mocking him in pantomime during the film's famous flogging scene.

While *The Rogue Song* was being filmed, Lionel Barrymore always stopped work at five o'clock sharp in order to go to his home a few blocks from the studio where his wife, the former Irene Fenwick, would be waiting. Once a great beauty as well as a talented actress, she was now an invalid. In Hollywood, known the world over for its marital infidelities, Barrymore's devotion to his wife was legendary. When she died, his spirit broke. Ironically, he too became an invalid, but in his final acting roles he made his wheelchair part of his acting technique.

Meanwhile, his restless leading man, was keeping up the appearance, at least, of fidelity. With Mrs. Tibbett at his side, he used his free time to troop all over the area: Bel Air, Westwood Village, the San Fernando Valley, and the original Hollywood district. It was during a walk in the exclusive neighborhood of Beverly Hills that Larry and Grace spotted a stately English farmhouse[12] at 933 North Rexford Drive. It was on a corner lot of about an acre and had six bedrooms, a large living room, a family room, dining room, kitchen, enclosed patio, and maid's room.

Brimming with excitement, Grace stared at the two-story house and spied a discreet *For Sale* sign posted in one window. She wanted to buy it immediately. The Tibbetts had been renting various houses along Sunset Boulevard, but now, for the first time since the cottage at La Crescenta, the family might live comfortably together in their own home. To Grace's delight, negotiations to purchase the house on North Rexford Drive from Mrs. Florence Sterling were completed on 23 August 1929, and the Tibbetts moved in. Larry's architect friend Lloyd Wright contracted to handle the additions to the master wing and the service way, and to build a swimming pool.[13]

While Larry worked on *The Rogue Song*, his daily work routine seldom varied. At dawn, Earl, his chauffeur and gardener, would drive Larry in Larry's town car to the studio at Culver City, where he remained until five o'clock, when Earl would drive him home again. The twins were included as extras in crowd scenes; the nine-year-olds had the time of their lives "working" on the film.[14]

That summer Larry and Lloyd Wright took the twins and Wright's stepson in Larry's La Salle touring car on a camping trip in the Sierras, to Convict Lake. Richard Tibbett recalls the less-than-idyllic experience:

> We had our fishing gear, sleeping bags, and new .22 Winchester pump rifles. We camped on the shore for two or three days and nights and Dad and Lloyd showed us kids how to fish and hunt small game. Dad told us ghost stories at night, by the campfire, about the convict who escaped and ended up hiding at the lake—hence the name of the lake. By now Dad and Lloyd got tired of having us kids around. They found somebody to baby-sit us nearby, and they took off for Reno for some gambling and womanizing. They came back three or four days later and took us all home.[15]

Larry was in greater demand than ever for concerts, even while filming continued. He gave well-attended recitals in San Francisco's Masonic Auditorium and at the Bohemian Grove. He also sang at the Hollywood Bowl. Although opera remained his primary focus, his concerts continued to be infinitely more rewarding financially.

And his recitals took him away from the ever-vigilant Grace to trysts with Jane, who had become absolutely necessary to him in the two years since they had met. He loved her passionately and totally, as he had never loved another woman. He even carried Jane's photograph in his wallet. He made no effort to conceal all this from Grace, whose fits of jealousy in this Southern California paradise of beautiful women had now become so obvious that cameraman Schoenbaum wrote to his daughter Vera Gebbert in Washington, D.C., "Mr. Tibbett is a kind genius with a magnificent voice and a rather jealous wife who sits on the set day after day, so Catherine Dale Owen, the leading lady, won't snatch Mr. Tibbett away."[16] His astute observation is borne out by a group photograph of *The Rogue Song*'s cast and crew—and grim Grace. She looks as out of place as a lone bulldog among borzois, but she was not going to leave Larry's side.

With his role in *The Rogue Song* completed, Larry and his family returned to New York in early autumn of 1929 to the career that he loved most. As he again traveled the 3000 miles from California to New York, he was riding high. At the Met he was receiving bigger and better roles. This season he was to emulate his father as a sheriff: he would be Jack Rance in Puccini's *The Girl of the Golden West*. His recital schedule was heavier than ever, and his concerts brought in an increasingly large income.

In addition, if *The Rogue Song* were a success, he would be known as a movie star across the nation, even in the smallest towns that had moving picture houses. Louella D. Parsons, Hollywood's influential gossip columnist, was already proclaiming him a second Rudolph Valentino. Plans were set for *New Moon*, his second film, which would costar the beautiful Metropolitan soprano Grace Moore. Soon he would command truly astronomical fees everywhere—fees as high as the dizzying prices of stocks at the exchange.

By 3 September 1929, when stock values reached their highest point, Rudy Vallee had made popular what any opera singer would call nonsinging—crooning. That Vallee's voice could be heard at all was entirely due to the new electrically amplified microphone. His songs perfectly captured the carefree spirit that characterized the times, just as his later hits, such as "Good News" and "The Best Things in Life Are Free," would convey the desperate post-crash optimism.

As Larry began rehearsals at the Met late that October, he could not doubt that, like the country itself, he was firmly established on the path named in one of his favorite songs—the glory road.

On Monday, 29 October 1929, the Metropolitan Opera season opened with Puccini's *Manon Lescaut*. Tullio Serafin conducted a cast that included Bori, Gigli, and Giuseppe de Luca.

The previous week the stock market had made an appalling and unprecedented drop, particularly on Thursday. The rush to sell was so astonishing that the ticker tapes reporting the figures to aghast speculators ran far behind the actual prices of the stocks being traded on the floor of the exchange.

On Tuesday, the day after the opera opened, the company was on its usual visit to Philadelphia. Thus the New York house was dark—as black as that same Tuesday came to be called in American financial history. Frederick Lewis Allen vividly described the devastation that took place on Wall Street:

> The Big Bull Market was dead. Billions of dollars' worth of profits—and paper profits—had disappeared. The grocer, the window cleaner, and the seamstress had lost their capital. In every town there were families which had suddenly dropped from

> showy affluence into debt. Investors who had dreamed of retiring to live on their fortunes now found themselves back once more at the very beginning of the long road to riches. Day by day the newspapers printed the grim reports of suicides.[17]

Even the conservative *Commercial and Financial Chronicle* for 2 November 1929 allowed that "the past week has witnessed the greatest stock market catastrophe of all the ages."

At the opera house, however, the atmosphere was relatively calm. People said that the downtrend was only temporary. Hadn't one of the Met's chief supporters, J. P. Morgan, bought heavily into the market to prevent it from falling further? On that same 2 November, they went ahead with the revival of Puccini's *The Girl of the Golden West*, presenting a matinée with Jeritza, Martinelli, and Tibbett.

The baritone found the opera, with its odd blend of Italian and Italianate American styles, highly diverting. Using his father as model for the Western lawman, he sought to portray Sheriff Jack Rance as realistically as possible. He described his experiences with the revival in *The Glory Road*:

> Puccini's opera is beautifully done, but, after all, it is an Italian's conception of the Wild West, and the music is by no means Western in manner or feeling. . . . The cowboys didn't act like any cowboys I had ever seen—either around Bakersfield or on my uncle's ranch in the Tejon Mountains, where, as a youngster, I had done some cow-punching myself. For instance, in the celebration at the end of the opera the director had these supposedly tough cow hands throw their arms around one another and express their jubilation by kissing each other on the cheek in the best Latin manner.
>
> In the scene where the sheriff enters the cabin, searching for Johnson, the bandit, the director told me to come in crouching, with my six-shooter held at arm's length in front of me. I obeyed, and felt more like Annette Kellerman doing the Australian crawl than I did like a sheriff.
>
> "This will never do," I said. "The sheriff would enter standing erect, on the alert, with the gun held at his hip so he can swing it quickly to any part of the room."
>
> "Poof!" the director said. "What does an opera singer know about sheriffs?"
>
> I told him what I knew about sheriffs.
>
> "Oh," he said apologetically, and shrank away from me. "Oh. Then we shall do it your way."

> Upon my advice he eliminated the cowboy osculation in the last act, too, and forever after seemed to be a bit afraid of me. I believe he did not entirely understand my English. He thought I was the one who had done all the killing I had told him about, and he guessed he had better be good to me or I'd run amuck and shoot up the Metropolitan Opera House.[18]

The new production of Puccini's Western was a success (although the *Herald Tribune* complained that Larry's costume and makeup made him resemble a slick country preacher[19]), and the Metropolitan's season continued serenely. In spite of the fact that opera was a luxury likely to be severely affected if a true depression set in, the well-to-do who supported the Met seemed to be little concerned, although the economy had not rallied.

In January 1930 Larry set out on a concert tour. Lionel Barrymore had telephoned that the premiere of *The Rogue Song* would take place at Grauman's Chinese Theater in Hollywood on 17 January, but the concert schedule created a conflict. Since Larry could not change the bookings on his tour, Grace and the twins would represent him at the opening. Even though the boys, now nearly 10 years of age, had just had their tonsils removed and were suffering from postoperative infections, the three boarded the Chief and headed west.[20]

Five days later, their train steamed into Pasadena. They were rushed to Grauman's by car behind a phalanx of motorcycle police, arriving just in time for the showing. In a press conference after the screening, Grace made it known that her husband was on a concert tour of the East Coast, which was why he could not be present. Then she pointedly added that they had taken title to a lovely house in Beverly Hills and had already moved in, no doubt hoping to bring an end to the gossip that all was not well in the Tibbett household.

The Rogue Song, the first color musical motion picture, was a smash hit. Soon reviews of the film appeared in newspapers across the country. Declared the *New York World*:

> *The Rogue Song*, Metro-Goldwyn-Mayer's adaptation of the operetta *Gypsy Love*, may be put down unequivocally as one of the great achievements of the cinema. Of course, it need hardly be said that Lawrence Tibbett made it so.[21]

The Richmond (Virginia) *News Leader* echoed the praise:

> *The Rogue Song* at Loew's this week is essentially Lawrence Tibbett's picture—and very rightly so. Seldom, indeed, have the mo-

> tion pictures enlisted the talents and abilities of a star of such magnitude and versatility, for Mr. Tibbett is first of all a great artist, in all the essentials of that much misused word, and after that he is a charming person and a very fine actor.[22]

On 21 March 1930 Lawrence Evans wrote Grace from New York:

> The business here on *The Rogue Song* has been marvelous! It played to excellent business during the first four or five weeks, only the week-day matinée showing any decline over the first three weeks. It is still doing about as much business as most of the other pictures, and will run until sometime in April anyway. It is a great record it is setting out there at the Chinese Theater![23]

Regrettably, all prints of *The Rogue Song* seem to have been lost. RCA Victor, however, did release two 78-rpm discs of four songs from the picture, as they later released recordings of songs from *New Moon*, *The Prodigal* (later renamed *The Southerner*), and *Cuban Love Song*, other movies of Larry's.[24]

While together at their Beverly Hills home in February and again that summer, the Tibbetts entertained almost continuously. A single page from a personal scrapbook has a dozen separate clippings from the *Los Angeles Examiner* detailing dinners, luncheons, box parties, and yacht cruises the Tibbetts hosted. Grace had a head-to-hip photo published and a report that she had returned from a "fortnight's sojourn in Mexico." There is also an item, on the same page, of Larry getting writer's cramp from signing autographs in a theater lobby, and the Tibbetts' maid calling the police to rein in two of the Tibbetts' dogs who were disturbing the neighbors.[25]

For most of the remaining 1929–30 opera season, Larry, his reputation now tremendously enhanced by his film success, continued his circuitous concert tour schedule. He returned to New York to sing for the first time at the Met one of his most moving and successful roles, the elder Germont in Verdi's *La Traviata*, performing at the matinée of 19 April 1930 with Bori and Gigli. The last night of the season was a gala concert, and he sang, significantly, Jacques Wolfe's popular adaptation of the spiritual form, "De Glory Road," with Stewart Wille at the piano.

In spite of the harsh economic times, Larry's stock was never higher as he hit his own glory road back to Hollywood to make *New Moon* with Grace Moore. The blonde Miss Moore and the trimly mustachioed Mr. Tibbett were both enormously attractive. Both had beautiful singing voices, and both took a casual delight in liaisons, enjoying them whenever the opportunity arose.

Moore worked hard to be a legend for her myriad fans, but she had perhaps even more detractors, who absolutely refused to take her seriously as an artist. Charles O'Connell, director of RCA Victor's Red Seal division, was among the latter group, describing her temperament as "passionate without tenderness"; he wrote of Miss Moore in 1947, the year she was killed in a plane crash:

> I have mentioned as a requirement of the great artist deep love for the art one serves. This I am afraid is a qualification that Grace doesn't possess. In the first place she doesn't really love music, and in the second she has no willingness to serve music; she rather expects it to serve her, as indeed it has done and done well. Fundamentally, Grace is not concerned with artistic achievement per se.[26]

Tender she may not have been, but on the set of *New Moon* that summer of 1930, her passion extended to her handsome costar, who reciprocated with gusto. And although *New Moon* proved a bust at the box office, she and Larry enjoyed every moment the production allowed them together. Grace Tibbett's jealousy soared; for some reason, she was especially disturbed by this particular affair. Jane Burgard—who was then in San Francisco and still deeply in love with Larry—may also have heard of the offscreen romance; in any case, Larry's roving ways never seemed to affect their relationship.

The film *New Moon* was based thinly on Sigmund Romberg's 1928 operetta, *The New Moon*. Unaccountably, the setting has been moved to Russia, and the silly script must be taken on faith. Again there was no pre-recording, so Larry sang anew during each take, simply squandering his high As. He is a charmingly natural presence on screen; even today on video, it is easy to see his appeal.

Moore, somewhat fleshy for modern tastes, sings beautifully but is a bit too placid, playing her role straight as written and not adding much of her own zesty personality. Unfortunately, there are not enough scenes of Tibbett and Moore together, onscreen at least, to awaken the audience's interest in them as a couple. The film was also called *Parisian Belle*, to increase ticket sales to those to whom "Paris" was a synonym of "naughty."[27]

At the Tibbett family home on North Rexford Drive, Larry and Grace continued their useful habit of nonstop social entertaining, to escape being left alone with each other. A multicolored tent was set up next to the house through which caterers moved like clockwork, bearing trays of food and, above all, bootleg drink. Prohibition laws were everywhere and by everyone openly defied.

The Tibbetts' parties were welcomed and well attended by their widening circle of friends: actor Charles Farrell—Janet Gaynor's leading man—and his wife Virginia; Rupert Hughes; Leslie Howard, who before *Gone With the Wind* would become Grace's lover; Richard Day, who would be another of Grace's lovers; Nelson Eddy and Jeanette MacDonald. The British colony in Hollywood was represented by such actors as Clive Brook, Ronald Coleman, Nigel Bruce, Madeleine Carroll, and Basil Rathbone, who, with his wife Ouida, remained close to Larry long after the singer's Hollywood years.

As lately as 6 October 1994, on the obituary page of the *New York Times*, there was some interesting late-breaking news concerning Larry's heady Hollywood days and one Lina Basquette, "silent-film star and dog breeder," who had died at age 87. Apparently, when not busy with her nine marriages to seven husbands, she indulged in affairs with the rich and famous, among them Nelson Eddy, the prizefighter Jack Dempsey, "and the Metropolitan Opera baritone Lawrence Tibbett." Under the circumstances, it is hard to tell whether Basquette belonged to Larry's collection—or he to hers.

This movie-making was highly lucrative, and unlike the nation as a whole, Larry continued to ride high financially. So he signed with the Met to appear in only the second half of the 1930–31 season and remained in Hollywood that autumn of 1930 to begin shooting on his third film, *The Prodigal*. Although his salary at the Met remained modest ($550 each employed week[28]), the high fees paid for his numerous recitals, as well as for appearances on the Atwater-Kent radio hour, record royalties, and above all the large amounts he received in Hollywood, were beginning to add up. The income of the once poverty-stricken baritone, who had been grateful for $10 church jobs, now approached the half-million-dollar mark annually.

But no amount of money could ease the strains at home. In early January 1931, with filming complete and as the baritone was preparing to return to New York, his marriage finally came to an end.

Half a century later, Richard Tibbett, one of Larry's twin sons, recalled the night of the break. His father had come home late that evening, and Grace confronted him, screaming bitterly about his affair with Grace Moore. His parents' voices mounted ever higher, a mingling of fury and unloving sarcasm, until finally Larry left the house and Grace rushed to her bedroom, where she made her decision.

The next day, when the twins, now nearly 11 years old, were driven home from school by the family chauffeur, a more composed Grace was waiting for them. She told them that she and their father were getting a divorce and that she was leaving home immediately. She said that they, the twins, were to remain at home, where their governess, the chauffeur, the cook, and the downstairs maid would take care of them. Then, her face the color of alabaster, she climbed into her convertible, started the engine, and without a backward glance or wave of goodbye to her sons, drove away.[29]

Larry Jr. offered his own insights into the dissolution of his parents' marriage:

> Mother had no culture or polish and Dad's society contacts were terribly hard on her. She was a high-strung woman. She had an extremely crude voice, she was brash and noisy—but very smart. Mother liked to talk a lot, she was more of a talker than a listener. Dad, on the other hand, listened to what other people had to say. Mother was very aggressive; she really was a difficult person to live with. Dad was a total Don Juan.[30]

Rupert Pole—the son of Larry's Shakespearean mentor Reginald Pole, a friend of the twins, and one of author Anaïs Nin's two concurrent husbands—also had his opinion of Grace and Larry's marriage:

> It was believed that Larry was blackmailed into marrying Grace, that Grace got Larry to marry her at a weak moment. Larry was never meant to be married. His marriage to Grace was a miserable mistake. Grace did love him, as much as any woman can love a man, and he took advantage of that. He knew she loved him and got her to do all sorts of favors for him before they were married. He treated her churlishly.[31]

Kurt Weinhold, who would become Larry's manager, gave his perspective on the relationship between Larry and Grace:

> Naturally Tibbett had been ambitious. He was a very poor California boy who suddenly discovered that he had a voice. Like many young American boys, he had married entirely too early to the wrong woman. Grace was a very abrasive character and probably very jealous. She had good reason. Tibbett was a ladies' man and enjoyed the company of women. If Tibbett had a few words with an attractive colleague, Grace would upbraid him in public,

> reproach him for not making enough money in the beginning, and sound like a real martyr. Grace made unwarranted remarks and she didn't care how or when she made them. When Tibbett became more famous, he enjoyed the adulation of many important women, no doubt about that. He was an extrovert of the first order. He was never bashful. He now had the opportunity to enjoy life to the full, and as Grace had no social graces whatever, they began to drift apart.[32]

That drift had now become a full and welcome break, but a series of personal crises—psychological as well as emotional—would soon send Larry reeling.

Larry returned to New York to ready himself for the Met, taking the twins with him and enrolling the two boys in school. But Richard and Larry Jr. were still young and needed someone to look after them. Preferring not to involve a stranger, Larry asked his mother, Frances Ellen, to join them and perform the maternal duties, and she willingly agreed. Hadn't she helped out many times before? Indeed, their grandmother had been the one loving constant in the lives of those hapless children, pulled apart by their parents' conflicts. The boys adored her and called her Nana.

She had scarcely unpacked her bags at the Savoy Plaza, where Larry had installed them all in a suite, when both Richard and Larry Jr. came down with winter colds. They passed their colds on to their grandmother. On 21 January 1931 Larry sang Amonasro to the Aida of Elisabeth Rethberg and won his usual acclaim. He had to hide his worry as he sang, for his mother's cold had turned to pneumonia. In that prepenicillin era, little could be done to arrest the dreaded illness, and three days later Frances Ellen died. She had been in her son's household less than two weeks. On the coroner's certificate, hypertension was given as a secondary contributor to her death.[33]

This was a terrible blow to Larry. From earliest childhood, his mother had been his security, his protection. After the violent death of his father, she had kept the family together. Behind any success Larry may have achieved lay his mother's encouragement and unflagging faith in him.

With Larry's marriage to Grace and the arrival of the twins, Frances Ellen had turned her devotion to her grandsons. She sensed that they would never receive the proper parental attentions from Grace, an unloved wife, or from Larry, an unloving husband with a wandering eye, absorbed in his own career. The twins treasured their walks with Nana in the park and the way she tucked them into bed at night. Although she had long recognized the disaster of her son's marriage, she never took sides and always showed great warmth to her daughter-in-law.

A scant two days after his mother's death, Larry had to sing the elder Germont in *La Traviata* opposite the Violetta of Rosa Ponselle. These two American-trained artists, neither of whom had European experience, gave a most moving performance.

Following a scheduled Sunday evening concert at the Met in which he sang what had become old favorites, "Eri tu" and Valentin's aria from *Faust*, Larry flew in a private plane to California, where his mother's funeral took place at Forest Lawn Cemetery in Glendale. The twins had gone on ahead from New York by train, and Grace came from Reno, where she was establishing the necessary residency for the divorce.

Over the coffin draped with white orchids, Larry, tearful and upset, flew at Grace in a rage. If she hadn't abandoned her children and gone off to Reno, leaving Nana to care for them, his mother would never have caught the cold that developed into pneumonia. "My mother's death is your fault!" he shouted accusingly, deepening the already profound pool of bitterness between them.[34]

After Frances Ellen's funeral, Grace returned to Reno to complete the six-month residence requirement necessary to apply for Nevada's easy divorce laws; she also traveled periodically to Palm Springs, where she stayed at El Mirador. An undated letter Grace wrote to Larry during this period begins with mild chitchat then continues:

> I am seeing a lawyer Tuesday. . . . My dear sweet lovable person, be calm, have no fears. My friendship and belief last a lifetime. I shall do all in my power to grant the wish of your heart with as little trouble, embarrassment, and hurt to you and those connected with you. Only trust me and have faith in me, particularly now that I am totally dependent on you.

Then, in language that was almost a threat, she made it clear that she was still Mrs. Lawrence Tibbett to the world and would continue to live accordingly.[35]

Grace knew that she had the upper hand. Aware that her husband was in love with another woman[36] whom he wanted to marry, she could make unlimited personal demands for the divorce, and she did. Perhaps if Frances Ellen had lived, Grace could have been persuaded to be less vengeful. But Nana and her moderating influence were gone. Larry Jr. put it this way:

> Mother agreed to the divorce because there was a lot of money there. You might say she stuck it to him and he really had to pay. He paid well for his freedom. And he was very much in love with Jane. At the end there was a lot of fighting between the two of them. People get a divorce because they don't get along.[37]

So Larry's second personal blow of 1931 came swift and sure at the hands of his estranged wife. He could have his freedom under the following conditions:

One: Grace would have sole title to the house on North Rexford Drive. The deed also covered two parcels of valuable land adjacent to the house. In addition, she wanted two of their four cars, the Packard convertible and the Ford.

Two: Larry would pay Grace $4000 a year for the care and education of the twins during their minority. The agreement also included a life insurance policy for $65,000 in trust for the twins as beneficiaries. (Grace later sued Larry to increase the stipend and lost.)

Three: Grace would receive an alimony of $2000 per month for as long as she lived, whether or not she remarried. She also demanded $5000 upon her execution of the settlement.

To all these terms Larry wearily acceded. Years later, when Doris Wittschen, Larry's secretary, asked him why he ever agreed to such a one-sided settlement, he replied, "I wanted Grace to stop making such a nuisance of herself. I told the lawyers to give her what she wanted—as long as I was finally rid of her."[38]

The settlement rankled a long time. On 23 December 1940 Larry wrote a letter to his son Richard; after declaring himself against joining college fraternities, especially if there is no money to pay for them, he continued:

> I am enclosing a Christmas check to you for $100. I should like to see you use this present to pay for half of your semester's tuition at the University. Naturally, I am sorry that I cannot do more at this time. Your mother should have enough remaining out of the $300,000 in cash and property which she has received from me to fulfill her proper obligation to complete your education. I mention these facts, Richard, for the fact that I believe you are now man enough and responsible enough to be in possession of the

> facts. I told your mother the other day when she telephoned me that since Larry [Jr.] was here in New York I am willing for the time being to assume his educational and living expenses. These expenses are, as of course your mother knows, rightfully hers and in assuming Larry's expenses I am doing more than my share. If your mother has not sufficient money left over from the $300,000 to pay for your education, she should then mortgage some of her property to do so. All this money and property was not hers alone but part of it was given for you boys and your education and should have been handled so as not to have placed that education in jeopardy. Therefore, I don't see how either you or your mother should expect me to mortgage what I have in order to make up for her ready cash.[39]

In truth, Larry would never really be free of Grace until the day he died. Letters continued back and forth, his ex-wife asking for money and Larry parrying. Every morning from nine to twelve she would work on her writing; she then drank through the remaining hours of the day. By evening she would be feeling sufficiently maudlin to telephone Larry on any excuse: the alimony check was late, or the twins needed new clothes, or their riding horses needed shoeing. Long after the divorce, Grace would telephone Larry's office in New York City. As Doris Wittschen remembered,

> I always had to be on guard when she called. There was really no reason why she should have called anyway. But she did. I never knew what was going to happen, what she had on her mind when she phoned. Sometimes she would call at the weirdest hours.[40]

Larry Jr. confirmed this:

> Mother was in love with Dad all her life, but she used to bug him something terrible, particularly when he was married to Jane. She'd call and reverse the charges. She'd want to talk to him, usually after she'd had a few drinks. Actually, she made a real nuisance of herself.[41]

In the end, although she adored Larry, Grace Mackay Smith was his millstone—his nemesis. And he had not been particularly good for her, either.

Following their grandmother's funeral, the twins returned to the house on Rexford Drive, beginning a period of rootlessness that would last until their college years. Between 1931 and 1938 they attended a succession of boarding schools and then high schools in the East and West.[42] Larry never visited them at school. For the most part, they spent the summers in camps, and between boardings, they were installed back in the house in Beverly Hills, which they shared with various housekeepers and a changing parade of cooks, chauffeurs, and gardeners.

Larry had raced back from the funeral to New York to resume his engagements with the Met in the second half of the 1930–31 season. He had new challenges to face, both vocal and dramatic, and an entirely new life to forge. He remembered off and on that he had sons, but he didn't bother himself about them too much, other than to moralize to them by letter, as he had done to their mother years before.

The circumstances surrounding Larry's next performance as Amonasro must have provided a diversion from the harrowing times he had recently been through. This *Aida* was scheduled for the same evening on which he had also agreed to do a broadcast concert from the studio of a radio network.

Since the Ethiopian king does not appear onstage until the second scene of the second act of the opera, Larry had decided that there would be time enough to fulfill both engagements. His only worry was that if he waited until he returned from the broadcast, he might not have enough time to apply the extensive body makeup required by the role before his entrance. His solution was to fully make up for the character and don his leopard-skin costume before leaving for the broadcast.

That evening a terrifying individual, fiercely brown of face, beard, and form, strode from the Metropolitan Opera House into the pre-theater crowds on Broadway. He wore a woolly gray wig, a barbaric crown of horns, savage-looking earrings, and an array of tiger-tooth necklaces. Over it all was a Bond Street topcoat. Thonged sandals covered his feet.

People stared, gaped, gasped, and scrambled in all directions; some fascinated onlookers followed the strange being to a waiting taxi. A policeman had to clear a path through the traffic, but despite the reassuring presence of the officer, stops at Broadway's red lights brought volleys of stares, pointing fingers, and startled exclamations. Nevertheless Larry's two performances that evening took place exactly as scheduled.[43]

Gatti, faithful to his policy of encouraging native works, continued to bring American opera before the public. In February 1931 Larry created the title role in a new work, Deems Taylor's *Peter Ibbetson*, based on George du Maurier's romantic novel of childhood sweethearts who, tragically separated, continue to meet one another in their dreams. Tibbett played the braggart, cad, and egoist, Colonel Ibbetson. The lovers, Peter and Mary, were sung by Edward Johnson and Lucrezia Bori; Serafin conducted.

Peter Ibbetson proved the most successful American opera yet produced by the Metropolitan, but by general consent, it was distinguished by its libretto rather than by its music. Taylor's work was pronounced "unoriginal" and even "monotonous," but the choice of du Maurier's still fascinating story was considered a masterstroke. Larry's portrayal of Colonel Ibbetson was called "powerful and convincing" and his acting was said to have "genuine theatrical value."[44] "The inevitable temptation to call [the opera] *Peter Tibbetson* was not resisted," quipped Kolodin.[45]

Beginning in 1931, it was customary at the Metropolitan to submit Saturday afternoon broadcasts to what were known as "air checks," recordings of the live performances taken over a direct telephone line. Some time later some of these air checks—and even direct recordings from the radio broadcasts—appeared as "pirate" recordings, which the cognoscenti could obtain for their collections.[46] Thus generations not yet born when Larry and other singers of the era were in their prime can hear, in recordings of full-length performances, what would otherwise be only tales of legend.

Gatti scheduled *Peter Ibbetson* for several seasons, and an air check of excerpts from 17 March 1934 has captured a compelling Larry, the strong spine of the opera, with Bori and Johnson in extremely stylish form. Without question Gatti and his casts gave the American operas their best shot at popularity. The basically romantic music of *Peter Ibbetson* does seem overcome by the words, but it grows on the listener with repeated hearings, as does the music of Taylor's earlier *The King's Henchman*.

That same February of 1931 Larry received another lift when his film *The Prodigal*, renamed *The Southerner*, opened to critical acclaim. This item—headlined "Tibbett Puts Musical Across" and penned by a Mollie Merrick in the flavorful Hollywood-reporter style of the time—appeared in the 24 February 1931 edition of Des Moines, Iowa's *Tribune Capital*:

> Hollywood, Cal. Sometimes I feel sorry for these men who make pictures. No sooner do they come to the conclusion that musical

> films are out—and they get that way from studying box office sheets, believe me—then lo and behold the fickle public seems to take to musicals all over again.
>
> But a true sign that the weather vane of local approval is swinging musicwards again is the word that . . . Lawrence Tibbett will make two more pictures. This titan of the screen—for no great artist ever took a gelatin public so completely by storm as did Lawrence Tibbett—will go right on producing melodious stories for the fan's approval.
>
> His most recent picture, "The Southerner," is said to meet the approval of the sternest objectors on the M.G.M. lot. It opens with "The Glory Road," [sic] a spiritual with which Tibbett created a furor in his concertizing last year. A most unusual spiritual and one which was a hazardous venture even for concert audiences. It speaks well for movie men's courage and their faith in this artist's personality and art, when they opened a cinema story with this song. Esther Ralston plays opposite Tibbett.
>
> The song itself is full of the recitative which is Tibbett's strongest asset. It caught hold all over the country—was an instantaneous success on the radio—so found its way into "The Southerner," the tale of an American prodigal which is considered by many one of the outstanding bets of the musical year.

The Prodigal is a trivial film. Larry works very hard to create the character that the scriptwriters neglected to develop; he is charming but sings very little, and only the role of the mother, played by Emma Dunn, has any life. Others in the cast were Roland Young, Cliff ("Ukelele Ike") Edwards, Hedda Hopper, and Stepin Fetchit.

In March 1931, Grace kept up a somewhat fanciful account of the coming divorce to her childhood friend, Dorothy ("Crony") Cutting, in a vein that was both self-pitying and touching: the afflicted and blameless martyr who is managing, but just, to survive.[47] Her first letter was sent from Palm Springs:

> Dearest Crony—
>
> Life has played a little Hell with me of late.
>
> Jan. 10th to be exact my beloved Lawrence asked me calmly and quietly for a divorce. Two weeks later our dear mother died and left a gap and a heartache nothing seems to heal.
>
> The day before I left New Jersey to bring her body living to rest, Lawrence changed his mind about letting me publish our

> story, which took me a year to write and for which *The Woman's Home Companion* signed me up for the unheard of fee of $20,000. All this happening within a month has broken, at least temporarily, my spirit. I am down at the desert—trying to be healed—Oh God what beauty surrounds me here—what a healing touch is the spirit of the great open—and yet within me my battle is alone. I only know that if I had not been his wife I would have died. I loved him so desperately. At least I was spared that. I had fifteen years' association with him—12 married ones and they made of me anything which I am now. If this freedom means his happiness it shall be his.

The second letter was mailed two weeks later from the Riverside Hotel in Reno, not far from the river into which, traditionally, newly divorced wives pitched their wedding rings when a judge declared they were no longer bound to their husbands.

> Dearest Crony—
> There is no news. Twelve days have gone of my lonely sentence here. It is a pathetic place where 2000 women are trying to forget.
>
> My radio, a heavenly view of calm and kindly mountains help me to forget the adjustment that is trying to take place within me. I leave here if all goes well September 15th. Until then I am doing my level best to put up with my isolation and like it.
>
> The twins came over and spent the afternoon with me. I was so glad to see them.
>
> They will soon be going south for school. They will stay with their father until I finish here.

Larry's refusal to allow the publication of Grace's account of their life together may have been his revenge for the one-sided divorce settlement. Grace was furious about it for many years. His refusal may also have stemmed from a desire to end his marriage as privately as possible. But Larry was a public figure, and the glare of publicity was unavoidable.

With the Tibbett divorce out in the open, *Motion Picture Magazine* asked, "Did Hollywood wreck the Tibbett romance?" It answered its own question with a terse, inevitable "Yes."[48] Several Hollywood magazines portrayed Larry as a "mad genius" who was beset with unholy ambition, while Grace, as she had been since her earliest days at La Crescenta, was styled the hardworking wife and mother.

Most appalling to Larry was an account that his old friend Arthur Millier, best man at his wedding, wrote of Larry's marital life in the 2 August 1931 issue of the *Los Angeles Times*. Millier had decided to cash in on his intimacy with the Tibbett family, with writing that has a macabre poetry all its own. His melodramatic article concluded breathlessly:

> And what about Tibbett? Will he be happier? Are actors ever happy? When the klieg lights sputter into whiteness and the cameras turn, he will have no time to think of happiness.
>
> Once he stood on the tip of San Jacinto's peak looking down on the world and up at the thunder.
>
> "We don't love enough. We don't live enough. There is only life and death streaming through what we call love."
>
> Picture it out for yourself if a man like that can be what we plodding mortals call "happy."[49]

Larry was understandably furious. "Why did Arthur have to do this to me?" he raged. "I would have given him the money for this piece of junk."[50]

The divorce between Larry and Grace, on the agreed grounds of Larry's cruelty, became final on 15 September 1931. Though he was still financially bound to her as the mother of his sons, Larry was now legally free. Jane's divorce from John Clark Burgard, also in Reno, was not final until 14 December. She told the newspapers on that day that she was definitely not going to marry Mr. Tibbett.

On New Year's Day 1932, Lawrence Tibbett married Jane Marston Burgard in New York City. At last, Larry had made a marriage of true love, and a splendid new life began for them both.

Chapter 6

TO THE HEIGHTS

"Lawrence Tibbett Weds Mrs. Burgard." The photograph accompanying the headline in the 2 January 1932 issue of the *New York Times* showed the couple standing before an ornate door in the apartment of Hunter Marston, Jane's brother, where they were married. The beautiful Mrs. Tibbett, reported the newspaper, had worn a gown of sapphire-blue velvet trimmed with ermine and a matching hat. Her corsage was of white orchids. The noted baritone wore a blue serge suit with a white carnation as a boutonniere. Because of his operatic and concert engagements, the wedding trip would be postponed until late spring. The bride and groom would make their home at the Hotel Pierre in Manhattan until they found a suitable apartment.

It was a relief to Larry to put 1931 behind him. December had dealt him one final blow: his fourth motion picture, *Cuban Love Song*, which had been shot during the heat of his legal wranglings with Grace, almost as an afterthought, had opened to universally bad reviews. *Variety* wrote that the film suffered endlessly from incoherent action forced upon what was otherwise strictly a narrative. There was "maybe too much singing" and an "unnecessary and unrealistic" shot of Tibbett in double exposure, singing a duet with himself.[1]

Larry would later write that he had been "shy and awed at the prospect of appearing with such famous women as Jeritza, Alda, Ponselle, and Bori, but the only leading woman who really had me scared to death was Lupe Velez," his costar in *Cuban Love Song*. When they met, he complimented her on her voice, about which he knew nothing, and sang a Spanish love song to her. This calculated approach tamed the spitfire, and in the end, Larry wrote, "I have never worked more peacefully with a leading woman."[2]

Cuban Love Song, which costarred Jimmy Durante, is a strange film. "Cuba" is too obviously a studio lot in Hollywood, Durante's comedic talents are all but wasted, and male chauvinism is rampant in the Tibbett character. Larry and his Navy ship are based in Cuba, and there he meets Velez, playing her Spanish bombshell persona. The magic between them is immediate, and from that point on the film rises to a higher level of emotion and realism. In the touching final sections Larry shows strong, mature acting. Period piece though it is, *Cuban Love Song* holds charm for audiences even today. But it was poorly received in 1931, and Larry was discouraged. Although he and Durante became and remained friends, it would be three years before Larry returned to Hollywood to make another film.

The year 1932 was kinder. Not only did it begin with the happiest of nuptials but by the end of the first month, on 28 January, Larry achieved his greatest triumph ever at the Metropolitan Opera House.

In March 1857, Giuseppe Verdi confounded Venetian audiences with his 19th opera, *Simon Boccanegra*, a gloomy work with a confusing story that presupposes a working knowledge of the bloody medieval struggle between the Guelphs and the Ghibellines. Twenty-five years elapse between the Prologue and Act One, and the soprano changes names before the audience has met her. The opera found favor with the critics but was rejected by the public. Baffling though the libretto might be, the character of the wise but vulnerable Doge Boccanegra, a buccaneer who rises to become the ruler of the Genoan empire with ultimately tragic results, possesses almost Shakespearean dimensions.

Twenty-four years later, before Verdi agreed to compose *Otello*, he asked his new librettist (and former critic) Arrigo Boito to revise the text of *Boccanegra* and tried again with it. The revision had its premiere at La Scala in 1881 and was enthusiastically received. It was still dark, however, with long, almost Russian scenes scored for only low voices, and it languished another half century until the author Franz Werfel, who had written a biography of Verdi, promoted performances in 1930 in Berlin and Vienna and the following year in Naples. For these productions the libretto was further clarified.

The revivals did not go unnoticed by Gatti. Since he had the services of a superb baritone who was also a great actor, as well as an exceptional supporting cast, he decided to mount the opera for the first time at the Met. Onstage with Maria Müller, Martinelli, and Pinza, under Serafin's baton, Larry brought Simon Boccanegra to life. His portrayal was a total triumph. According to W. J. Henderson, writing in the *New York Sun*, he "achieved one of the signal artistic successes of his career by presenting a finely wrought characterization in which admirable singing and acting, appropriate costumes and skillful make-up were harmoniously combined." Henderson further commented that Hollywood had taught Larry "much about dress, facial expressions and gesture. He is now one of the best actors on the operatic stage."[3]

Lawrence Gilman in the *New York Herald Tribune* was even more rhapsodic:

> Mr. Tibbett makes [Simon] an engrossing and impressive figure, almost a great one. His denotement of the Doge's magnanimity, his courage and his tenderness . . . his imperial dignity, his tragic pathos, is quite the finest thing that Mr. Tibbett has accomplished in opera. This is a remarkable embodiment in its truth, its power, its authority, its ease, its fluency and grace.[4]

For Larry, this artistic success was no accident. He had prepared for the Doge's role with the same relentless zeal with which he had approached the part of Ford in *Falstaff*. Conductor Serafin (whose last renowned "student" would be Maria Callas) had coached him again, and their intense collborative study of the character had borne ripe fruit.

On the afternoon following the *Boccanegra* premiere, Larry again sang Colonel Ibbetson. In the Sunday concert he sang three songs and, with Martinelli, a duet from *La forza del destino*. The unhappiness that had hung over his personal life for years was at last dispelled. Now content and productive, he could concentrate entirely and triumphantly on the tasks at hand.

Although 1932 was a boom year for Larry, for the nation as a whole it was the worst since the stock market crash of 1929. The Depression had deepened, and President Hoover seemed unable to bring about any kind of economic recovery. This, however, was an election year, and if the country voted Democrat Franklin Delano Roosevelt into the

White House, perhaps this patrician New York governor would be able to effect a turnaround.

Still the lines at soup kitchens around the country lengthened; once well-to-do men and women sold apples on the fashionable streets of Manhattan's Upper East Side. That autumn Mr. and Mrs. Lawrence Tibbett moved into a flat renting for $1000 a month at 120 East End Avenue, at the corner of Eighty-fifth Street, in one of New York's grandest apartment buildings.

The apartment overlooked Manhattan and the East River. Several blocks to the West, in Central Park, were row after row of what appeared at first to be wooden crates—until one noticed the smoke coming from bent stovepipes attached to their tops. Human beings in ragged clothes passed in and out of the structures; these "Hoovervilles," where the dismally poor existed under the picture windows of the rich, had sprung up simultaneously around the country.

The Metropolitan Opera offered its own study in contrasts. Once inside the gilded auditorium with its gold brocade curtain and red plush seats, operagoers could forget the Depression—particularly on Monday evenings, when ladies appeared aglitter with precious gems, their arms encased in shoulder-length white kid gloves, and sat in the front seats of the exclusive Diamond Horseshoe boxes while their escorts, in tailcoats and white ties, sat or stood discreetly behind them. The all-male members of the Opera Club, in their side section on the tier above, were always immaculate in white tie.

Backstage, however, the management was finding it increasingly difficult to finance the season. Had it not been for Gatti's years of penny-pinching, and above all for his Emergency Fund, which had swelled to a million dollars before the crash, the company might have already gone under. Even so, as 1932 progressed, the dismal threat of closure loomed ever larger.

In March 1932 Gatti scheduled the first of a number of fund-raising benefits. They were planned with a great deal of imagination, juxtaposing serious music with comic capers. Stars such as Lily Pons, Grace Moore, Lauritz Melchior, and Tibbett, together and sometimes clowning on the stage, could be counted on to sell the seats for the galas even as attendance at the regular opera performances declined.

The baritone finished out the season with more Boccanegras as well as Dapertutto, Amonasro, and the elder Germont. For the following season Gatti asked the leading singers to take pay cuts. The very existence of the opera company was now threatened by the national economy. Bori, Ponselle, Richard Crooks, Pinza, and Tibbett complied, but not Gigli, who thus ended his association with the Met and returned to Italy, singing "Giovinezza." Maria Jeritza also left the Metropolitan at this time, though not for financial reasons. Larry became a member of a committee to raise money for the Met.

With opera and concert engagements concluded, Jane and Larry set sail for Europe and their delayed wedding trip. This was Larry's first time across the Atlantic, although most of the repertoire for which he was celebrated, apart from his successes in new American operas, was European and in European languages.

In Spain, the Tibbetts met Titta Ruffo, who had retired from the Met in 1929. At a party in their mutual honor, the two baritones sang together and praised each other's vocal accomplishments. In Switzerland, Larry spent some time with the American composer Louis Gruenberg, who was completing his opera *The Emperor Jones*, scheduled for the Met and for Larry during the 1932–33 season. The Tibbetts also visited many of the opera houses on the Continent. Upon his return to New York, the baritone insisted to reporters that American singers were the equal of Europeans.

The effect of the Depression on the Met became apparent when a considerably truncated season opened on 21 November 1932, more than three weeks later than usual. Larry's Boccanegra was accorded the honor of opening night, and he later appeared as Valentin, Amonasro, and the elder Germont, by now familiar roles for him. Then, at the matinée of 7 January 1933, he created a role that many regarded as the apex of his career. This was Brutus Jones, in the world premiere of *The Emperor Jones*. Gruenberg had based his opera on Eugene O'Neill's play about a former Pullman-car porter who, having set himself up on an island in the West Indies as a brutal, posturing dictator, is finally forced to flee by his vengeful subjects.

Critics disagreed as to the merits of the short, harsh, melodramatic work. To Pitts Sanborn of the *World Telegram*, the opera was at its most effective when the composer allowed the characters to speak their lines over the accompaniment of distant drumbeats. "The orchestral commentary," he wrote, "for the most part sounded less like the issue of an inspired imagination than like a remembered conversation."[5]

Olin Downes was more positive. He praised Gruenberg for achieving a masterly contrast of mood and proportion in his music, the approach of which he variously described as headlong, fantastical, and "prodigiously sure." He declared that the role of the title character as written was "worthy of the greatest singer and dramatist, and the highest traditions of the musico-dramatic stage." Evidently Larry fit the bill; Downes called Larry's reading of the part "his supreme achievement."[6]

Indeed, the critics voiced unanimous enthusiasm for Larry's portrayal of the half-mad, fugitive Emperor Jones. In her book *Twentieth-Century Music*, Marion Bauer would write, "It is a one-man opera. Lawrence Tibbett made the most of a character part such as never before has come to a singer to perform."[7] But it remained for Lawrence Gilman, critic of the *New York Herald Tribune*, to pull out all the stops in his praise of Larry:

> We were indebted less at yesterday's premiere to the brilliant performance of Mr. Lawrence Tibbett as Brutus Jones, the Negro bad man and fugitive Emperor, who dominated the proceedings, from the moment he appeared, blustering, insolent, preposterous, in his blue military coat with the brass buttons and gold chevrons and his bright-red breeches until, an abject and ghost-ridden savage, praying, pleading, whimpering and hysterical, shorn of this thin caking of sophistication, he shot himself with his cherished silver bullet, an atavistic sacrifice.
>
> One hesitates to apply to the achievement of a gifted and serious artist the cheap word "triumph"—a word debased by facile and irresponsible employment. But one needs not hesitate to use the word concerning Mr. Tibbett and his Emperor Jones as enacted at yesterday's performance.
>
> It was, beyond question, his afternoon, his and O'Neill's—though this lonely and inimitable genius was nowhere to be seen, and was reputed to be far away. Mr. Tibbett's imaginative grasp and embodiment of a cruelly exacting role, his power of spacing and his control of climax, the long, inexorable crescendo of his progressive panic and degradation, were accomplished with a great artist's economy and reserve and cumulative power.
>
> The thunderous tribute which the young American received from the great audience (which filled the house to the last square foot of standing room) was as unmistakably heartfelt and irresistible as the most fanatical of operatic patriots could have wished.[8]

In those enlightened days, Larry's appearing in the stage jungle with a bare torso could be accepted. But his taking of curtain calls without first getting dressed was both controversial and quite good publicity.

Soprano Rose Bampton, who sang and recorded with Larry over the years, called his Boccanegra remarkable, but his Emperor Jones was "just out of this world. What a great voice it was in quality and tone, and he was a great actor—tremendous, really. He was strong in everything he did."[9]

The film of the O'Neill play *Emperor Jones*, starring Paul Robeson, also opened in 1933. Both Larry and Robeson possessed the intellect to learn from the other, and it would be interesting to know if the great actors had influenced each other in their impersonations. The final scene from the world premiere broadcast has been issued on CD by Pearl in passable sound. Aside from his flawless diction, in dialect, and his amazing ability to make music of the lines that are straight play dialogue, Larry extends himself to the utmost dramatically: he seems to go almost beyond himself, but with absolute discipline and art.

His commercial recording of Jones's monologue "Standin' in the need of prayer" was made in January 1934 for RCA Victor. It has been reissued many times since and remains a classic. In the late 1950s a young baritone who wanted to learn the monologue for his repertoire borrowed the vocal score of the opera from the library and found that what Tibbett sings on the recording is adapted quite freely from what Gruenberg had written. The bass-baritone George London had recently recorded "Standin' in the need of prayer," and so the student asked him where he had gotten his arrangement. London laughed his warm, deep laugh. "From the Tibbett record," he said.[10]

What a long way the gawky baritone from California had come since he first arrived in New York City 11 years earlier. Professionally, he was now a vocal artist of the first rank, and his career was firmly established.

His social progress, too, had been meteoric, and with his second marriage, he embarked on a highly sophisticated, nonstop social life on an elevated plane. At first, Jane had been apprehensive that her new husband, a singer, would not be accepted by her family and friends. But her brothers, particularly Hunter, liked Larry enormously and welcomed him into the Marston family and its exclusive circle of friends. The people Larry and Jane entertained at their luxurious East End Avenue apartment were artists, financiers, blue bloods, and celebrities from all fields. Fascinating and diverting as this social whirl must have been, it would eventually add to his undoing.

For even more than a professional athlete, a classical singer must keep up rigorous physical training. The singer's voice, his or her most precious asset, is contained wholly within the body, which must always be protected and nurtured. Most singers try to keep regular hours and at least avoid continuous party-going and late-night occasions, especially during the season of appearances. This is admittedly difficult on the evenings of performances, since singers wish and need to unwind after the adrenalin rush that comes from singing before a responsive audience.

In an earlier age, the soprano Olive Fremstad was so keyed up after her New York performances that, according to her secretary, she had to calm down with a fast walk along Riverside Drive before she could eat a bite of her supper. Then her secretary had to read aloud to her before the soprano could fall asleep.[11] Singers continue to have their individual methods of winding down and coming back to the world after their performances. Rest, as well as relaxation, should be part of it.

The temptation to attend parties given by his wife or admiring friends, or to go to receptions hosted by out-of-town concert sponsors, was too great for Larry. Singers must eat, and many do so after the work is done, at such parties and receptions. There is a limit, however.

According to Larry's son Richard, the baritone did not eat at all on the afternoon of a performance, preferring instead to sleep. Weight was not a problem for him as he kept himself in shape with his rowing machine and, on non-performance days, he "loved salads, and was a nut for fresh vegetables, particularly corn on the cob, but wasn't much for desserts."[12]

But what about drink? Singers have been known to drink, even to drink to excess, and there have been many famous cases of those it hurt and those it did not seem to affect. Larry, from his earliest childhood, had been close to two-fisted drinkers, including his own deputy-sheriff father and saloonkeeper uncle. During his young manhood and first years in New York, Prohibition had given alcohol consumption an unprecedented allure. He was probably too poor to be able to drink much then, but as his career progressed, and particularly when he entered the social orbits of New York and Hollywood, liquor became more and more easily available to him. Grace Tibbett also liked to drink, and Larry and Grace, in pushing each other on to intoxication, found an easy way to mask the pain of their relationship. Now, with an heiress on his arm and Manhattan at his feet, Larry had more glamorously inviting occasions to drink than ever before.

The apartment Larry and Jane shared on East End Avenue, built by Vincent Astor, was cavernous and sumptuously laid out. Reached by private elevator, it had a dining room that comfortably seated 40 guests.

The apartment included a huge pantry and kitchen, four maid's rooms, and a butler's chamber. From the windows stretched dramatic vistas of the city that Jane's handsome new husband, the lionized young baritone, had conquered.

Tibbett was the perfect enticingly theatrical addition to her monied world, the young Gary Cooper who complemented her Marlene Dietrich–inspired hats and Valentino dresses in striking shades of red and blue. Larry Jr. described his stepmother:

> She was a very well-organized woman, and whatever money could afford, she had. She had a masseuse come in every day and do her back. She lived the good life. The masseuse would arrive about 11; then she was ready for lunch at an expensive place in New York City—21 or the Colony. She was on the "Ten Best-Dressed Women" list for 10 years. She spent about $50,000 a year on clothes. She had the very best of care.
>
> She loved to party. Dad tried to beg out lots of times, but she was too strong-willed for him. She made him go and he went. She moved in high society in New York: the Astors, the Vanderbilts, the sponsors of the Met. Jane traveled in what we now call the jet set. She had expensive tastes and did everything she wanted to do. She watched her diet scrupulously.
>
> She was a very formal person. She was a leader. She had people doing all sorts of things for her, secretaries and other employees. She never did any work at all, it was always done for her. People waited on her and she knew how to give orders.[13]

Appearances were everything to Jane. Tenor James Melton's daughter remembered that when her father died, Jane insisted his widow borrow one of her black hats and nearly opaque veil for the funeral. Jane also lent her apartment for the post-funeral gathering. "She knew just what was needed—before, during, and after. In her friendly but opinionated manner, she insisted on just what my mother needed."[14]

With the apartment, and with Larry at her side, Jane could make the most of her talents. She was beautiful; she had never known anything but wealth and privilege. Although her speaking voice was nothing out of the ordinary, she was quite well-spoken.[15] The quintessential hostess, she could graciously bring charm and amusement into the lives of a whole gathering of people, all to the accompaniment of superb food, fine wines, and a steady stream of strong spirits.

Neither of the Tibbetts was particularly politically minded, but Jane, the daughter of a staunchly Republican family, moved in circles that regarded the new man in office, President Roosevelt, with almost paranoid intensity as "that man"—a betrayer and a threat to their abundance and to his class. Jane and her friends burlesqued Eleanor Roosevelt for her looks, her mode of dress, and her "parlor pink" espousal of causes that aided the poor. In contrast, Larry, a Democrat from a working-class background, admired the president for his political skill and his humanitarianism. Wisely, Larry and Jane did not often discuss politics together.

And so, beginning in the autumn of 1932 and continuing through the Depression years, parties and larger parties with hundreds of guests came to be routine in the Tibbetts' apartment. All the seductions of a high-flying social life—rich food, plenteous drink, late hours, and lovely, available women—became the norm in the life of the gregarious baritone. He had not ceased his womanizing when he had fallen in love with Jane, and neither did his marriage to her alter him. He continued to relish sexual escapades. These were "recreational," without emotional depth, and were enjoyed as such by his partners and accepted by all in his social milieu, including his wife. Though he appeared at ease among his high-powered friends, he was new to their game. If he felt intimidated or even slightly panicky in some of the situations in which he found himself, there was always a drink at hand to steady him.

After a performance, Larry "always preferred to go home and rest," but how could he rest in a home where he would invariably find a party in full swing—and Jane waiting to show him off to their guests "like a trained bear, in spite of the fact that he had to sing in an opera or concert the next day."[16] Larry did not begin smoking with any seriousness until he married Jane, herself a heavy smoker. She was also a serious drinker. Larry Jr. remembered:

> [Jane] really directed my father. Dad was a nice guy; he put up with it. She had a habit of showing him off like a puppet at her cocktail parties. Eventually he got used to it and began to enjoy it, but in the beginning he dreaded it. He never drank very much until he married Jane. He was a good guy, and he went along with her. This was not in his best interest, especially after a performance at the Met. Then he would return home and start to party.[17]

Larry's new life did not yet impinge upon his concert and opera appearances. His breakneck schedule at the Metropolitan for the month of February 1933, at the height of his career, included Mercutio in *Roméo et Juliette* on 3 February, the all-encompassing *Emperor Jones* on 8 February, a repeat of *Jones* on 11 February, and Valentin in *Faust* on 13 February, to say nothing of opera rehearsals and pre-concert run-throughs.

After his performance on the 13th, he immediately boarded a train for a recital in North Carolina on the 15th, then one in Georgia on the 17th and another in Virginia on the 20th. Then he took the train back to North Carolina for a concert on the 22nd, went further south to Alabama for the 24th, and on to Florida for appearances on the 26th and 27th, with another on 1 March. After each concert appearance he would undoubtedly be toasted as the guest of honor at a reception. With glass in hand, he would charm the adoring guests and unwind.

Although Jane was now in the early months of pregnancy, the much sought-after couple entertained when Larry was home, or they would go out to parties given by other members of their circle. On the rare night without a party, Larry might repair to Toots Shor's, a favorite watering hole for sporting people, where he got along famously with the proprietor. Larry placed great emphasis on manliness, and he considered drinking with his cronies to be one of the manly arts.

At Toots Shor's, in the company of pals such as his lawyer Henry Jaffe, Larry would knock off four glasses of wine within an hour and chase them down with an Irish Mist. If the conversation lagged, more orders for the still-contraband wine and spirits could be counted on to loosen everyone's tongues and set them to telling the latest ribald jokes.[18]

Ideally, a singer should rest between engagements, eat properly, abstain from heavy drinking, and shun public places and drafts to avoid picking up a cold. On the day of a performance, he should rarely speak and avoid wide temperature fluctuations lest they cause phlegm in his throat or mucus in his sinuses, which would mar the beauty and ease of his singing. In short, Larry was leading an exhausting and perilous life, far from the ideal.

On 17 August 1933, Jane gave birth to her fourth son, Michael Edward. Larry had half-hoped for a daughter he could name after his mother, but his baby boy was another high point in a memorable year.

On 9 November 1933, the American Academy of Arts and Letters presented its gold medal to Larry in a formal ceremony in its auditorium. Nicolas Murray Butler, chief officer of the academy and president of Columbia University, made the presentation. Standing beside

Butler, dressed formally and with a gold chain across his chest, was Governor Wilbur Cross of Connecticut, also an officer of the academy. The citation noted that Larry was a leader in the campaign for English-language opera and a master of diction. He was the first singer to receive the medal, which, since the inaugural award to actor Walter Hampden, had always gone to actors. (In 1944, another singer-actor, Paul Robeson, would be awarded the medal.)

Larry, in a cutaway coat and striped pants, stood stiffly next to Dr. Butler and delivered his words of acceptance in a deep, resonant voice:

> Dr. Butler, Governor Cross, ladies and gentlemen of the academy: I thank you for the great honor you have bestowed upon me, by granting me the Medal for Good Diction on the Stage.
>
> As you can well imagine, receiving the medal is a thrilling and happy moment in my life, and I am grateful you felt I was worthy to receive it. I shall treasure it always.[19]

That night, during a flight to San Francisco for two performances of *The Emperor Jones*, Larry examined his medal. It was gold-plated and roughly the size of a quarter. On one side, the "Spirit of the Drama" appeared in the conventional Greek robe, with a small wreath in her hair and sandals on her feet. She was walking forward, bearing the familiar masks of comedy and tragedy, as well as a branch of laurel. Her wind-blown cape and forward movement suggested progress. On the reverse was the Academy's Pegasus, like Larry, soaring above the clouds.

Larry's schedule was as hectic that November as it had been the previous February: a concert in New York on the 2nd; one in New Jersey on the 3rd; and concerts on the 5th, 6th, and 8th in Washington, D.C., Virginia, and Mississippi. He then rushed back to New York overnight to accept the academy's medal on the 9th, followed by the slow cross-country flight to begin rehearsals for *Emperor Jones* with the San Francisco Opera.

The opera met with some boos at its San Francisco premiere.[20] Alexander Fried of the *San Francisco Chronicle*, who in 1928 thought Larry's Scarpia less a satyr than a Puritan father gone wrong, called Gruenberg's score for *Jones* not eloquent, never glorifying diction into really thrilling utterance.[21] Larry's portrayal of Jones was again a great personal success.

The baritone again appeared in this work on 17 November 1933, sang Tonio in *Pagliacci* on the 21st, and, with soprano Claudia Muzio as Violetta, performed as the elder Germont in *La Traviata* on the 24th.

On the 27th he gave a San Francisco recital. On the 30th he reappeared as Brutus Jones. And between 2 and 15 December, he sang seven concerts on a Western tour, devoting 13 days to the usual bumpy train rides, bad food, and uncomfortable hotels.

It was on this particular concert tour that Larry heard the news that the Eighteenth Amendment had been repealed and that Prohibition was no more. Liquor would continue to flow as before, but now it was legal.

Larry's schedule that autumn was enough to fell a horse, let alone a vocalist with a delicate instrument to protect and the need to expend a tremendous amount of energy in each performance. Yet Larry not only survived this killing pace but flourished. As rugged as the man, seemingly unaffected by climatic changes and invulnerable to the effects of tobacco and alcohol, his rich, sonorous, utterly expressive voice continued to enthrall audiences wherever he sang. His vitality seemed limitless—until the inevitable problems arose.

In 1934 the Tibbetts acquired a second residence, called Honey Hill Farm, in Wilton, Connecticut, between Norwalk and Danbury. It was a perfect establishment for a gentleman farmer and a fine place to bring up four growing boys, the three from Jane's second marriage, and Michael, the child of their present union. The twins born to Larry and Grace were only occasional visitors due to the terms of the divorce and Larry's lack of interest. For all, the farm was a welcome contrast to the professional and social duties of the city apartment; it was a place to enjoy the outdoors, to do physical chores, and to let off steam.

The original one-story house was built in 1711, set on 50 choice acres with a three-quarter-mile frontage. Additions over the years had added two more stories, and the house now had 15 rooms and several outbuildings. Larry retained the architect Aymar Embury to remodel the buildings and to modernize the entire farm. When in 1935 the renovations were completed, the east wing, which had been a barn, housed a 55-foot-long two-story studio and music room. It also boasted a fireplace seven feet high.[22]

Larry was euphoric while collaborating with the architect. His vision included a temperature-controlled wine cellar, and they turned the old farm buildings into contemporary structures, both functional and aesthetic. Larry derived much satisfaction from working a true farm, one that raised its own hay and grazed three cows, a pig, a goat, chickens, and a workhorse. The Tibbetts also raised eight dogs at a time for the benefit of the Seeing Eye Foundation.

Fields of corn flourished at Honey Hill Farm, as Larry had developed an insatiable appetite for fresh corn. There was also a quarry and land for growing vegetables; more than 30 of the 50 acres were set aside for apple and pear orchards, which blossomed exquisitely in the spring. In keeping with their lifestyle, the Tibbetts sold most of the eggs and vegetables raised on their farm to the Stork Club and the 21 Club in Manhattan.

Though Honey Hill provided Larry with the outdoor life he enjoyed, he was still first and foremost a consummate professional singer. Mornings from eight o'clock until noon were devoted to studying repertoire with his accompanist Stewart Wille. Only after that would Larry don his work clothes and happily toil in the fields until sundown. When he was away on concert and opera appearances, the farm was managed by a professional farmer.

Since every New Year's Eve carried over to the first of January, their wedding anniversary, Jane and Larry had given annual parties at their New York apartment to mark both occasions. The guest list for these gala events was so sparkling that they were always fully covered by the media. Later, the celebrations were held at Honey Hill Farm, where they were smaller and intended to accommodate friends who lived in the Wilton and Norwalk area: Met tenor Mario Chamlee and his wife, soprano Ruth Miller; tenor James Melton; violinist Jascha Heifetz; composer Deems Taylor; Grace Moore, now married; coloratura Lily Pons and her husband, conductor André Kostelanetz; Frank Chapman and his wife, contralto Gladys Swarthout; and the former diva Geraldine Farrar. If there was snow, the party would invariably conclude with mile-long downhill toboggan runs. Jane would put as much planning and thought into these affairs at the farm as she had done for the large East End Avenue soirées.

On the Fourth of July the whole family usually gathered, and Larry shot off fireworks from "Brünnhilde's Rock," which was fun for all. But at the few dinners they all had together, the boys had to wear shirts, ties, and suits and were not allowed to talk.[23] Larry saw his twin sons once or twice a year, when they came to him. Though he was genuinely fond of them, he did not project much warmth to them or to the younger Michael but remained reserved and seemingly aloof. Perhaps he thought it unmanly to give overt demonstrations of love to other males. He accepted Jane's children as his own, with the same conservative friendliness.

Inevitably, this mélange of assorted children from various marriages was burdened with tensions, which the three self-absorbed parents did little to dissipate. One of the twins, Richard, has said "I never had attention, love, instruction, concern, or guidance from my father, and very little from my mother. [I spent] countless nights of crying [and] was set apart by servants, town cars, notable father, and guarded isolation."[24]

Larry Jr. saw much to admire in Jane and even compared her favorably to Grace. As he recalled,

> I particularly remember meeting Jane for the first time. I sensed immediately that Dad would marry Jane; I could tell by the way they looked at each other. They both wore signet rings that, when opened, revealed tiny photos of each other. As young as I was, I felt instinctively that Jane was different from any woman I had ever seen with Dad. She was tall, beautiful, and very much high society. When I was with Jane, it was a lot different from being with Grace, my mother. I guess Jacqueline Onassis was as close a look-alike to Jane as I can remember. Jane was a snob, of course, but she was invited everywhere. The people in Jane's set had their days all plotted out for them in advance.[25]

Larry and Jane's domestic life was complex. It was complicated by the tugs and pulls of their utterly different backgrounds, by the confused relationships of their children, and above all, by the dominating whirl of nonstop social engagements. Through it all, the baritone tried to hold on to his priorities. He once said to Larry Jr., "You know, son, my first love in life is music, the second is Jane, and the third is my children"—a daunting message to a child, to learn he is third on his father's list.[26]

The Metropolitan's 1933–34 season opened later than usual, on 26 December, with Larry as Peter Ibbetson. So badly had the Met been hit by the Depression that many thought it was a miracle Gatti had opened the doors at all, even for so truncated a season. To raise money, he again produced imaginative evenings of concerts. At one of these, Tibbett sang "Ol' Man River" from *Showboat*.

Somehow Gatti found the money to introduce the season's only novelty, the world premiere of an opera by Howard Hanson, a composer born in Wahoo, Nebraska, and director of the Eastman School of Music in Rochester, New York. This was *Merry Mount*, set in Puritan New England. Pitts Sanborn of the *World Telegram* summed up the plot as "the brief invasion of the pious shores of Massachusetts by some boisterous cavaliers, who set up a big, bad Maypole and dance around it like unregenerate heathen."

Sanborn continued: "*Merry Mount* is almost a one-part opera and that part is Wrestling Bradford." And who created the role? Lawrence Tibbett, exhibiting "once more his intelligence and skill as a singing actor, as well as splendid courage and endurance."[27]

Merry Mount was the 15th American opera presented by the persistent Gatti. Yet because it seemed to critics nearer to oratorio than opera, with little lyric power, this musical product of the United States, like its predecessors, appeared destined for oblivion despite the vocal and dramatic power that Tibbett brought to it.[28]

From the air check of the 10 February 1934 premiere, we can judge that *Merry Mount*, which is melodic and powerful, is one of the American operas most worthy of a major revival. Tibbett, in this performance, is towering. His diction is extremely clear, even with this flawed recording's primitive sound, and he reads his lines as the definitive actor he was. His voice has a tremendous richness and command.

An air check also exists of a 10 March 1934 *Pagliacci*. As usual, Larry owns the Prologue, and he conveys a strong undercurrent of jealousy and evil throughout. He was a stickler for reality as Tonio: Helen Jepson sang her first Nedda with him a season later, and Larry told her beforehand to hit him with the whip and, if she could get close enough, to bite him on the ear. "Well, I didn't really hit him with the whip, but I did bite him. Offstage he laughed and said 'You really got me!'"[29] With Queena Mario and Martinelli, this is a good performance all around.[30]

With *Peter Ibbetson*, *Merry Mount*, and *Pagliacci*, the other operas Larry appeared in that season of 1933–34 were *Emperor Jones*, *Simon Boccanegra*, *La Bohème*, and *Faust*. Now in the prime of his career, Larry's concerts sold out wherever they took place. Whatever their sacrifices in those economically depressed times, audiences managed to scrape together enough money for tickets to hear the magnetic artist.

In June 1934, upon returning to Honey Hill Farm after a concert tour, Larry received a phone call from Mrs. August Belmont (née Eleanor Robson), the former actress for whom George Bernard Shaw had written *Major Barbara*. In precisely enunciated words, this member of the board of the Metropolitan Opera informed him that the board of trustees of New York University was awarding him an honorary doctorate in music as the "foremost American singer of his era."[31]

Larry attended New York University's commencement ceremonies in Manhattan on 13 June. Dr. Kingsley, dean of the Graduate School of Arts and Sciences, delivered a flowery commendation:

> Lawrence Tibbett speaks a universal language, the eloquent discourse of music; even as he honors us by his presence, we honor him for his services to an age that sorely needs the soothing and inspiring agency of song superbly rendered. He is presented for the degree of Doctor of Music.[32]

The new chancellor, Harry Woodburn Chase, then soberly intoned:

> Lawrence Tibbett: As an American who has achieved high distinction in your art, as one who has set and has worked for high standards in your profession, as one whom the community delights to honor, I now confer upon you the degree of Doctor of Music by the authority invested in me by the Council of New York University.[33]

Larry was the recipient of several honorary degrees, but he would always feel acutely uncomfortable surrounded by academicians. He intensely disliked their speech and manners, which he considered pompous (and what did he think of the speech and manners of social soirées?). He preferred the stage of an opera house, where, for him, life was real.

Nonetheless receiving the honorary doctorate gave him a pronounced lift, adding to his joy at being a young 38-year-old bursting with health and at the height of a marvelous career. In addition, the boys had returned to the farm for the summer, and the baby, Michael, was a robust and charming one-year-old.

Summer vacation was a relaxed and peaceful interlude during which the older boys did the chores, haying and weeding and feeding the livestock. For this they were paid a dollar an hour. Toward the end of August, Larry jubilantly began to harvest the sweet corn he adored. At a single sitting, he could devour the juicy golden kernels from nine or ten ears.

At one point Larry chartered a sailboat for a family outing. Jane was not amused but went along. A storm hit and they ran aground on a sandbar, where they remained until they were rescued by others. Jane never went sailing again.[34]

Larry Jr. remembered another touchy moment at the farm:

> I really caught hell. [Jane] was serving sweetbreads, and I can't stand brains. She always had servants: a butler, a first maid, a second maid. Anyhow, here was a dish of brains on the table ready to be eaten, and I couldn't stand it. She made me eat it, and I threw up right on the table.[35]

On 18 September 1934 Larry began a weekly engagement on the *Packard Radio Hour* where he sang, among his selections, some arias in English translations. The program was interrupted late that year when he went back to Hollywood to shoot his fifth film, *Metropolitan*, but then picked up again.[36] It is safe to say that his name and voice became even more famous throughout the country from these appearances. Many air checks of his singing on this program, originally ordered by him, were published "privately" but are now in his commercial recording discography.

He still had time for a long concert tour before the Metropolitan opened, again at a late date of 22 December 1934, this time with a production of *Aida*. The cast included Elisabeth Rethberg, Martinelli, Tibbett, and Pinza.

Two weeks later, in a Saturday matinée, Larry sang the elder Germont in *La Traviata* opposite Rosa Ponselle and the tenor Frederick Jagel, Americans all. Broadcasts of the Met's Saturday matinées, which had commenced in 1931, had now become a staple of America's musical life, and indeed would help to save the Met from bankruptcy as opera lovers from all over the United States and Canada sent contributions in response to intermission appeals for donations.

The air check from the 5 January 1935 broadcast of *Traviata* has Larry's Germont entering in high moral dudgeon. He coldly but clearly presents to Violetta his argument against her involvement with his son—only to melt under her charm. With truth and honesty he projects the conflicting emotions. Ponselle, who was not particularly focused up to that point, finds her full force in the confrontational duet.[37] In his big aria, "Di provenza," as always when he sang it, Larry is authoritative and finds unexpected dynamics and emphases that make the overfamiliar music sound quite new.[38]

On 28 January, Larry sang his first of what was to be many Scarpias at the Met, although it cannot be said he made Scotti forgotten in the role. The cast that evening included Lotte Lehmann and Martinelli. On 16 February the broadcast was *Boccanegra*, minus the Prologue. This opera was broadcast (and recorded) again on 21 January 1939 with almost the same cast, and the same conductor, Ettore Panizza, but the earlier performance seems more alive. Larry and Pinza spit their duet at each other with animal excitement, and the Council Chamber scene is pure magnificence. Panizza's conducting is also less quixotic in 1935, and Martinelli's voice sounds less as if it had been squeezed out of a toothpaste tube.

RCA commercially recorded two excerpts from *Boccanegra* in 1939, the father-daughter duet with Larry and Rose Bampton (listen to Larry's final *pianissimo* high F, which has spooked baritones ever since), and the great Council Chamber ensemble. With Larry in the lead, these are landmark discs.

John Dizikes wrote that by the 1930s Larry had "gradually gained control of his rich and vibrant voice" and now succeeded Antonio Scotti "as leading baritone of the house."[39] Larry Tibbett Jr. summed up his father in the simplest of sentences: "I often thought that my Dad was a genius."[40]

The 1934–35 Metropolitan season was the final one for the magisterial general manager Giulio Gatti-Casazza. Since he had taken the post in the autumn of 1908, he had served the Met well. With Arturo Toscanini on the podium, the two raised the curtain of their first season with an *Aida* that became legendary, featuring Emmy Destinn, American contralto Louise Homer, Caruso, Scotti, and Adamo Didur. Both Toscanini and Destinn made their Met debut that evening.

The wily general manager had taken what seemed to be a frightful gamble when he cast an American-born singer whose only prior experience had been in vaudeville, Rosa Ponselle (née Ponzillo), as the lead soprano opposite Caruso in Verdi's *La forza del destino*. That evening, 15 November 1918, made operatic history and proved to be another victory for Gatti. He showed the same shrewd ability to recognize a singer's potential when he offered a contract to a totally inexperienced young baritone from California named Lawrence Tibbet.

Gatti often gave leading roles to American singers, even singers without European experience. New Jersey–born Anna Case was Sophie in the Metropolitan premiere of Strauss's *Der Rosenkavalier*, and tenor Paul Althouse of Pennsylvania sang the False Dimitri in the premiere of *Boris Godunov*. Gatti's first allegiance, however, remained to ethnic Italians.

During his long tenure Gatti tirelessly promoted the cause of American opera. Even in his last season, on 24 January 1935, he presented an

American work, *In the Pasha's Garden* by John Laurence Seymour, again with Larry in a leading role and with the radio singing star of the Paul Whiteman Orchestra, Helen Jepson, making her Met debut. Jepson later recalled, "Larry was so supportive that night. He helped me on the unfamiliar stage and made me feel at home."[41] Kolodin noted that "Tibbett performed the Pasha better than the part warranted,"[42] and Lawrence Gilman claimed the baritone "walked away with the show, after his habit."[43] But poor Frederick Jagel, as Larry's wife's lover, got buried alive in this one, literally. The opera was a disaster and quickly forgotten.

Gatti's final gift to operatic America came in the last months of his tenure, when he presented a nearly unknown Norwegian soprano as Sieglinde in the 6 February 1935 broadcast performance of *Die Walküre*. This was the peerless Kirsten Flagstad, whose later performances, particularly when she was paired with that force of nature called Lauritz Melchior, always sold out and did much to prevent the Met from sliding into bankruptcy.

A few weeks after Flagstad's debut, members of the Metropolitan participated in a "Farewell to Gatti" concert, which was also planned as a benefit to help the company's ailing finances. Larry was the only member who sang, not in duets or ensembles, but alone, performing the *Pagliacci* Prologue.

When Gatti sailed home to Italy with his second wife, Rosina Galli, the premiere danseuse of the Met (who was not at all pleased by her enforced retirement), Rosa Ponselle threw a shipboard party for them on the S.S. *Rex*. It was 27 April 1935, and emotions ran high.

Helen Noble, for many years telephone operator at the old Met, wrote in her memoir *Life with the Met* a moving description of the event:

> The Italian chefs outdid themselves for, of course, Gatti, Galli and Ponselle were their idols. The food covered long tables in the main salon and was in such fascinating and colorful shapes that it looked much too handsome to disturb. There was also an open bar and plenty of champagne.
>
> We all found it hard to say goodbye. Mr. Gatti looked so tired and sad, we felt we must not add to his sorrow by breaking down. Let's all be gay and foolish, we said to each other, and of course the champagne helped! But the tears came anyhow. Goodbye, Mr. Gatti! Good luck, Mr. Gatti! Come back to see us, Mr. Gatti![44]

But Gatti never returned to America. He died at his villa in Ferrara, Italy, on 2 September 1940, having never really overcome his ache over leaving the Met.

In the spring of 1935, Larry sang on two special occasions. The first was the Gatti farewell concert, and the second, on 12 April, honored the 50th anniversary of impresario and conductor Walter Damrosch's first New York concert. The latter gala was the complete third act of Wagner's *Die Meistersinger*, performed in English.[45] Larry sang Hans Sachs, and Jepson was Eva. Critics praised Larry's voice, acting, nobility of bearing, and superb diction. It was then believed that he would sing the complete role at the Met, but he never did.[46]

A recording exists of Larry singing Sachs's Fliedermonolog (mislabeled where it appears as the Wahnmonolog), from the *Packard Radio Hour* of October 1934. The reading is meltingly beautiful and deeply human. His diction is of course impeccable, and though sung in English, his Wagnerian style is totally idiomatic.

Although Larry never sang Wotan in an opera house, his majestically tender interpretation of the Farewell from *Die Walküre* can be heard on a commercial recording made with Leopold Stokowski and the surging Philadelphia Orchestra in 1934, part of Stokowski's interesting experiments with Wagner as sung by atypical voices.[47] Larry sang the Farewell in concert with orchestra three times in the summer of 1939, the last in Grant Park in Chicago. He also sang it with piano accompaniment.

At about this time Larry resumed his unusual relationship with Doris Wyckoff, the daughter he never had. He had continued to send her roses every Christmas. She was now an 18-year-old undergraduate student at New York's Barnard College, and on the urging of her roommates, she had announced her presence to the celebrated opera star with a prim little note. He called immediately and insisted that she come to hear him in *Merry Mount* that very evening. While her amazed fellow students watched from their dormitory windows, his town car drew up at the door to sweep the dressed-to-the-nines coed off to a Tibbett performance at the Met. Larry bowed to her personally at the curtain calls.

Thereafter Larry invited her to rehearsals and put a box at the Met at her disposal for the Saturday matinée performances. He also plied her with books on opera. He accepted an invitation to a Sunday tea at the college's Johnson Hall with Doris and her fellow adoring undergraduates. All this the wide-eyed, unsophisticated girl from West

Virginia accepted with enthusiasm and wonder. "He was gracious, friendly, fun, and very nice," she recalled. Twice Doris helped Larry and Jane out of a spot by baby-sitting.

In 1993 Doris Wyckoff exclaimed, her wonderment unabated, "I still see him vividly in front of me, so friendly, just like your neighbor, the man next door. He was a friend."

Though Larry's sexual pursuits of women were unflagging, this was not the case with Doris Wyckoff. Once she expressed gratitude to him for all his considerations and added that she didn't know why he should be so kind to her. He answered, "My dear, if it gives you as much pleasure as I think I see in your pretty brown eyes, that's all that matters."[48]

Here must have been the real-life expression of all the tenderness that can be heard in Larry's singing of the father-daughter duets from *Boccanegra*, *Rigoletto*, and even *Traviata*. Virile yet gentle, lustful yet restrained, Larry was indeed a man of paradoxes. In short, a complete man and artist.

Part Four 1935–1940

Chapter 7

PERSONAL TRAGEDY

In mid-October 1935 the *Los Angeles Times* published a letter—headlined "Why I Quit Hollywood Forever and Why I Have Returned"—to coincide with the opening of Larry's latest picture, *Metropolitan*. In it, he explained why he had resumed the movie career on which he had for a time turned his back:

> When I left Hollywood four years ago to rejoin the Metropolitan Opera, I pledged myself never to return. Now I am back and glad of it.
>
> At the outset, let it be clearly understood that it wasn't the money that brought me back. There is more to be made on the concert or operatic stage, while radio pays as well for a smaller outlay of time and effort.
>
> The truth is that four years ago, Hollywood had not advanced far enough in the handling of sound to do full justice to the operatic voice. Today, an amazing degree of perfection has been attained.[1]

Larry had come back to Hollywood in late 1934 to work on *Metropolitan*, produced by Darryl Zanuck at 20th Century Fox and costarring Virginia Bruce. During the shooting of the film, Larry and Jane leased a palatial home in Beverly Hills near Sunset Boulevard. It was close by the house on North Rexford Drive in which the quixotic Grace carried on a high-powered social life of her own, laced heavily with drink—more or less the same kind of life that her former husband led in New York, but with far less financing.

Following her divorce from Larry, Grace had abruptly married one of her cousins; he was gay, and the marriage was quickly annulled.[2] The steady companion of the first Mrs. Lawrence Tibbett was now film actor Ramon Novarro, quite a feat for a woman who could lay so little claim to personal beauty in that unreal world where appearances were paramount. Her starry circle still included Leslie Howard, Charles Farrell, and Janet Gaynor, and both Louella Parsons and Hedda Hopper had been added to the mix—separately, no doubt, as these two Hollywood gossip columnists were implacable enemies.

After tending to social matters, Grace devoted her time to her writing. Although Larry had prevented publication of her memoirs, her poetry frequently appeared in E. V. Durling's columns in Hollywood; her own social commentary was published in an Encino newspaper and included in the scenarist Rob Wagner's columns about the movie colony. She claimed that her life was guided by the daily horoscopes written by her close friend Myra Kingsley. In the odd way that lives have of crossing, Kingsley and her husband, arts patron Howard Taylor, were neighbors of Larry and Jane Tibbett's at their Manhattan apartment.

While he was filming *Metropolitan*, Larry had a chance to see something of the twins, who nominally lived with their mother, though in fact they spent most of their time in one boarding school or summer camp after another, visiting Grace only on holidays. According to Larry Jr., "After [the] divorce, she had boyfriends, so we couldn't live with her. Frankly I don't think she wanted to be bothered. You know, it's work, bringing up kids."[3] Richard adds, "I was completely under the control of headmasters, governesses, summer schools, and camp counsellors until I went to college in 1938."[4]

Larry sporadically tried to be a father to his sons by mail, neatly typing letters on "Lawrence Tibbett" letterheads. On 2 March 1935 he addressed "an unpleasant one" to the 15-year-old twins, berating them for their poor marks in school. "You are due a good straight talking to, and I want you to carefully consider every word I say," he pontificated. One piece of advice to Larry Jr. revealed the father's thinking on one facet of his profession: "If you intend to be an actor, Larry, you had better begin to put something in your brain besides a desire to show off, or else you will be a cheap 'ham' actor not worth your salt." He concludes by announcing that he is withholding their allowance for that month and will continue to withhold it until their grades improve.[5]

Looking more like Clark Gable than ever, Larry takes charge as an actor and a personality in *Metropolitan*, his fifth film. Unfortunately, the script is extremely old-fashioned, although it does occasionally try to be honest to music and to opera. Larry's singing is magnificent, especially in a memorable *Pagliacci* Prologue that is, rightly, the climax of the film. Certainly one cannot fault Larry here or elsewhere in his existing body of film work as being excessively "hammy" or charge him with overacting, though he no doubt would have modified his style for modern audiences.

In spite of generally good reviews, *Metropolitan* was a flop at the box office,[6] and no one was more aware of it than Zanuck. As a result, he sought to settle Fox's two-picture contract with the star, which called for a payment of $100,000 per film. Larry was adamant, however, demanding that the terms of the contract be fulfilled.

Producer Zanuck was furious. Calling in young Otto Preminger, who had not yet directed his first Hollywood feature, Zanuck asked, "Otto, are you ready to make a film?" Preminger replied in the affirmative, and Zanuck snapped back, "Good. I have this son-of-a-bitch Lawrence Tibbett who's made one film for which I've paid him a fortune. I don't want to lose still more money on him, so you can practice on this son-of-a-bitch."[7]

The movie was a B picture, *Under Your Spell*, filmed during the summer of 1936. According to Preminger, it was not at all bad, principally because Larry, contrary to expectations, worked well with him as the director. This, Larry's sixth and last film, was released in November 1936.

Critics were shocked to see it given second billing in a double feature (*Give Me Your Heart* with Kay Francis and George Brent was the lead feature). Larry himself summed up *Under Your Spell* with the pungent phrase "Under Your Smell." Still, the film did feature two arias, both big production numbers done in costume: again Figaro's aria "Largo al factotum" from *The Barber of Seville* (also featured in *Metropolitan*) and "Le veau d'or," Mephistopheles's Calf of Gold aria from *Faust*. The latter allowed audiences an opportunity to hear Larry sing an excerpt from a role that he never performed onstage, a basso role at that, and to wonder if he had been influenced in his interpretation by Chaliapin, with whom he had sung in his first, jittery *Faust* performances.

Back in New York City, Larry was given the honor of appearing on the opening night of the Metropolitan Opera season for the fourth time, on 16 December 1935. The work was *La Traviata*; in the cast were the beloved Lucrezia Bori as Violetta and the tenor Richard Crooks as Alfredo. (Larry had recorded a pious *Crucifixion*, the John Stainer oratorio, with Crooks in May 1929.) Before the year was out, on 28 December 1935, he took on a new characterization that stretched his essentially lyric baritone. This was the role of the malignant and maligned jester in Verdi's *Rigoletto*.

On 18 January 1936, the matinée of *Tannhäuser* was broadcast. Larry was the Wolfram, and an air check survives. Throughout Larry employs a deep timbre, almost like a bass. This does not prevent the few climactic high notes from being firmly projected from a high head position.

His first act is unremarkable because of conductor Bodanzky's slow tempo (conductors often tend to slow Wolfram's music down so much that he appears to be a wimp), but the second-act song contest takes fire. It is a real competition, a hard-fought battle, the result of close collaboration between the conductor, Lauritz Melchior as Tannhäuser, and Larry. Deep compassion and a gorgeous Song to the Evening Star distinguish Act Three.[8] An unstoppable Melchior and a radiant Kirsten Flagstad also make this a truly great performance. It appears that discs of this performance became generally available when Larry loaned his personal copy of the broadcast transcription to Edward J. Smith, who had a business of releasing "private" or "pirate" recordings.[9]

Also in the 1935–36 season, on 27 January 1936, Larry sang the title role in Puccini's *Gianni Schicchi* for the first time. Toward the close of the Met season, however, his attention was diverted by the totally unmusical problems of the rights of labor versus those of management—to strikes, to what might be called trust-busting, and eventually, to a labor union.

Until 1936 vocalists under contract to the Metropolitan Opera functioned under severe restrictions. They were required to obtain the management's permission before singing a concert away from the Met; they were charged a commission for the use of the Met's name in their concert advertising; and they were required to pay the Met $200 when they sang with another opera company. At the Met itself, they had little to say regarding the selection of roles they were scheduled to perform, the rehearsal time allotted to prepare for their roles, or the number of performances they were expected to sing in a season. In addition, the Metropolitan must grant its permission before a singer could appear on radio (later television), and it took a commission from those fees.

Larry's mother, Frances Ellen McKenzie Tibbet. Photo by Wolfe & Doerr, Los Angeles.

The notorious outlaw
Jim McKinney.

Bert Tibbet, Larry's uncle and
his father's avenger.

City Marshal Jeff "Four Eyes"
Packard.

The Chinatown joss house, shortly after the shootout took place. Photo by C. A. Nelson, Bakersfield, California.

The backdoor of the joss house. Photo by C. A. Nelson, Bakersfield, California.

Larry at 14, ca. 1911.

Larry in *The Chimes of Normandy* at Manual Arts High School, 1913.

Larry (Mercutio) as he appeared in the 1914 program to Manual Art's production of *Romeo and Juliette*.

Larry at 18, on the family ranch in the Tejon Mountains during the summer of 1915.

Dashing and armed, sometime before his military service.

In the merchant marines, 1918.

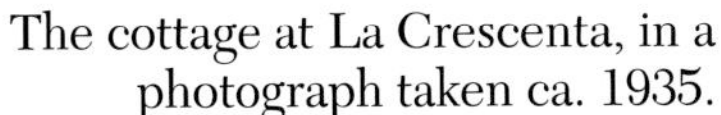

The cottage at La Crescenta, in a photograph taken ca. 1935.

Helen Moss, Larry's coach and first accompanist.

AEOLIAN HALL, 29 West Forty-Second Street

NOONDAY MUSICALE

UNDER THE DIRECTION OF

THE LA FORGE - BERÚMEN STUDIOS

ARTISTS APPEARING:

JEAN JOHNSON, Mezzo-Soprano LAWRENCE TIBBETT, Baritone
ALBERT RAPPAPORT, Tenor ERNESTO BERUMEN, Pianist
ERIN BALLARD, HELEN BLUME, HELEN MOSS, Pianists

and

THE DUO ART PIANO

Friday, November 3rd, 1922, at 12 o'clock noon

ADMISSION WITHOUT CHARGE

A ticket to Larry's first professional New York appearance.

Larry and Grace in an early Evans and Salter publicity shot. Photo by Bain News Service.

Playing in the sand with the twins, ca. 1921. Larry is holding Larry Jr.

Nana with the twins, Larry Jr. (left) and Richard, ca. 1924.

The young concert baritone, 1926. Photo by Hoover.

Tibbett and friends in Atlanta during the Met tour, April 1927. Top row, left to right: James Wolfe, Julia Claussen, Florence Easton, Rosa Ponselle, Louis Hasselmans, Giulio Setti, Louise Hunter, Louise Lorch. Bottom row: Armand Tokatyan, Larry, Edward Johnson, Edward Ziegler.

Larry and accompanist Stewart Wille rehearsing at the Bohemian Grove, late 20s.

Another view of the bohemian, Laguna Beach, California, 1928.

Dorothy Potter, Larry, and Doris Wyckoff in the photograph snapped by Stewart Wille in Charleston, West Virginia, 11 May 1928. Courtesy of Doris Wyckoff.

The autographed photo Larry gave to Doris Wyckoff that same day.
Photo by Lumiere, courtesy of Doris Wyckoff.

The cast and crew of *The Rogue Song*, 1929. First full row, left to right: Charles Schoenbaum, Catherine Dale Owen, Lionel Barrymore, Larry, and Grace. Courtesy of the Museum of Modern Art, Film Stills Archive.

Larry and Catherine Dale Owen in a publicity still for *The Rogue Song*, 1929.

Larry and Grace Moore in a publicity still for *New Moon*, 1930.

Hollywood! Larry, Louis B. Mayer, Ramon Novarro, Grace, and Charlotte Earle (mother of the painter Eyvind Earle), ca. 1930.

Cartoon by Ham Luske, 1930, captioned "News Item: Lawrence Tibbett sings from the time he gets up in the morning until he goes to bed at night." From the book *The Movie Musical*, edited by Miles Kreuger, courtesy of Dover Press.

Larry Jr., Larry Sr., Grace, and Richard at the Pasadena railway station, summer 1930.

Larry in *The Prodigal*, 1930.

With Lupe Velez in *Cuban Love Song*, 1931.

With Virginia Bruce in *Metropolitan*, 1935.

Young Jane with her family, the Marstons.

Jane Marston Burgard Tibbett, all grown up. She was extremely fond of this photo and gave a framed copy of it to Larry as a Christmas present.

Larry and Jane aboard their chartered yacht, the *Rhodos*.

Baby Michael inspects his father's golden throat, 1934.

Larry greeting Eleanor Roosevelt at the Mayflower Hotel in Washington, D.C., 9 November 1935.

Larry at 40.

Larry as Emperor Jones, 1933. Photo by Morton, courtesy of the San Francisco Opera Archives.

Dino Borgioli, Claudia Muzio, and Larry in *La Traviata*, 1933. Photo by Morton, courtesy of the San Francisco Opera Archives.

Larry in *I Pagliacci*, 1933. Photo by Morton, courtesy of the San Francisco Opera Archives.

After a performance of *Rigoletto* at the Metropolitan, 11 March 1939. Left to right: Larry, Lucrezia Bori, Jan Kiepura, Lily Pons, Edward Johnson, and Irra Petina. Courtesy of Marta Eggerth and Marjan Kiepura.

Larry and Jane with Margaret Truman after a performance of *Rigoletto* in Washington, D.C., 22 November 1945. Photo by E. L. Robinson Jr., Philadelphia.

Larry with his and Jane's collection of Russian enamels. Photo by Larry Gordon.

Colleagues at the Met surprise Larry with a backstage silver anniversary party, 21 January 1949.

Larry, one year after his 1950 retirement from the Metropolitan Opera.

Larry as the Reverend Davidson in *Rain*, Pocono Summer Theater, Mountain Home, Pennsylvania, 2 July 1951.

As Captain Hook to Veronica Lake's Peter Pan, 1951.

At the American Guild of Musical Artists dinner, 25 February 1954, Deems Taylor turns over to Larry a book containing tributes from friends around the world, while Jane looks on.

Larry at his booking for drunk driving, 29 September 1954. Photo by International News, courtesy of the Bettmann Archives.

At Manhattan's Stork Club, 22 April 1955. Left to right: Horace G. Brown Jr. (Grace's third husband), Joan Blondell, Robert Hays, Marion Davies (the present Mrs. Brown), Larry, and Josephine Hughes.

Similarly, the concert field was dominated by the absolute monopolies of agent/managers with near incestuous relationships with orchestras, sponsors, and presenting organizations. Here too performers faced a morass of rules, rates, and strictly circumscribed opportunities.

It has been facetiously suggested that the American Guild of Musical Artists (AGMA) originated on a golf course in New Jersey, between a mashie and a niblick, but in fact a musicians' union was not a new idea. Earlier attempts to organize singers in the operatic and concert fields had been led by two tenors, John McCormack and Edward Johnson, the latter who would become general manager of the Metropolitan Opera. Together they sought to organize a union in 1923 but failed. Soprano Lucrezia Bori, Larry's close friend, attempted to link opera singers to the already existing Actors' Equity and also failed, as had failed the earlier Met soprano and highly successful concert artist Alma Gluck.

So Larry, after a long period of study and reflection, decided for the first time in his career to step outside the usual confines of the opera house or concert hall and organize singers into a union of their own. Maybe he had never forgotten his original Metropolitan contract, which had just about indentured him to the company. He was joined in this effort by Jascha Heifetz, the renowned violinist, who, even before Larry, had worked on behalf of instrumental concert soloists. Although poles apart in heritage and temperament, Tibbett and Heifetz embodied the basic principles that would guide the union. AGMA would attempt to do for its members, solo classical music artists, what Actors' Equity had, with great pain, accomplished for actors: forge a union that would fight for and win improved economic and working conditions for its members.

The absolute power of certain men over the artists the union would represent may have spurred them on. One tour de force was Sol Hurok; another was Arthur Judson, a concert manager and a virtual one-man monopoly. He founded and controlled the Columbia (radio) Broadcasting System, managed the New York Philharmonic and the Philadelphia Orchestra, and headed up Columbia Artists, the management firm with whom artists had to be associated in order to receive engagements. He also controlled Community Concerts, which arranged concerts in hundreds of towns throughout the United States. "The whole system of concert presentations was controlled by Columbia. What Tibbett and Heifetz wanted was to form a union to do something about Columbia."[10]

In early February 1936, seven artists met at the Tibbett apartment in Manhattan, where the first steps were taken to form the guild. Four of the group were appointed to draft a constitution and by-laws, and after many meetings, those documents were approved by all. On 11 March 1936, the artists, now numbering more than a score, met and voted themselves a union, electing Larry their first president. They approved a temporary board of governors and officers, set a date for the first general meeting, and selected a lawyer to handle the legal incorporation of the union. With Tibbett and Heifetz, the pioneers who nurtured the guild were Richard Bonelli, Mario Chamlee, Frank Chapman, William Daly, Eva Gauthier, George Gershwin, Alma Gluck, Charles Hackett, Frederick Jagel, Frank La Forge, Queena Mario, James Melton, Ruth Miller (Chamlee), Gregor Piatigorsky, Frank Sheridan, Albert Spaulding, Gladys Swarthout, Deems Taylor, Donald Voorhees, Paul Whiteman, and Stewart Wille.

An article on the founding of the union, written by Quaintance Eaton, appeared in the 25 May 1936 issue of *Musical America*. A lengthy declaration by Larry opened the piece: "We decided to make haste slowly. . . . If everyone hailed us as perfect, we should be suspicious." By the time the article ran, 113 members were enrolled in the union. A further sampling of charter members includes Leon Barzin, George Cehanovsky, Agnes De Mille, Florence Easton, Anna Hamlin, Howard Hanson, Helen Jepson, Giovanni Martinelli, Edith Mason, Lauritz Melchior, James Melton, Nathan Milstein, Lucy Monroe, Grace Moore, Eugene Ormandy,[11] Lily Pons, Rosa Ponselle, Fritz Reiner, Artur Rodzinski, Lanny Ross, Alice Tully, Fred Waring, and Efrem Zimbalist. The first executive secretary of the new union was the widowed Mrs. Herbert Witherspoon.[12]

Why did Larry and Jascha Heifetz succeed in organizing a union when the efforts of others had come to naught? In 1936, various factors throughout the United States helped to create a climate more favorable to the creation of unions in general and AGMA in particular. Economic conditions were extremely poor, and the Committee of Industrial Organizations (CIO) had emerged after its break with the more craft-oriented American Federation of Labor (AFL). Larry's own lofty stature in the arts certainly contributed to its success, as did the support of Heifetz and cellist Gregor Piatigorsky, who led scores of instrumentalists into AGMA.

The younger, up-and-coming artists were gratified that Larry and the other established and well-known artists—those who were big enough not to need the daily protection of a union—were fighting for *them*. Larry was enjoying a major career on the stage, on radio, and in films; yet he insisted that the next generation had to have the finances and the time to study and make their careers.[13]

Kurt Weinhold, who as an artist's manager was affected by the existence of a union, offered these comments:

> Tibbett was not the real initiator of AGMA. That was Jascha Heifetz. He started AGMA rolling. But Heifetz was smart enough, even though he was the overall promoter of AGMA, to get Tibbett interested in AGMA. Heifetz [was] a very cold person, hardly one to draw others to him. He felt that a singer at the Met, like Tibbett, would make a much better front for AGMA than he would. It was he who prevailed on Tibbett to take the presidency of AGMA. When I tried to argue Tibbett out of it, Tibbett would argue back that I knew that the unions in Germany had done well for German singers so AGMA would also do well here.[14]

Hy Faine, executive secretary of AGMA from 1946 to 1970, thought differently:

> Tibbett was the leading force in the formation of AGMA. As a person he was very dynamic, highly respected; he had convinced the instrumental artists like Piatigorsky and Heifetz to join with him in starting AGMA. Unquestionably, Tibbett was the founder and spearhead of AGMA.[15]

Faine went on to list the abuses eliminated by AGMA:

> The basic agreement limited the amount of fees that could be charged and the length of the contract and set up a system of arbitration between the bureaus and the artists. There was a standard form of contract they had to adhere to, and they could not put anything in that they wanted. As long as the contract was in effect, the manager could not get rid of the artist client. Each performing field had its own standard form of contract.[16]

Novel then; basic today.

Once the guild was in motion, with Larry as president, he discovered that much of his limited free time would be spent persuading singers and other artists to join AGMA's ranks. He soon decided to issue a pamphlet entitled "Questions and Answers About AGMA." In the foreword he touched on the fundamental problem the union faced:

> The emergence of AGMA on the musical scene is not the fruit of impulse or inspiration, but rather the logical result of a tendency which has been making itself felt with increasing insistence—the tendency toward organization in the business procedures of musical activity. Within the past few years the business side of music has become a vast industrial organization. This in itself is natural and acceptable because organization is the philosophy of the age and is necessary for progress.
>
> But until now, the artist has been laggard in responding to this tendency. While the business associates of the artist were fast consolidating their position in strong business organizations, the artist remained as he had been. He may, perhaps, be excused for this, because art has always been conceived to be an intensely individualistic occupation, and the artist has not been trained to think for himself as part of the social community.
>
> To those of us who formed AGMA, the solution seemed to be the awakening of the artist to the need of organization on his own part. We believed that the artists could join together for collective action on matters on which they all had a common vital interest without jeopardizing those individualistic aspects of musical artistry which it might be desirable to retain.[17]

As AGMA evolved into a craft union of solo musical artists, its growing roster of members reveled in the diversity of skills represented within its ranks: singers, instrumentalists, dancers, band leaders, composers, and vocal coaches. As Hy Faine observed, the very idea of performers, highly individualistic, highly competitive, and primarily concerned with their own artistry and their own careers, joining together for the betterment of themselves, was unique on the American scene.

Once AGMA had become a reality, Larry applied to the AFL's Associated Actors and Artists of America (Four A's) for a charter. Its president, Frank Gilmore, turned down the application on the grounds that a tiny existing union with a membership of 200, the Grand Opera Artists' Association (GOAA) had already obtained a Four A's charter for musicians. Undeterred, Larry immediately opened negotiations with Elizabeth Hoeppel, the president of GOAA, with the objective of merging the two unions.

Madame Hoeppel, a contralto, had come to the United States from Germany in 1923 hoping to find the streets of America lined with opera houses, if not paved with gold. Instead, she discovered about five: two in New York, the Metropolitan and the Hippodrome; and one each in Boston, San Francisco, and Chicago. To be sure, a number of touring opera companies were operating, even several made up of black singers, but with the exception of Fortune Gallo's tenacious San Carlo Opera Company, they presented only sporadic performances and were at all times subject to sudden bankruptcy and extinction.

Elizabeth Hoeppel's eyes shone when she called to mind her meetings with Larry. She remembered a tall, extraordinarily attractive man with a deep, resonant voice and genial manners. But she also remembered the steel in him whenever they reached an impasse, which was fairly often. After all, the GOAA would not surrender its charter lightly since most of its members were from the old opera companies of Europe, which had long been unionized. Nevertheless, Hoeppel realized that the artists' mutual security would be enhanced by merging with a potentially larger union than they could ever hope to become. She was finally persuaded to relinquish GOAA's charter to AGMA.

When asked to comment upon AGMA's success, Hoeppel replied thoughtfully: "I think AGMA really succeeded because Lawrence Tibbett was one of the few singers around who had the stature to keep the producers in line. After all, he was so popular all over the United States that no one dared to challenge him."[18]

Like most neophytes in the labor movement, AGMA was initially weak and nearly helpless against its powerfully entrenched opposition, the employers. Often it lacked even the basic funds with which to remain afloat. Larry and Jane, along with a few other affluent members, had to maintain the infant union with loans or outright contributions.

Once it had absorbed GOAA, AGMA went after the Grand Opera Choral Alliance (GOCA). This was a small but lusty group of choristers who had gone on strike against the Metropolitan during the long-ago season of 1905–06, demanding better working conditions, more pay, and recognition of their union. The strike went on for three days before management gave in. Soon after, GOCA was joined by the choristers of the Chicago City Opera and of the San Carlo. In 1938, the Four A's revoked GOCA's charter, transferring it to AGMA, but not without causing a bitter fight among members of the locals. It is possible that some choristers did not want to merge with AGMA, associated with Tibbett, because they blamed the baritone for the death of one of their members in 1937.

Perhaps more than a third of the operas presented by a company in any given season feature dueling or stabbing scenes with sharp objects. This stage violence occurs in such standbys as *Carmen*, *Faust*, *La forza del destino*, *Otello*, and *Il Trovatore*, not to speak of Wagner operas such as *Lohengrin* and *Tristan und Isolde*. Even though real weapons are never used, it seems remarkable that so few mishaps occur during performances. Yet a fatal accident involving Larry took place at a rehearsal on 27 January 1937.

He had just completed a season at the San Francisco Opera where he sang his first complete Iago (on 20 November 1936, to Martinelli's first Otello), as well as Rigoletto, Tonio and Gianni Schicchi as a double bill, and Scarpia. Following his Chicago debuts as Iago and Rigoletto, he was back at the Metropolitan for the 1936–37 season, learning another role in English for another American opera. This was *Caponsacchi*, based on Robert Browning's narrative poem "The Ring and the Book," a tale of jealousy and murder in old Florence. The composer was Richard Hageman, also a Metropolitan conductor, whose popular concert song "Do Not Go, My Love" many singers included in recitals.

The plot called for Larry, as the evil Guido, to stab his father-in-law Pietro to death while his wife Pompilia (sung by Helen Jepson) looked on. One of the choristers, the veteran bass Joseph Sterzini, as an assisting "hired assassin," was required to pin back Pietro's arms while Larry thrust the dagger into the heart of the old man, performed by the bass John Gurney.

Because wooden or soft rubber weapons looked unrealistic on the stage, the Metropolitan equipped the performers with blunt-edged metal daggers and swords. When wielded too vigorously, these props can inflict minor cuts or bruises. But never in the history of the Met had there been a serious mishap or a fatality until Sterzini's hand somehow came between Tibbett and Gurney. Tibbett's stiletto inflicted a deep cut between the chorister's thumb and index finger.

The bleeding was copious, and the first aid inept; no one knew how to apply a tourniquet. And the ambulance was first erroneously dispatched to the Metropolitan Life Insurance Company in lower Manhattan. By the time an emergency vehicle pulled up at the opera house, Sterzini had bled a long time. He was possibly diabetic and already weak from loss of blood. Five hours later, at 5:15 p.m., he died. The dagger was never found.[19]

The following day, District Attorney Cossetino of New York County absolved Tibbett of any blame. A medical report disclosed that the unfortunate victim of the accident had long suffered from a heart ailment and that his death could have occurred at any time. Although the shock from the wound may have been a contributing factor, it was not the direct cause of death.

Although Larry habitually made a great show of masculine ruggedness, his was a generous and compassionate nature. He was appalled by what had happened. He and Jane, who was equally distraught, attended the funeral. Just two evenings after Sterzini's death, Larry had to appear in *La Traviata* with a full complement of choristers, some of whom, if they did not condemn him as an out-and-out murderer, regarded him as a man of violence who was careless of other people's lives.[20]

If some regulars in the company now held the baritone in low esteem, certainly many others remained devoted to him. At the opera house, artists could be haughty and self-centered, but Marie Klein, of Brooklyn, had heard only of Larry's kindly consideration of others, including the non-singing staff.

> During the mid-thirties, my mother worked at the Metropolitan Opera as a cleaning woman, and managed to hear many rehearsals at Sherry's [the third floor bar areas used for rehearsals during the day] by singers such as Rethberg, Martinelli, Pinza, Tibbett, etc. Most of them were deeply engrossed in their own work (and themselves) and noticed no one, but Tibbett always found time for a few words and some small talk with the maintenance staff.[21]

Caponsacchi enjoyed the usual fate of American operas mounted at the Met: it was performed twice that season of 1936–37 and was never heard from again. Kolodin wrote,

> The dramatic power to sustain interest in the theater was absent, either in Arthur Goodrich's libretto or in Hageman's elaboration of it. Tibbett's overstrenuous Guido seemed designed to overcome this deficiency, but the results were mere bluster.[22]

Also in that season, Larry sang his usual Tonio in *Pagliacci*, the elder Germont, and Aida's father Amonasro, as well as two demanding Rigolettos. Even more arduous was his first performance of all four villains in Offenbach's *The Tales of Hoffmann*, including Dr. Miracle, a role often given to a true bass. Kolodin hated the production and wrote of Larry in the roles, "An inclination to sneering laughter and stagy postures made much of Tibbett's work an embarrassment to observe."[23]

The air check of 23 January 1937, the second performance, can only be called effortful. Vina Bovy sings the four ladies and rises above the gloom that otherwise permeates the proceedings. Larry makes an immediate impression with each character he plays, so extraordinary is his presence and the dark vocal color he chooses for his villains. Following performance practice when one singer takes on all four roles, he pitches Dapertutto's aria half a tone down, but his lengthy preparation for the high G is excruciating. It is clear that he understands the other villains, but they don't come to life. Are they physically overplayed, a danger with their characterizations? René Maison, the Hoffmann, is also uncharacteristically leaden. Perhaps it was an off day for conductor Maurice Abravanel.[24]

At the close of the season, Larry decided to extend his horizons. He had conquered America; it was time to find out what singing in Europe would be like. In early May 1937, Larry and Jane boarded a luxury ocean liner that would take them to a string of concert and opera engagements on the Continent, where Larry would face audiences steeped in Old World musical traditions. In Great Britain, France, and Austria he would be singing in the native language of the country; in Hungary, Czechoslovakia, Norway, Denmark, and Sweden his audiences would hear songs in English, maybe for the first time. Europe was yet another in a series of challenges that Larry neatly met and summarily dispatched.

Aus meinen grossen Schmerzen
Mach ich die kleinen Lieder.

Out of my great sorrows
I make my little songs.

So begins the poem that Heinrich Heine wrote and Robert Franz set to music. The song was a concert favorite and no doubt familiar to Larry. What the baritone could not know as he and Jane set sail in the highest spirits was that these words would soon apply in a close personal way to him.

As the British Cunard liner the *Queen Mary* headed into the Atlantic, Larry and Jane had only one regret: they were giving up their summer on the farm. When school was out, the two older Burgard boys were set to go to a summer camp in Oxford, Maine, and the Tibbett twins to a camp in a different part of the country. Only the two youngest, Peter Burgard, who considered himself Larry's son as he grew up, and little Michael Tibbett, not yet four, would remain at the farm with their governess, Bernice.

It was prudent to send the older boys off in different directions. They had entered their adolescent years and when they were all together, trouble usually broke out. "The Great BB Gun War," as the family called it in years to come, was a memorable case in point.

Larry, who enjoyed hunting small game, had given each of the older boys Daisy BB guns; he foolishly considered the guns a good way to prepare them for the sport. These were not toys, but pneumatically operated rifles that could shoot small lead pellets with the zing of real bullets. Manufactured chiefly for target practice, they could do real damage if handled carelessly.

One day in early 1937, after Larry, Jane, and Michael had left for the farm, the twins and the three Burgard boys got into a heated argument at the New York apartment. One of them remembered the BB guns, and the war was on. BBs began to zip and ping all through the apartment, cracking windows and expensive art objects.

When Jane's personal housekeeper, the prim and starchy Teresa Vojio, came upon the scene, she received a stinging pellet on her backside. Screaming, she ran from the room and telephoned the farm. Larry told her to call the police then leaped into his station wagon, but it would take him two hours to reach the apartment.

Teresa, frantically ducking as pellets buzzed by her like angry bees, put a hysterical call through to the police. Her fright, coupled with momentary lapses into her native Finnish, confused the police sergeant, who assumed that a gang of robbers had invaded the Tibbett residence. He promptly dispatched a full squad of New York's finest, heavily armed, to 120 East End Avenue. When Larry arrived, everything was under control. The boys were huddled together, quaking apprehensively under a police officer's stony gaze, their BB guns now piled harmlessly in the center of the room.

Grimly, Larry lined the boys up. When he slowly drew his heavy belt from his work pants, they realized what was in the offing. One by one they were ushered into the bathroom, where one stinging whack followed another. This episode marked a low point in family relations but was always joked about in later years.[25]

But now the churning steamship, trailing a wake of white in the exquisite blue, was putting such scenes far behind Larry and Jane, and they settled effortlessly into the pleasures of first-class seaboard living. All around them during the five-day crossing the talk was of the upcoming coronation of King George VI, which was to take place on 12

May 1937, six days after their ship docked at Southampton. There was delicious gossip, of course, as the previous king, Edward VIII, had abdicated the throne of England in December 1936 to marry the divorced commoner Wallis Simpson.

Seated at the captain's table for supper, Jane Tibbett nearly died of envy as half her dinner companions claimed to have been invited to the coronation in Westminster Abbey. Imagine her delight when—upon arriving, along with 20 pieces of luggage, at London's Claridge's hotel—she received a call from Prime Minister Neville Chamberlain himself, inviting the Tibbetts to the ceremony.

While Jane busied herself with their social schedule, Larry saw to arrangements for his forthcoming concerts and opera appearances. The baritone felt uneasy because Stewart Wille, his regular accompanist, was not with him. The pianist, suffering from severe earaches that impaired his hearing, had begged off this trip. Long before, Larry had realized how much Wille's support meant to him. The two men, highly artistic and individualistic, complemented each other to a degree rarely heard on the concert stage. This time, fortunately, most of Larry's European concerts were to be given with full orchestra, so Wille's absence would not be devastating.

On 14 May Tibbett appeared at Covent Garden for the first time, as Scarpia in *Tosca*, with Gina Cigna and Martinelli in the cast. The *London Times* found him "powerful in voice and gesture," but several other London papers were critical of his performance. The *Daily Telegraph* and the *Daily Herald* found his acting better than his singing, and the *Spectator* attacked his lack of subtlety, preferring Scotti's "refined mental sadism."[26]

But in London—as in America—Larry's electric appeal involved his audiences to an astonishing degree. The famously undemonstrative British cheered him with one ovation after another, and long lines of autograph seekers and well-wishers queued up for him each evening at the stage door. On 11 June he sang Amonasro in *Aida* (with Cigna, Stignani, and Martinelli), and here even the critics were on his side.

When Eugene Goossens's opera *Don Juan de Mañara* was accepted for performance by Covent Garden, the composer, who placed Larry on a par with Mario Sammarco and Scotti, requested that Larry create the title role. Larry agreed, learned the role, and sang the world premiere on 24 June. The idiosyncratic composer and music critic Leon Dudley (who went by the name Kaikhosru Sorabji) wrote that Larry gave "a very distinguished performance,"[27] but the opera itself was not well received: seven onstage murders was considered a bit much, even in the country that gave the world Jacobean revenge tragedy. A second performance of *Don Juan* followed four days later.

Larry's Iago in Verdi's *Otello* was shown to London on 26 June; Eidé Norena and Martinelli appeared with him. Once again, the public seemed to like the baritone more than the critics did. He also gave several well-received recitals. In *The Gramophone*, the mysterious "Beckmesser" (who may have been Walter Legge) wrote that Larry's line of tone was straight and solid as a piston rod,[28] while in the face of his glorious high notes, Ernest Newman wondered if Tibbett might not really be a bass.[29]

As president of AGMA, Larry also devoted his time and energies to visiting the offices of several British musical and theatrical guilds in order to introduce the American union to them. Thus he prepared the way for better future relations in the world of the performing arts, which had rarely been without troubling international issues.

Ever aware of Larry's need for diversion and relaxation, Larry's manager Lawrence Evans had wisely limited Larry's schedule of concerts and opera appearances, and Jane too had planned their London itinerary well, leaving her husband enough leisure time to be a tourist as well as a visiting opera star from America. While shopping at Harrod's, the two ran into Jane's friend Marjorie Merriweather Post, of the Post cereal family, and Larry and Jane were happily able to accept her invitation to join her on her yacht *Sea Cloud* for a cruise to the Soviet Union. There she planned to meet her husband, Joseph E. Davies, who was serving as American ambassador to the U.S.S.R. Other guests aboard the yacht were to be Clare Boothe Luce and her daughter, Anne Brokaw.

The prospect of sailing delighted Larry. His sea legs were shipshape from cruising on his own chartered yacht, the *Rhodos*. But compared to the *Sea Cloud*, the *Rhodos* was a rowboat. The Post ship, commissioned in 1931, was a 316-footer with a breadth of 49 feet. It had four square-rigged masts (the tallest rising the equivalent of a 20-story building in height), 30 sails, and a crew of 72. On windless days, four auxiliary diesel engines drove the vessel at a speed of up to 15 knots.

Marjorie Post herself had decorated the *Sea Cloud*'s main salon, which contained exquisite *objets d'art*, antique furniture, and Sèvres porcelain, glued in place to safeguard it against the shifting of the sea. The staterooms had regular beds, open fireplaces, and gold and marble bathroom fixtures. Thick carpeting covered the floors, and oak panels gave the rooms a rich, glowing appearance. Upon seeing this floating palace, Queen Maud of Norway herself had exclaimed to Marjorie Merriweather Post that she too lived like a queen![30]

On the appointed day, Larry and Jane joined Marjorie and her guests aboard the yacht. The coastline of the United Kingdom gradually vanished as the *Sea Cloud*, sails full, ploughed northward toward the Skagerrak, the Kattegat, and the Baltic Sea. The destination was the eastern end of the Gulf of Finland, where the passengers would debark at St. Petersburg.

Larry and Jane eagerly explored this historic Russian city, its streets, palaces, churches, and museums. One day, after buying an assortment of antiques and enamels to add to their collection, they were driven to a collective farm on the city's outskirts. While they were crossing a field of hay, a group of *muzhiks* started singing "The Song of the Volga Boatman," their scythes swinging rhythmically in time to the music. Impulsively, Larry joined in the chorus, and as his baritone swelled, the workmen stopped their work and looked up in astonishment. Jane focused her camera and snapped several pictures. One shows Larry surrounded by the Russians—listening intently, smiling broadly—as he sang.[31]

When they returned to their hotel, a telegram was waiting: MICHAEL HAS POLIO. STOP. NOW OUT OF DANGER. STOP. AWAIT YOUR INSTRUCTIONS. It was signed by Bernice, the children's governess.

During the summers between 1936 and 1939 the incidence of poliomyelitis, or infantile paralysis, had reached epidemic proportions in the United States. No one knew its causes, only that the disease came on in the heat of summer and seemed to flourish wherever there was swimming. It struck mainly at children. The scare was such that healthy children panicked in their beds at night, imagining a numbness creeping up their legs.

The first symptom, however, was a fever, followed by a sore throat and finally extreme fatigue; paralysis of the limbs or the entire body developed afterward, while agonized parents looked on helplessly. No vaccine was available, nor was there any real cure to restore the use of the young limbs or entire bodies wasted by the affliction.

The telegram's message deeply shocked both parents. It had happened to their son. There was no question but to cancel everything and return to America. But they were half a world away, and even though the days of air travel had begun, the journey home would be excruciatingly long. "Now out of danger," Bernice had telegraphed, but was it true? Polio not only paralyzed, it killed! They left immediately.

Exhausted and heartsick, they finally reached home and heard the governess's story. Though the day had been chilly, the boys had demanded their usual swim, and she had taken them to a beach near Stamford, Connecticut. That evening both boys had developed a fever, and the next morning when Michael attempted to get out of bed, he had tumbled to the floor. Peter too had experienced some difficulty in walking, but in the unpredictable manner of the disease, this soon passed. Little Michael was now paralyzed from the neck down.

Jane, beside herself with fury, accused Bernice of negligence and instantly fired her. A registered nurse was sent for. As it turned out, Mary Cummerford had the warmth and devotion the child desperately needed. For the next two years, she would feed and bathe him and sleep protectively on a cot by his bed. It was she who would stand beside him as he attempted to move in the heavy iron braces he was forced to wear—the only way then known to deal with polio.

A week after their return, Larry and Jane had their first violent quarrel. Many years later, as an adult, Michael remembered the scene and recalled his feelings in detail. His father declared that since Michael was out of danger, they might as well return to Europe and carry out his contracts. His mother had exploded, "Damn your contracts! Our child is lying in the next room like a rotten apple and you're worrying about contracts! What kind of father are you? Grace let you get away with this, but I won't. If you leave now, you leave alone. I'm going to remain here with Michael."

Though helpless and still in much pain, it was four-year-old Michael who settled the matter. He knew that his nurse would give him far more attention than his social-butterfly mother and singing-star father were capable of doing. Since Nurse Cummerford was with him day and night, he pointed out, they needn't worry about his safety. If they insisted on staying, they would only be in the way.[32]

And so the following week the Tibbetts again boarded ship, this time for Copenhagen, where Larry resumed his tour. Out of great sorrows, he made his songs.

Chapter 8

MORE TRIUMPHS, UNTIL . . .

Larry's reception in Scandinavia was free of the carping of the London critics. A concert in Denmark on 15 September 1937 was enthusiastically received, and the King of Denmark presented Larry with a set of silver, 173 pieces in all.[1] It was the same for a concert in Oslo on 21 September, to which Oslo's *Aftenposten* sent both a music critic and a film critic, both of whom waxed rhapsodic. The music critic praised Larry's expressions of humor and called him a fine and noble artist whose tone rang out, whose voice was even throughout his range, and whose attention to the text was strong. The film critic was impressed that Larry's operatic colleagues Kirsten Flagstad and Kaja Eide (Eidé Norena) had sent Larry flowers before the concert and urged that the singer's films be revived in Oslo, since now that the Norwegians had seen and been charmed by him in person, they would rush to see him in the cinema.[2]

On 24 September Larry sang *Rigoletto* at the Royal Opera in Stockholm with Hjördis Schymberg and Jussi Björling. The reviewer for *Svenska Dagbladet* admitted being very suspicious of Larry's reputation but now, having heard him, found not only that Tibbett was great but that his greatness was at the right level. His bel canto was ideal, and his actions were economical. "[At the Royal Opera] we have louder voices but no one who can compete in vocal finesse or musical dramatics. . . . The evening was a great success for Lawrence Tibbett."[3]

The critic for *Dagens Nyheter* also reported he knew of the Tibbett reputation and therefore expected a lot. Tibbett delivered:

> His tragic jester was a masterful accomplishment. Although his stately figure spoke against him, he nonetheless looked like Rigoletto. His entry was almost overlooked, and during the first part of the first act we hardly noticed him, but from [the Monterone scene] on, the figure came alive and dominated the stage, not because he was a famous guest but because this old opera was in the hands of an artist who could realize the possibilities of the role without going too far. His rich voice can sound like a cello and a bassoon; his phrases have power and elegance.[4]

In the entire review only two lines concerned Björling and Schymberg.

Frank Hedman, producer of Bluebell of Sweden Records, was at that performance. In 1988 he wrote from Stockholm:

> I have been a regular opera-goer since childhood. Jussi Björling was a great favorite of mine, and I heard him in most of his repertoire. In 1937 I had become a travel agent, working for Thomas Cook & Son in their office opposite the Stockholm Opera. In the autumn of that year it was announced that Lawrence Tibbett would make a guest appearance as Rigoletto opposite Björling's Duke. Tibbett had for years been a singer whose records I collected, not the least the Victor album of *Porgy and Bess*. I purchased two tickets for my mother and myself and enjoyed one of the best performances ever of *Rigoletto*. The love of singing displayed by the two leading singers, and their great artistry, made the rest of the cast better than they usually were.
>
> The following day Mr. Tibbett entered Cook's office and ordered a rail ticket from me. He noticed that I recognized him, and he smiled at me. But I was too shy to tell him I had heard him at the Opera the night before. What did one say to an artist one admired? In time I came to understand one may say almost anything, however trivial, if the words are sincere.[5]

Larry was a media event in Stockholm. Large notices in the papers accompanied his every appearance. Lundholm's Piano Store took out a large advertisement with a head shot of Larry and a quote from him about the Steinway piano: "Lawrence Tibbett on Steinway."[6]

Svenska Dagbladet reported that Larry's concert was met with huge ovations, that female admirers filled the hall, and that flowers had been sent over from the Royal Opera Ballet. The critic also noted that the variety in Larry's concert program was almost too much. Larry sang Handel, Italian opera arias, and German, Russian, and American songs. High points were the *Pagliacci* Prologue, Iago's Credo, the Loewe ballad "Edward"—just about everything. The only thing that struck the reviewer as less than successful was Strauss's "Morgen."[7]

Larry also sang a Scarpia in Stockholm. The opera company held a banquet for him at which Björling spoke, and at another occasion, King Gustav V presented Larry with the *Litteris et Artibus* gold medal. That event had its lighter side, as protocol required a silk top hat for the ceremony and Larry had not brought one with him. The one finally found for him was several sizes too small, as the comical photo published by *Svenska Dagbladet* proves. In the accompanying interview, Larry says that the king asked him to take care of Jussi Björling, who was about to make his American debut. "I promised to do my best if he needs help," was Larry's reply.[8]

At the conclusion of the Scandinavian leg of his trip, Larry bumped into Nellie Walters of Columbia Artists at the railway station in Stockholm. He was surrounded by all sorts of luggage and was handling it himself. Miss Walters asked Larry where Jane was and why she wasn't helping. Larry wiped his brow and said, "She's down at the bar."[9]

On 5 October, Larry made his Paris debut as Iago with Norena and Martinelli, his partners from the London performance of the opera. *The Excelsior* reported he "belonged to the race of the great lyric tragedians. . . . One admires the wide variety of his resource, from the fierce . . . Credo to the whispered venom in Otello's ear." *Le Temps* praised his ability to "direct all the drama" on the stage and his "generous voice."[10] He sang another *Rigoletto* there on 21 October.

In Prague on 7 October he sang *Rigoletto* and won a standing ovation. The *Prager Tageblatt* called Larry's performance "an achievement bearing the hallmark of genius."[11] On 11 October Tibbett sang *Rigoletto* in Budapest and was forced to encore "Cortigiani." The critic for the *Pester Lloyd* was amazed by Larry's voice "which could do simply everything."[12] He won still greater praise for a Budapest recital on 15 October. George Jellinek heard Larry in Budapest at that time and described his voice as "like gold, as smooth as lava."[13]

The Viennese were less impressed. Budapest had received him ecstatically, but Vienna was negative and chauvinistic.

Larry's visit to Vienna began with a banquet on 8 October. The next day he sang Iago in Italian while Joachim Sattler, Maria Reining, and the rest of the cast performed in German. Time had not allowed for proper rehearsals, and the performance received mixed reviews, with critics blaming the management. The *Neues Wiener Tagblatt* reported that Larry "was neither a vocal Croesus nor a fascinating bel cantist. . . .

His baritone is approximately good middle class." The critic for the *Neue Freie Presse* thought he lacked "star quality," and expressed preference for Vienna's own Alfred Jerger. *Der Morgen* considered Larry "typically American . . . a kind of socially polished Mephistopheles."[14]

The critics hailed Larry's skill at singing lieder in German at a 14 October concert. The *Neue Freie Presse* was astonished by this "quite unexpected" triumph. The *Anbruch*, in its November issue, recorded that Larry received a "stormy ovation."[15] A *Rigoletto* on 17 October had critics faulting the company's directors for failing to provide an adequate supporting cast for such a distinguished guest.[16]

Larry was back in London by late October. On 24 October he sang in Queen's Hall. The *London Times* admitted he was indeed a great singer, but criticized his operatic mannerisms, which were said to spoil the effect of his singing. The reviewer also objected to Larry's use of English translations for lieder and his effort to emphasize the drama within the various selections. A recital on 4 November in Glasgow was received with more praise, the *Herald* singling out his fine diction and "his ability to negotiate long phrases."[17] Whatever England's reservations about Larry's singing at the time, that country's record producers lead the field in rereleasing his recordings, both commercial and "pirate," in carefully remastered digital format.

The Berlin *Stimmwort* of October 1937 carried a detailed assessment of Larry's concerts during his first European tour in an article titled "Lawrence Tibbett as a Concert Singer."

> I had the good fortune of hearing Lawrence Tibbett in recital in Copenhagen. Until then I had known the world-famous baritone only from motion pictures. It made me very happy that, this time, reality did not prove to be disappointing—as it usually is. On the contrary, the true Tibbett is revealed to us only by hearing him in person. This is why I write the following comments with enthusiasm.
>
> He is not the usual type of singer with broad, high chest, stout figure, short neck. Slim and elegant, he walks onstage in a lively and elastic manner and with a very courteous smile. As soon as the accompanist plays the first chords, however, his entire attitude changes. Concentration of body and soul flows into his tone, resulting in a magic influence on the watching listener.
>
> This transformation is an unconscious one, without any pose or mannerism. It is as if inspiration comes to the singer. It is not he himself who sings, but rather the inspiration, singing through him. In addition, the range of his singing abilities is enormous. All

means are at his disposal: sense of humor, both the gracious and the ironic.

I thought no one would ever be able to sing the "Song of the Flea" better than Chaliapin did. Since Tibbett possesses similar vocal qualifications, I expected him to imitate Chaliapin in this song. He did it all in his own way, however, and just as ingeniously. His buffo style is outstanding. I have heard the aria from *The Barber of Seville* sung by all the famous artists such as Forsell [teacher of Björling, Svanholm, and Joel Berglund], Schlusnus, and others. It seemed to me that Tibbett surpassed them all.

There is a rare fragrance in his cantabile when he sings Lully's aria from *Amadis*, "Bois épais"; and above all in his rendition of the "Evening Star" by Richard Wagner.

Even more than in charm, humor, and mild elegy, Tibbett reveals himself in great dramatic parts, so that I can well understand his being equally esteemed as a concert and as an operatic singer. Compared with him, all the singers with merely beautiful voices—performing well-studied arias and songs—seem very insignificant. Nature contra routine, imagination contra boredom!

An artist who is able to express himself with such intensity is bound to have a natural voice of rare qualities. Such renditions would not be possible unless nature had provided a well-fit instrument. This seems to be true with Tibbett's voice to a high degree. . . .

In the first place, the range of his voice is extraordinarily large. This is why Tibbett can sing a ballad for bass by Brahms just as well as Figaro's aria from *The Barber of Seville*, which is written for a tenor-bass. His low register, though lacking somewhat in sonority, is all the same produced with concentration of sound, and it is sustained in an even volume, like a cello tone.

Tibbett's diction is outstanding. He seems to seize the consonants in a pincer movement. His parlando is of utmost clearness even in the prestissimo passages. His breath control is perfect—and this is, so it seems to me, not so much the result of conscious breath technique but of an automatically working and well-balanced compression. There are not breathy sounds—each tone is concentrated, and the vowels, in general, are round. No striking dualism is noticeable—as it is with so many outstanding singers whose tone-production is round and full on the open vowels while the *i*'s and *e*'s are pointed. Also the pureness of the tone is not intermingled with throaty and guttural sounds; Tibbett's tone is free—although with all his high qualities not overlarge. His voice is well fit for a Wolfram—not for a Wotan.

This does not mean that his voice is not strong. The fact that

> one never hears an unsteady sound or a tone off-pitch makes his singing very enjoyable for the listening musician. How rare this is! Tibbett proves the words of Müller-Brunow: "Technique is a fruit of the tone production."
>
> Since Tibbett's tone production is beautiful and free, his technique is bound to be excellent. This enables him to do everything: an exquisite legato, a portamento in the way Caruso did it—and a coloratura like pearls.[18]

Larry concluded his first European tour in late November of 1937. "He is full of his reminiscences," *Opera News* reported soon after:

> For two months he averaged a performance of some sort every other day. Twenty-seven concert appearances took him from Oslo to Bucharest. He sang Rigoletto in Prague and Baron Scarpia in Vienna, with operatic stops in between.
>
> "Those European audiences certainly know their opera with an intimacy that Americans do not possess," he admits with a smile. "And they put it up to the singer every time. On the other hand I feel that American concert audiences are every bit as experienced as those abroad."
>
> "My work in the movies was the best advance publicity a singer could have. I firmly believe that no small part of my capacity houses was due to curiosity as to the man those people had known on the screen. Only in London and Vienna did I detect a certain condescension to the movies," Mr. Tibbett said.[19]

And as Frank Hedman related from Stockholm, the *Porgy and Bess* recordings hadn't hurt his advance publicity, either.

Upon his return to the United States, Larry's first engagements were in Chicago for *Otello* and with Björling in two performances of *Rigoletto* in November 1937. He returned to the Met on 22 December for his first New York Iago and the Met's first *Otello* since 1913. *Opera News* reported:

> Mr. Tibbett's acquaintance with Iago dates nearly a score of years back, from the time when, at the age of 21, he acted the part in Shakespeare's play. He studied the lines with his friend Reginald Pole, and later with Granville Barker.[20]

The artistic partnership between Larry as Iago and Giovanni Martinelli's Otello in this opera became one of legend. They sang the opera first together in San Francisco, then Chicago, London, Paris, New York, and Cincinnati. Their Desdemonas included Elisabeth Rethberg, Edith Mason, Eidé Norena, Maria Caniglia, Irene Jessner, Helen Jepson, Stella Roman, Rose Bampton, and Vivian Della Chiesa, and the conductors varied as widely, but the tenor and baritone stayed together, garnering cheers and admiration for their portrayals.

In this Met premiere, after an earlier uncertainty about Cigna and Norena, Rethberg was the Desdemona, with Panizza conducting. Pitts Sanborn wrote in the pages of the 4 January 1938 *World Telegram*:

> Mr. Tibbett's Iago has evidently been worked out and developed with infinite care. Subtlety, finesse, polish were there; now a bubbling volatility, now a dour and meditative air. Acting Mephistophelean in half-tints was this villain; whatever the evil, a figure of buoyancy and grace; timeless in essence, redolent of the Renaissance.
>
> Singing and acting were Tibbett's usual forte. The Credo went well, and better still "Era la notte"—a masterpiece of color, shading, and phrasing. A blind man would have been at no loss to follow the progress of this Iago.

Oscar Thompson commented in the *New York Sun*:

> Subtler Iagos than that of Lawrence Tibbett undoubtedly have walked the same boards. But one may question whether parts of the music, particularly the narrative of Cassio's dream, "Era la notte," have been more beautifully sung. The Credo was delivered with sting and power. And there was no evasion of the upwards curve to high A-natural, commonly indicated rather than sung. The pictorial was not slighted by Mr. Tibbett. But some bits of stage business were unfortunate.[21]

Also in the 1937–38 Met season he sang with little success the title role of Puccini's *Gianni Schicchi* in English.[22] His schedule also included the elder Germont (with Norena, later with Jepson as Violetta), Wolfram, Rigoletto (with Pons and Kiepura), and excerpts from *Pagliacci* in a Sunday concert. The season ended with a Silver Jubilee Concert in honor of Giovanni Martinelli, which concluded with the "Si pel ciel" duet from *Otello* sung by the honoree and Larry.

No sooner had he concluded his first European tour than Larry began to plan a second tour for the spring and summer of 1938, this time of Hawaii, Australia, and New Zealand. Why Australia? Soprano Marjorie Lawrence, an Australian native who had joined the Met in

1934, had presented an irresistible challenge to Larry. As she later wrote in her autobiography, *Interrupted Melody*:

> Musicians, particularly singers, whose powers are waning and those who fall short of being the best should not go to Australia and hope to satisfy Australian concertgoers. . . . And singers who have recorded should not venture into the Commonwealth to sing unless their art be at least as perfect as it was when they made their recordings. The mass of Australian concertgoers wants everything from a singer: a good voice, the best songs, a platform personality, and a cast-iron constitution.[23]

Melba's often misquoted (and suspect) dictum, "Sing 'em muck," did not apply Down Under.[24]

A good voice, the best songs, a platform personality, and a cast-iron constitution? Larry had them all—and would need them for this grueling seven-month tour. Following appearances in Hawaii (a geographically convenient port-of-call they would revisit on their way home), Larry and Jane arrived in Australia, where the audiences welcomed them joyously. No sooner had their ship steamed into Melbourne harbor than a dirigible appeared overhead with a huge sign swinging from its cabin: "Welcome, Lawrence Tibbett."

Over the next months, despite his heavy schedule of lengthy recitals, Larry made time to hear the vocal auditions of many young hopefuls, trying to spare them the disappointment he had felt when, as a beginner in Los Angeles, Mary Garden had promised to hear him and then could not. He advised them to study—or to forget their dreams, if they lacked real talent.[25] In a handwritten letter to Richard from Melbourne, Larry offered more of the same—the uplifting sermonizing he believed sons required of their fathers. After apologies for forgetting the exact date of Richard's high school graduation, he gave his impressions of Australia.

> This is really a thrilling young country. I have been having a tremendous success. Broke all records for consecutive concerts in Sydney. Thirteen of them and two more booked for next month. Melbourne promises a like record. With all the success tho I'm homesick to see you and our other boys and the good old U.S.A.

Larry had promised to send a watch as a graduation gift, but it would have to wait, he wrote, "until I return in the fall."[26]

Claude Kingston, the impresario for many of the artists who toured

Australia at that time, described the country's concert scene in his autobiography:

> What a roll of fame it was between the two world wars! Paderewski, Chaliapin, Kirsten Flagstad, Yehudi Menuhin, Moiseiwitsch, Amelita Galli-Curci, Percy Grainger, Heifetz, Clara Butt, Lawrence Tibbett, Richard Crooks, Tito Schipa, Jan Kubelik—practically every man and woman who stood for anything in the high-grade entertainment world."[27]

On Larry's tour the artist's drinking worried Kingston, but it never interfered with Larry's concert appearances or with the quality of his voice. He was once late for a dinner, as he was sleeping off his afternoon cocktails, but he made it, and he never missed a concert. Kingston offers little about the concert tour itself, mentioning only that Larry was paid 70 percent of the gross concert receipts—"His share read like a figure in the national Budget"—and making much of Larry's undeniable appeal. "The Tibbetts really were a pair of charmers."[28]

Like most women of her class, Jane carried a large quantity of jewels with her on her trips, a necessity for the social occasions she would encounter along the way. Usually, once aboard ship, she locked the jewels in the purser's safe. At the conclusion of this tour, however, aboard the Matson-Oceanic liner *Monterey* out of Hawaii, she simply put her plush-covered jewelry box in an unlocked drawer of her stateroom bureau. As the ship neared Los Angeles harbor, she discovered that her jewelry, valued at $50,000, was missing.

Authorities were notified immediately and G-men boarded the ship as it sailed inside the breakwater. Six hundred passengers were held for hours while their staterooms and baggage were searched; the G-men finally allowed them to debark, and the ship proceeded up the coast to San Francisco. The search narrowed to the crew, and a messman was arrested for the theft. He led them to a life preserver, inside which was found hidden a portion of the missing jewels, valued at $20,000. The messman went to jail, but the remainder of the missing valuables was never recovered.[29]

While Larry and Jane were traveling the world, Michael was at home, struggling to regain the use of his legs. He had undergone three operations but even with iron braces strapped to his legs, he could still barely walk a step. Seeing his young son thus, upon his return, was the last straw for Larry. He finally lost patience with the doctors and decided, over the objections of his friends, to seek out Sister Elizabeth Kenny, an Australian nurse who had had considerable success in treating polio; her recently opened institute in Minneapolis featured her revolutionary technique of applying hot, moist compresses to the affected muscles in conjunction with massages and exercises.

Larry first heard of Sister Kenny and her accomplishments during his Australian tour, but he had been wary of making drastic changes in Michael's care until both he and Jane were convinced that their son's overall condition was not improving. They were now convinced.[30]

Thus it was on his sixth birthday, 17 August 1939, that Michael met one of the most important persons in his young life. After a brief examination of his slight body, Sister Kenny turned to the attending physicians and cried, "You butchers! Just look what you've done to this child!" She was so angry that she could barely hold back her tears. "If these parents will let me, I'm going to take this child to my institute and try to save him—if I can."[31] Larry and Jane agreed straightaway, and Michael spent the next 18 months at the Kenny Institute in Minneapolis.

Sister Kenny was a large, well-proportioned woman, standing just over six feet. She had a round face, a broad, flat nose, extremely expressive blue eyes beneath heavily penciled eyebrows, and a full head of curly hair, prematurely white. Her mouth had a downward thrust, which lent her face a perpetual look of bulldog aggressiveness. She was born in 1896 in New South Wales, and although she received little formal education, she managed to apprentice herself as a nurse to several doctors and was accepted into the Australian Army Nursing Service during World War I. In the following years, even as her unorthodox but successful methods of treating polio among Australian children increased her reputation around the world, her pugnacious personality infuriated the medical establishment wherever she went. In 1940 she left Australia permanently and established her headquarters at her institute in Minneapolis.

Michael was one of her first patients from the United States. On the day he arrived at the institute, he wore iron braces from waist to ankles and hobbled awkwardly toward Sister Kenny on crutches. She towered over him as he approached. Her first words to him were a terse command: "Drop those crutches, Michael Tibbett!" He did.

Kenny and her therapists set to work on Michael immediately, applying hot, moist packs to his back and legs daily. Then, positioning him face down, they would knead and stretch the atrophied muscles until he felt them tingle. Sister Kenny helped Michael learn to isolate the groups of muscles that had been affected. Putting her hand on a particular muscle, she would urge him to concentrate, saying, "Think where my hand is, Michael. Think about trying to contract this muscle." Gradually, Michael was able to make each muscle flicker, then tense briefly, then contract for a longer time. One by one, his muscles came back to life.

Almost imperceptibly, other parts of his body began to function. First he could twitch his toes, then he could turn his upper torso around in bed an inch at a time. At first he was awed by all this focus on his muscles, then he began to accept the results with pride. Michael progressed so rapidly that Kenny displayed his "before and after" photos to the Minneapolis Medical Association, but the doctors still refused to accept her methods and continued to treat their young patients with casts and iron braces. Sister Kenny, on the other hand, had faith in the use of mind over metal where polio was concerned. When Michael left her institute after a year and a half of treatment, he wore neither crutches nor braces. He did have a pronounced limp but managed to walk unaided and upright.

Michael remembered how Larry and Jane stared with disbelief as he carefully walked down a staircase, unassisted by so much as a handrail. Frantic with worry, they had rushed to Minneapolis after Walter Winchell inserted an item in his column announcing in error that their son had suffered a relapse and was critically ill.

The Tibbetts were so impressed with Sister Kenny's work that they contributed heavily toward the construction of a second building at the Kenny Institute. Larry turned over to her the proceeds of several concerts, and in the early 1940s he was appointed chairman of the fundraising drive for the Sister Elizabeth Kenny Foundation in the New York area. Jane was eventually appointed the head of the foundation's women's division in New York City.[32]

Larry's older sons were entering young manhood. Richard Tibbett enrolled at Cummock Junior College and then the University of Southern California, both in Los Angeles.[33] His twin had graduated from the Santa Barbara School for Boys and had come to live with his father and stepmother in New York while he pursued a career in the theater. The attractive younger Larry closely resembled his father and also possessed a pleasing light tenor voice, suited to musical comedy. Larry Jr. sometimes went to the Met for his father's performances and hung around backstage in the dressing room until curtain time. Years later, his recollections were vivid:

> After Dad finished preparing his makeup, Angelo Cassamassa, dresser for the male artists, would come in to help him get into his costume. After that, Dad would start vocalizing with his scales, and I would go out to my seat in the side parterre. After the opera, when the chauffeur arrived, we would go home together, not only to the inevitable receptions Jane cooked up but to meetings with fellow officers of AGMA.
>
> Believe me, in those days unions had a lot of problems to handle. All things considered, Dad was a very busy man. Money was coming in hand over fist, so when I asked him once why he helped to organize all those unions in addition to AGMA—American Federation of Radio Artists [AFTRA's precursor] and the Screen Actors Guild—when he really didn't have to, I realized my question was rhetorical. Dad was simply for the underdog, as he always had been—all the little people in the music and entertainment business.[34]

In the autumn of 1938, upon his return from his concert tour, Larry appeared in Chicago singing Rigoletto and Hoffmann's four nemeses. Then he, Martinelli, and Maria Caniglia opened the Metropolitan's 1938–39 season on 21 November with *Otello*, the house's unquestioned hit. It was broadcast and recorded on 2 December. Larry's Iago here is altogether amazing. On the recording his voice is completely in control, to be used as his intelligence commands it. He keeps it light—except where power is the better choice—and his *mezza voce* insinuates and floats. The Credo is sung with all the variations of an actor delivering a Shakespearean monologue, as is the later recounting of Cassio's dream. Since his teenage years, Larry had known instinctively that acting was part of the professional singer's art and he proves it with this legendary characterization.

RCA released excerpts from the opera with Tibbett, Martinelli, and Helen Jepson, a commercial set that gained a large circulation. Although not as exciting as a performance—the conductor here is Pelletier—this too is well worth hearing.

Other roles Larry sang that season were Scarpia, the elder Germont, Simon Boccanegra, Rigoletto, and a new role, Falstaff. As always, Larry's Scarpia was a rugged, erotic killer. (A former Metropolitan chorus member said she always expected him, as Scarpia, to bare himself and have an orgasm.) As Germont, acting an old man, Larry was high voltage even when he was seated. Before beginning Germont's aria and with just a look at Alfredo, he would stand still and make a profoundly human statement. As he sang, a dramatic sound that was perhaps not very pretty would a moment later turn into a dreamy legato. He had learned to use his voice with the most subtle effects, never losing sight of the psychology of each character he portrayed. He was one of the greatest singing actors ever, a complete performer, and there was not a musical or dramatic challenge he would not attempt.

His *Rigoletto* was broadcast on 11 March 1939, a particularly good performance with Lily Pons and Jan Kiepura taking turns in the spotlight and Gennaro Papi conducting. Here again, Larry is absolutely towering. Although there are those who say that this is the role that harmed his voice, the difficult music seems almost too easy for him, so well does it fit his voice. His acting is also fully nuanced.[35]

Jarmila Novotná called Larry the greatest Rigoletto ever. "There is no other singer I know who worked like that. I worked with [Max] Reinhardt, and he would have loved him. He was terrific, wonderful, the best actor ever on the stage."[36] Marta Eggerth, whose husband, Jan Kiepura, sang the Duke to Larry's Rigoletto, concurred. "Of course Reinhardt would have loved Larry, Reinhardt was a great director, but *all* directors would have loved Larry. He wore a small hump, not an overdone one, so that you would have sympathy for his character. He was a great actor. Whatever he did was reality, it was never false."[37] Patrice Munsel said that nobody understood the role like Larry did. She trailed off, with a despairing look at the ceiling, "Today's Rigolettos . . ."[38] "For Mr. Tibbett," *Opera News* reported,

> Rigoletto is a man of about 50, whose paternal tenderness is his redeeming trait. He is more of a lovable character than many who are played by baritones in grand opera, such as Iago or Golaud, two of Tibbett's favorites, though he does not reach the nobility of Simon Boccanegra, who remains Tibbett's favorite part.[39]

The new role in Larry's repertoire this season of 1938–39 had a familiar ring, but now he was Falstaff, not Ford, in the Verdi opera. He had prepared for this Met revival during the concert tour he had just concluded, spending his spare time in the balmy climes by brushing up his Shakespeare, reading the Bard's *Henry IV* and *The Merry Wives of Windsor*.[40] These were the days when certain special roles like Falstaff, Norma, and La Gioconda were almost sacred; to be cast in them at the Met was a hard-earned and universally acclaimed honor. Larry was only the third baritone to sing Falstaff in the house, following Maurel, who had created the part for Verdi, and Scotti. By all accounts Larry did not match his predecessors as the portly knight; perhaps he did not have the opportunity to perform Falstaff often enough. But Francis D. Perkins wrote favorably of the baritone's opening night performance, 16 December 1938, in the *New York Herald Tribune*:

> His singing is well-phrased, expressive, and artistic, and his actions showed an understanding of the role and good taste. . . . On yesterday's evidence it promises to become one of Mr. Tibbett's memorable impersonations.[41]

Kolodin was negative, faulting both Larry's singing and his costume.[42] Others in the opening night cast were Maria Caniglia, Marisa Morel, Irra Petina, Bruna Castagna, Charles Kullman, and John Brownlee; Ettore Panizza conducted.

In February 1939, Larry joined Kirsten Flagstad, Geraldine Farrar, Walter Damrosch, Leopold Stokowski, Frederick Jagel, and Jascha Heifetz in protest against the Daughters of the American Revolution's refusal to allow Marian Anderson to sing at Constitution Hall.[43] These wide protests led, as is well known, to the concert being given instead at the Lincoln Memorial that Easter Sunday, 9 April 1939.

That summer, Larry had a full concert schedule. He sang at the White House on 8 June for England's King George VI and Queen Elizabeth (with Marian Anderson and Kate Smith), and on 15 August he sang at the Hollywood Bowl for the first time in 16 years; Werner Janssen conducted. Later that month, on 22 August, he sang outdoors before 300,000 listeners at a free concert in Chicago's Grant Park.[44] In this busy summer, Larry also made an important radio broadcast for the Council Against Intolerance and fought actively against the proposed abolishment of the Federal Theater of the Work Projects Administration (WPA).

Lawrence Tibbett's national celebrity flourished with every news item, from feature story to gossip-column mention (true or fanciful), with every photo layout and even in cartoons. In a poll of 729,000 listeners taken in June 1939 by *Radio Guide*, Larry followed Nelson Eddy and Richard Crooks as the public's favorite "Star of Stars" male singer.[45] It is duly noted that Larry had a radio rehearsal before a Groucho Marx broadcast.[46] It is soberly announced that Larry is slated to sing Boris Godunov at the Met during the coming season, "the role that Ezio

Pinza had in the recent revival" (not at all likely).[47] The Tibbetts' estate, Honey Hill Farm, is closed "while the family sojourns on sunny sands."[48] The New York World's Fair is on, and "Lawrence Tibbett brings his own miniature camera to the Fair grounds and snaps pictures like any other wide-eyed tourist."[49] And this couldn't pass without notice: "Errol Flynn and Lawrence Tibbett were passengers on the United Airlines *Mainliner* which arrived from the Coast on Friday."[50]

This was the public face; the family face was different. That year, Larry and Jane gave up the apartment on East End Avenue. With the older boys grown and scattered for the most part, it seemed simpler for them to take a 16th-floor suite at the Savoy Plaza, which was centrally located at Fifty-ninth Street and Fifth Avenue. Their windows offered splendid views of Central Park, and the interior was described by neighbor Marta Eggerth as elegant and beautiful.[51] The Savoy had all the conveniences of first-class hotel service and was all the more attractive since Jane was a principal stockholder. Close friends hoped that the move to the Savoy would perhaps cut down on the party-loving couple's social life, but regrettably, this didn't prove to be the case. Guests continued to pour through the door and ice rattled and corks popped with the same reckless abandon as before. This suite, and the farm, were nominally also the home for Peter Burgard, Michael, and Larry Jr.

Older they may have been, but the twins continued to feel the pain of their father's inattention. On 1 December 1939 there was a men's homecoming dinner at the University of Southern California, where Richard was majoring in cinematography. The idea was to have famous fathers of undergraduates attend and speak. Groucho Marx and Edward Arnold appeared, but Richard sat in place of his father on the dais and delivered Larry's message.[52]

After appearances at the San Francisco Opera in *Rigoletto*, *Otello*, and *La Traviata* in October, Larry opened the next Metropolitan season on 27 November 1939 with *Simon Boccanegra*. Four days later, on 1 December, he sang a matinée as Wolfram, and three nights later, Rigoletto's "Cortigiani" at a Met concert. He sang a complete *Rigoletto* on 6 December then, with two days rest, the elder Germont on 9 December. He did not appear again until 16 December, when he sang Scarpia.

Next began a round of second performances of these roles, including a *Rigoletto* with Jussi Björling on 1 January 1940. He was away from the Met on a concert tour until 12 February, when he returned to sing another Scarpia. On 24 February he sang Iago, and then came another Germont with Novotná as Violetta on 1 March, concluding his 1939–40 New York opera season.

August 1940 brought a titanic union battle. It seemed that all the headline stars of the day, with Larry in the forefront, were in each edition of the national newspapers either calling each other names or banding together. The "Nine Old Men," as the ruling council of the AFL were known, kept postponing their decision on whether a craft union had raided a performers' union. A Supreme Court judge rejected a temporary injunction, and the battle raged on. In the end, performers had their own union and the stagehands theirs. On another front, Larry became president of the American Federation of Radio Artists, a union that he had helped found. He served as president from 1940 to 1945 and as a member of the board of directors until 1952.[53]

Larry lived for the moment: for him the past was dead and the future remote. Given this, and notwithstanding his demanding nature, did he take care of his voice? Some critics say that he did not; others claim he did. Unlike many singers, he was not so frightened by a sudden breeze that he never left home without a scarf and hat. He did not flee a room because it was too cool or damp. He smoked—everyone did and nobody worried about it. On the other hand, he did not talk for two hours before a performance, nor did he drink ice water.

But shunning ice water did not prove to be enough. After living on top of the world for so many years without a worry about his singing voice, which flowed so freely, so beautifully, something did happen to that voice. As a singer, he was never able to fully relax again.

No one has been able to prove exactly what happened, but the change became painfully obvious. Although he "was in absolutely superb voice at his Stanford concert on 24 January 1940,"[54] sometime soon thereafter Larry's voice began to sound dry, choked. He had trouble sustaining a line. The smoothness, the "lava flow" quality, was too often gone. He sang, he interpreted, but he suffered. So, often, did his listeners.

The basso Jerome Hines described the phenomenon of the late 40s, by which time Larry's vocal trouble were already deep-seated:

> The problem was pretty much as follows: Larry would commence to sing with strong, healthy sounds, but within four minutes into a role, his voice would begin to quiver and shake with muscle spasms, and the high notes would just crack and break up. While

> I was singing with him, I noticed that he was trying to keep his voice relaxed, but he couldn't. The voice would tire and simply break up. Then he would attempt to start every phrase with a lot of breath, but the voice would not respond, and the result would be a terrible chaos of sound.[55]

As Larry was so popular and well known, folk legends grew up about the problem. Many people still believe that Tibbett had a throat operation, as some will insist that he died of a brain tumor. Neither is true.

Some say he had a collapsed vocal cord (a condition that is itself a matter of controversy, although it is reported to have happened to George London). This is possible, but it does not appear consistent with the circumstances. In January 1949 *Newsweek* reported that Larry in *Rigoletto* a week before was "a completely rewarding and commanding figure on the operatic stage . . . a grand singing actor in the grand tradition of opera"; nonetheless, the same article noted Larry's singing problem and quoted a physician who called it "an uncommon form of spasticity of the larynx muscle."[56]

Many others would say it had to be his alcoholism. Drink did not help, and heavy drinking sometimes made his singing worse, but alcohol did not bring on the problem. It has been suggested that Larry first began to drink more heavily as a result of the tragic fatal accident that occurred during the *Caponsacchi* rehearsal, and certainly Larry did drink more heavily as a result of the difficulty he now encountered in singing. But then, every so often, moments recalled his past vocal glory.

Rupert Pole insisted that Larry was a light musical comedy baritone, almost a tenor, and forced himself into being a "big" operatic baritone, thereby hurting his voice.[57] This also does not stand up to recorded evidence.

Was it fear? Tibbett loved to sing, sang continuously, even tenor arias at his wife's parties—but now he could not predict what kind of sound would emerge from his throat. Soprano Helen Jepson knew Larry well professionally. He had sung, and helped her, at her Met debut and they sang in four other operas together. They also did joint concerts and recorded together. According to Jepson, "The last time I appeared with Tibbett was in *Traviata*, it must have been in the early 40s. He was having vocal problems—so was I. I took his hands. They were ice cold."[58] Fear definitely had something to do with Larry's problem, but only after it arose. Fear was not the cause, but, like drink, merely the effect.

Another theory is that Larry's voice became abused. The baritone George Cehanovsky traced the problem to a particular episode:

> During Tibbett's long career at the Met, and on the concert trail, he never missed a day on his rowing machine or, in other ways, consciously exercising and taking care of his physical body. Had jogging become the rage in his day, I'm certain he would have become a jogger, too. He knew, as any good singer knows, that there is a dependent relationship between body and voice. Now, in retrospect, since he literally worshiped his body, I've often wondered why he never had the same respect for his voice.
>
> Throughout 1937 he had no vocal difficulties at all, but early in 1938, when he went to Cincinnati to sing *Rigoletto* with Lily Pons, suddenly he was laid low with an attack of strep throat.
>
> I had always understood that if you attempted to sing while suffering from a strep throat, you could damage your voice irrevocably. Tibbett must have thought this injunction an old wives' tale because, with strep throat and all, he went through his scheduled *Rigoletto*, first in Cincinnati and then in San Francisco, putting on performances as no one before him ever had. But afterward, he was never himself again.[59]

But, Cehanovsky's late recollection notwithstanding and from all evidence of performance recordings, Tibbett was at the top of his form through the 1939–40 season. He was singing superbly. It appears that he then sang, in the spring of 1940, an outdoor engagement in bad weather with the throat ailment that Cehanovsky mentions, and then continued to sing, without proper rest. Hy Faine of AGMA specifies it was in Washington that Larry strained his voice.[60]

Richard Tibbett says: "I talked to Larry Jr., and he didn't know what caused the illness even though he was staying with Dad at the time. My own recollection, from afar, was that Dad caught cold singing at an outdoor concert and didn't take adequate care of his throat."[61]

Larry knew he was in trouble and was on the verge of canceling his opera and concert engagements for the rest of 1940, but he had recently begun working with a new vocal coach, Vito Mirsky, who seems only to have compounded the problem. Mirsky urged Larry *not* to rest, arguing that if Larry stopped singing, his voice would grow rusty, but that if he continued to sing, his vocal problems would eventually right themselves. Larry was so frightened of losing his voice, and Mirsky was so reassuring, that Larry decided to continue with his typically heavy schedule, except for the San Francisco Opera. He canceled his 1940 season there, where he was to have sung *Fanciulla* with Marjorie Lawrence.[62]

There is another theory, and it involves vocal technique, specifically the aspect of "open" versus "covered" vocal production. For purposes of discussion, terms must be defined: open production is said to be characterized by Italian baritones such as Ruffo and Gino Bechi; covered production by the American Leonard Warren. Open can eventually hurt, while covered is said to protect.

Many hold that there is a break in the range of every singer, male or female, which occurs as the scale is ascended. A vocalist has the choice of producing the transitional notes at which this change of register takes place—the *passaggio*—in two different ways. A baritone may choose to sing the E-flat or F-natural above middle C in the way he produces his lower range—open—and the sound will issue forth with a rousing, lusty quality, as if produced by the throat or the whole upper torso. On the other hand, if he sings these notes of the *passaggio* covered—in the nose or head, or the "mask"—the sound is more gentle and less virile.

Many insist that Tibbett, who placed such an emphasis on rugged manliness, sang as high as possible in the open manner, thrilling his audiences with the robust, bravado quality of the sound. But danger can lurk in the continuous emission of open high tones: the delicate vocal cords can eventually rebel at such ungentle treatment, causing the vocalist to sing flat and eventually to lose the high range altogether. Leonard Warren, for one, was enjoined never to sing in such a reckless, uncovered manner. Warren covered, and Warren still managed to be exciting. Yet it is always a temptation, when Rigoletto curses or Scarpia threatens or Iago exults, to sing big, loud, and open. What a great sound a baritone can get, and many do—for a while.

Did Tibbett shout at the top, and was that the root of his problem? A close listening to his available recordings makes one doubt this. As a fine technician, he had at his command all the tools of singing, and he used them all—including open sound production—most intelligently. Otherwise he could not have kept up the schedule he did for as long as he did before the crisis.

He did not cover in the careful way that Warren did, but head resonance was always present. In fact, his high notes often produced the same effect as stringed instruments (of course, the voice is a stringed instrument). Tibbett would cut off the note, but it would seem to continue resonating in the air. In his recording of the Porter's Song from Flotow's *Martha*, his normal resonance gives more of the feeling of a trill than his trill itself. Likewise, especially in the 1935 broadcast recording, at the end of the Council Chamber scene in *Boccanegra*, where Tibbett sings "Paolo," the whole head is resonating.

His voice placement was correct: forward and virile to be sure, but in the area of the nasal cavities. It was perhaps not as perfect as the placement of Jussi Björling or Helge Roswaenge, where the voice seems to support itself and float of its own accord out into the audience, but it was superlative.

Mezzo soprano Risë Stevens was emphatic on this point: "There was no way he sang from the throat."[63] The baritone Robert Merrill seems equally certain about the source of Larry's difficulties and also about his reaction to them: "No one who could sing *mezza voce* the way Tibbett did could possibly sing from the throat. No, it sounded like he had gotten into trouble physically and then blamed it on everything else."[64]

Larry should not have sung outdoors in bad weather with a sore throat, but having done so, he should have canceled his later engagements and rested. But to stop singing was almost unthinkable to him, and his vocal coach told him what he wanted to hear: sing—ignore the injury. Strapping, hearty Lawrence Tibbett could not be sick.

So he drank, and insecure in his singing, he drank still more. Drinking did not help the singing, and his now flawed singing did not help his drinking problem. Rumors flew about a purported throat operation.

The next season, Olin Downes reviewed Larry's 3 January 1941 return to the Metropolitan in *Rigoletto* for the *New York Times*. Noting Larry's weeks of absence attributed to "indisposition," he found him "more cautious than usual" in the role that he allowed in the same review had become one of Tibbett's greatest. For Downes, the impact and ring of Act Three's "Sì, vendetta" in particular was, in a word, insufficient.[65]

Of the *Pagliacci* Tonio on 9 January, Noel Straus wrote that although Larry's Prologue was magnificent, his tones thereafter were more often than not hollow and lacking in body. As for his acting, it was "filled with remarkably vivid detail . . . both touching and virile."[66]

But Larry was no longer consistent in his appearances, and what Straus heard on 9 January was different from Larry's performance on 1 February. We know because the broadcast of 1 February 1941 with Martinelli was recorded. It is clear that Larry no longer "owned" the Prologue and that he has a bit of effort with it, but any baritone today would kill to sing it the way he does. He is completely authoritative throughout the rest of the opera and does not appear to have what a singer of lesser stature would call problems, but he is not the Larry of the past. In the broadcast, Martinelli has a field day as Canio, his voice ringing freely. He and Larry ad lib the histrionics so much that they make Gigli sound like a Toscanini purist. Norina Greco is a full-voiced

Nedda and Frank (Francesco) Valentino a rich, passionate Silvio. Ferruccio Calusio conducts a memorable performance.

Larry sang Iago on 18 January and 3 February, and another Rigoletto on 8 February. He remained a great actor, an intelligent interpreter, and an authentic star. But his difficulties had been spotted, and his freedom was gone.

Part Five 1941–1960

Chapter 9

DON'T FENCE ME IN

Drink is everywhere, and when the drinker cannot refrain from helping himself to it time after time, he or she is considered an alcoholic. This is a dirty word to a great many people who love their liquor and could not possibly do without it but would never admit that such a term could be applied to them. Lawrence Tibbett now fell into this category and the term applied. According to the medical literature,

> The cause of alcoholism is unknown. Psychologic hypotheses have noted the frequent incidence of certain personality traits, including schizoid qualities (isolation, loneliness, shyness); depression, dependency; hostile and self-destructive impulsivity; and sexual immaturity. Families of alcoholics tend to have a higher incidence of alcoholism, and many clinicians now believe that alcoholism usually occurs in the context of a necessary genetic or biochemical predisposition. However genetic or biochemical defects leading to alcoholism have not been clearly demonstrated, although a higher incidence of alcoholism has been reported in biologic children of alcoholics, as compared to adoptive children. . . . Societal factors affect patterns of drinking and consequent behavior, the attitudes transmitted through the culture or child rearing. Alcoholics frequently have histories of broken homes and disturbed relationships with parents.[1]

Did Larry have an inherited tendency to drink? Certainly his rough-and-ready father had been a heavy drinker, not to mention his uncle, who ran "the best saloon in Bakersfield." And as far as disturbed relationships go, although in his book he called him his hero, Larry barely knew his father. Two of the baritone's three neglected sons—Larry Jr. and Michael—became alcoholics, and the alienated Grace Tibbett, who lived her adult life in defiance of her fanatically religious mother, finished out *her* existence as an alcoholic. Nor did Larry lack for personality traits that may have driven him to alcoholism; gregariousness, love of the fast life, and an emphasis on "being able to hold your liquor" were all part of the baritone's makeup.

Whatever the reasons, Larry continued to drink with persistent regularity, particularly when he was depressed over the condition of his voice. Since alcohol is not a stimulant but a depressant, it only added to his dark moods.

In the autumn of 1941, Larry appeared as Rigoletto with the San Francisco Opera. Everyone had been saying that Larry had lost his voice, so it was with great curiosity and anticipation that the critics watched and listened as Larry sang. They could not be supportive. The 21-year-old basso Jerome Hines, who had just made his debut and was on hand to hear the performance, recalled one headline that read "Vocal Tragedy for Lawrence Tibbett." "I remember wishing he had tried something a little easier," Hines commented years later:

> It was not a question of nit-picking when Larry sang. Robert Weede, a great baritone in his own right and Larry's understudy for this performance, was also an admirer of Tibbett. When I went backstage, Weede was holding his bent head in agony. He really suffered with Larry, even though he was a competitor. He hated to see such an enormous talent shattered.
>
> Yet it was when I heard Larry and Weede singing together, nine years later at the Met [in Mussorgsky's *Khovanchina*], that I understood why Tibbett, even with his voice in shambles, was a great singer, and Weede just a good singer. With that wracked voice trying desperately to come out, Tibbett was still on another level altogether. He still had that imposing sound, that celebrity sound.
>
> Even when he was in trouble, his singing was still something of another caliber. Weede was a very fine singer, a superlative technician, one of our truly great baritones. But he just did not have the vocal scope that Tibbett had, and of course, Larry was a fantastically talented actor, which also brought to his voice that star-class sound.
>
> Unfortunately, I did not get to know Larry at all during that

> run of opera although I was on speaking terms with him. I didn't run into him again until I came to the Met in 1946. Then I began singing with Larry quite a bit. Edward Johnson, the general manager of the Met, always had a great deal of compassion, as well as respect, for Larry, and bent over backwards to keep him at the Met during those years, even though Tibbett's voice was just not holding up.[2]

Hines went on to compare baritone John Charles Thomas and Tibbett, both of whom liked nothing better than to "raise the cup":

> I don't know whether Thomas was an alcoholic, but he was an Irishman who really liked his liquor. While he would drink plenty of it, it never seemed to affect him onstage or off. In my opinion, Thomas never abused his voice the way Tibbett did.
>
> Thomas was never a great actor; he was a ham, and he belonged in show business more than in opera. He was a very broad character, and notorious for singing tra-la-la because he could never memorize his lines. Now Thomas's voice was never as big as Tibbett's, but he was a masterful technician with a gorgeous voice, which he was able to sustain even through an alcoholic haze.[3]

In contrast, Larry, though a far greater artist, grew increasingly unreliable. His voice had a way of teasing him. Suddenly it would take on its old lustrous quality, and he could completely control it. But just as quickly and insidiously, it would shatter. To bolster his courage in the face of this uncertainty, he now drank before appearances, but he could not sing "through an alcoholic haze" unnoticed. His art was too refined.

After singing Iago in Chicago and his sole turn as Figaro in *Il barbiere di Siviglia*, Larry began his 1941–42 season at the Met with a matinée on 29 November 1941, returning to portray his old standby, the elder Germont in *La Traviata*. Jarmila Novotná was Violetta, and tenor Jan Peerce was making his debut as Alfredo. The scheduled conductor, Gennaro Papi, had died unexpectedly that morning and Panizza replaced him. *Traviata* repeated on 5 December. Larry—and the nervous Peerce—got through them.

It is not known how the Tibbetts spent the weekend after the 5 December performance. Most likely a late-hours party filled their Saturday evening, and they probably slept late Sunday morning, though on occasion Larry attended Riverside Church, with its striking tower looming over the Hudson River.

Social historians have recorded with some care, however, what the nation as a whole was up to on that first Sunday in December 1941. The newspapers that day reported that traffic accidents were up 16 percent above 1940, that 30 people of some importance were lunching at the White House, and that white shirts, regularly $2.50 or even $3.50, were on sale for $2. That afternoon, at 3:03 p.m. Eastern Standard Time, radio programs across the country were interrupted with the announcement that the Japanese had bombed the American naval installation at Pearl Harbor on Hawaii.

Calling 7 December "a date which will live in infamy," President Roosevelt went before Congress on 8 December 1941 to declare a state of war not only against the Japanese aggressors across the Pacific but also against the German and Italian Fascists on the other side of the Atlantic.

Larry Jr. was drafted immediately into the U.S. Army Signal Corps and was sent to the officers' training school in Fort Monmouth, New Jersey. Before his training was complete, he was assigned to El Centro, California, for duty. His twin, Richard, enlisted in the signal corps on 10 July 1942 and was sent to Camp Livingston, Louisiana, attached to the Third Army as a technican third grade. He was recommended for the officers' training school in Fort Monmouth, New Jersey, and was commissioned a second lieutenant, after which he was assigned to the signal depot in Dayton, Ohio.

For the moment, their father gamely tried to continue his career with another *Traviata* on 13 December and a Scarpia in *Tosca* five days later. On 23 December he was rushed to Doctors Hospital for an emergency appendectomy; he was not released until 3 January 1942. He hoped to return to the Met but had to sit out the rest of the season. It was just as well, for too often now Larry presented his audiences with sounds that were only faintly reminiscent of his once effortless, soaring baritone. The cancellations due to his appendectomy, of course, cannot be connected to his vocal condition, but inevitably the number of his opera and concert engagements was reduced.

Larry's shrinking performance schedule left him freer to devote his energies to the war effort. He was too old for active service, but he joined the executive committee of the United Service Organization (USO) and made numerous appearances before the armed forces, overseas as well as in the United States. He also sang frequently at Red Cross and war bond drives.[4] Whatever the state of his voice, he remained every inch a distinctly All-American star, and his patriotic audiences greeted him with gusto.

Jane too did her bit. She became active in arranging benefits for the Red Cross, the USO, and China Relief. Larry's secretary, Doris Wittschen explained:

> You see, she knew not only the society people but the performers—through Tibbett, who was her entrée. Through Tibbett, she could get hold of Guy Lombardo or Eddie Duchin. She had all those contacts which she could use, and properly, too.
>
> She was not a lazy woman, believe me. She was not one to stay in bed until noon. She was always up and out early. Tibbett used to scoff good-humoredly, "She's being busy again." All this busyness didn't seem to add up to much to him. But he didn't resent it. In fact, he liked society benefits. He was not at all a liberated male.[5]

As president of AGMA Larry also continued to work untiringly for the union, and this was a particularly trying time. James C. Petrillo, president of the American Federation of Musicians, decided that his union should represent all instrumentalists, solo artists included. Jascha Heifetz and Gregor Piatigorsky, among the founders of AGMA, were especially upset and a bitter fight ensued. Larry Jr. recalled:

> I'll never forget when my father took on James Petrillo of the American Federation of Musicians. There was a lot of publicity in the press about it. Dad was really afraid of being assassinated. We all breathed a big sigh of relief when AGMA and the AFM settled their differences and came to terms.[6]

With respect to Heifetz, perhaps the world's greatest violinist at the time, Petrillo, a violinist himself, came up with his classic line, "A fiddler is a fiddler."[7] The courts finally found for the Musicians' Union and Heifetz joined it, although he also retained his AGMA membership for many years after.

Larry's less productive antics made headlines in the *New York Times* in July 1942: "Tibbett Hurts Spine—Metropolitan Singer 'Taking It Easy' After Jumping Injury." The dateline was Wilton, Connecticut, and the item that followed confirms a way of life not particularly conducive to serious artistry. According to the report, the 45-year-old singer had slipped and fallen on a stone while broadjumping and would be resting at his Connecticut home for several weeks to ensure his complete recovery from the spinal injury that resulted. The accident happened on a previous Saturday, at a pool party held at the Southport estate of advertising executive Chester J. La Roche. No doubt alcohol was involved, and the men decided to "be boys again," in Larry's words. Larry was assured by his physician that if he rested for a while he would not have to miss any concerts, and yet he was forced to cancel at least one professional engagement, a radio appearance, on 28 July.[8]

In spite of such self-made setbacks, Larry managed to carry on and to keep up appearances. In November and December 1942, he was back in Chicago for *Aida* with Milanov and Martinelli, and Alexander Kipnis as Ramphis; *Traviata* with Novotná and Melton; *Otello*; and *Rigoletto* with Jan Kiepura as the Duke. His income tax return for the year 1942 listed modest charitable donations to a variety of organizations, including the National Foundation for Infantile Paralysis, the National Urban League, the Russian Cathedral, the Home of the Sages of Israel, the Town Hall 50th Anniversary Fund, the Greater New York Fund, the Travelers Aid Society, the New York Infirmary for Women, the Colored Orphan Fund, the Russian War Relief, the American Red Cross, and the local Boy Scouts.[9]

Larry had always inspired fidelity from friends and colleagues, and true to form, general manager Edward Johnson again engaged his services for the 1942–43 season. He offered Larry a new role, Don Carlo, vocally high-lying and dangerously heavy, in a revival of Verdi's *La forza del destino*. Before the premiere of *Forza*, Larry coped with a *Traviata*, an *Aida*, and two *Toscas*.

La forza del destino, on 9 January 1943, was not a success for the baritone. "There was a time," Oscar Thompson wrote in the *New York Sun*, "when Lawrence Tibbett would have outshone Mr. [Kurt] Baum in the tenor-baritone duets. But there was little freedom and much effort in his part of 'Solenne in quest' ora' and 'Le minaccie, i fieri accenti.'"[10]

The air check of 23 January 1943, with Jagel as the tenor, while not horrific, shows Tibbett making a noble attempt to tame music that clearly overmatches him. There are long phrases in the role of Don Carlo, and often the tessitura stays quite high, requiring a free technique with the voice floating on an unfettered column of air. This Larry could no longer do. The performance had other problems as well. Even Ezio Pinza as Padre Guardiano cracks wide open on a high note, something unheard of for him. Stella Roman is the fine Leonora; Bruno Walter conducts.

Although at the top of his form Larry would have been the perfect Don Carlo, he sang the role only four times in New York over two seasons and twice on tour. The young Leonard Warren took over the role and 17 years later died on the Metropolitan Opera stage while performing it.

In light of this and subsequent unsuccessful appearances, it is natural to wonder why Larry did not simply give up and withdraw from the stage. But his voice and musical art, combined with his tenacious character, had made him one of the most famous men of his day. How could he leave the "glory road" when he was still comparatively so young?

Elizabeth Cooper of San Francisco, one of Jane's closest friends, recalls that after a concert in San Diego sometime in the mid-1940s, Larry and Jane came to her house for the evening. Jane went right to bed but Larry stayed up talking to their hostess.

He was extremely agitated because the recital had not gone well. Pacing up and down, he railed bitterly about what had happened to his voice, describing what he believed to have caused its deterioration. He thought it was only a fault in his breathing. He ranted on, becoming confused and frightened, but after a while he calmed down and said softly, "You know, Beth, having once achieved the pinnacle of success, I am now scraping the bottom of the barrel of failure. I should be grateful that now I can pass on my experiences to the younger singers."[11]

Larry continued to unburden himself to his wife's friend. At one point she asked him what would happen if he stopped singing for an extended period of time and rested his vocal cords completely. At once the baritone countered with his coach Vito Mirsky's philosophy, that if he did not sing, his voice would get rusty. Larry desperately wanted to believe Mirsky's advice for, as he had written in *The Glory Road*, he "would rather sing than do anything else on earth."[12] If he did not sing, even sing badly, he would cease to feel alive.

There was no longer any doubt that Larry was seriously addicted to alcohol. Larry Jr. recalled that on one occasion at the Savoy, the Tibbetts entertained fifteen guests for cocktails, five of whom were French and three East Indian. Jane thought Larry knew who all the guests were, while Larry assumed that those he didn't recognize were friends of Jane's. Only after the guests had departed did the couple discover that neither had the foggiest notion who the French and East Indians were, or how they happened to be there.[13]

Meanwhile, with Johnson's support, Larry stubbornly pursued his singing career. In 1943 he joined the Cincinnati Summer Opera for three Scarpias and three Rigolettos. In the first role, the *Enquirer* found him "a commanding personality," in the second, "sensational."[14]

An idea began to take shape about this time. Although Jane was never much more than lukewarm about it, Larry loved the life at Honey Hill Farm. But, for part of the year, why not substitute the ocean for the rolling acres of land, and avocados for the apples that grew with such abundance in their orchards? Newspaper headlines blared that the Tibbetts were moving to Honolulu but in fact they had begun to search for a suitable vacation property in Florida. It would be 1945 before they found one.

In the 1943–44 season at the Met, Larry sang his final two performances of *Forza* and made a single appearance each in *Rigoletto*, *La Traviata*, *Pagliacci*, *Falstaff*, and *Tosca*. Continuing to carry on staunchly, he also premiered in New York that January a new role in an entirely different style, Golaud in Debussy's impressionistic *Pelléas et Mélisande*—but it was all uphill. His voice was continuously produced under strain. In her autobiography Eleanor Steber wrote:

> My longtime idol, Lawrence Tibbett, sang *Falstaff* with me in the first performance. He was a mere shadow of the giant he had once been, a gentle, troubled man, always gracious and friendly to me. Merely sharing the stage with him moved me deeply.[15]

Though Larry continued to perform in concert and at fund-raising benefits, his career was obviously flagging. Twenty-one years earlier, in 1923, he had sung such a terrible audition at the Metropolitan that he thought success would never be his. Fate intervened and he did reach the heights. Now fate stepped in again, in the strangest of ways.

Late in 1944 a miraculous agent in the form of a fellow vocalist appeared, and Larry's career entered a new dimension. This *deus ex machina* was none other than Frank Sinatra, "the Voice," whose ears stuck out from the sides of his head like seashells. During his reign the skinny kid from New Jersey was regarded, particularly by bobbysoxers, as a living god.

Sinatra had been a regular feature on the tremendously popular Saturday-evening radio show *Your Hit Parade*. But he tired of being pinned down by weekly broadcasts. To the dismay of his adoring fans, Lucky Strike cigarettes, the show's sponsor, announced that Sinatra would no longer appear each Saturday night, crooning America's favorite songs.

Imagine the horror of these young worshipers when they were further told that Lucky Strike had hired an *opera singer*, Lawrence Tibbett, to fill Sinatra's place. The Metropolitan Opera baritone had signed a six-month contract at $4000 a week to sing three songs on each program, about $1000 more than Sinatra received.[16] The contract also called for Lucky Strike to supply its chain-smoking new radio star with cartons of cigarettes each week. Vocalist Joan Edwards, the singing group "The Hit Paraders," and conductor Mark Warnow continued performing on the show, as they had with Sinatra.

From the outset, Larry had misgivings about stepping into Sinatra's shoes. He joked that he feared the show's live studio audience might hurl rotten fruit and vegetables in his direction. When he had first sung on the radio, in 1922 in Los Angeles, he had been assured that "millions" would hear him; years later he wrote that he had yet to meet a single person who had listened to him then. But the whole country seemed to be tuned in to his debut broadcast on *Your Hit Parade*, 6 January 1945. And though there was no fruit that first night, all Larry's apprehensions about taking over from Sinatra were confirmed when the mail from the vast home audience began pouring in. Nearly all who wrote condemned him for having dared to take Sinatra's place, with sentiments running along these lines: "This is to prove how much I hate you"—all caps, underlined in red ink, with the occasional emphasis only pink lipstick could provide.

Most members of the press praised Lucky Strike's replacement of Sinatra with an opera star, but there were dissenters. A columnist named Jean Meegan was one:

> The advertising agency in charge of the show was up in the air for a while on just who should make up the audience. They experimented with limiting attendance to servicemen, then took a whirl at admitting the general public. Now comes the announcement that the general public wins. The only limitation on attendance will be the studio's seating capacity.
>
> Tibbett, who never before had an exclusively "popular" program, says he was "scared a little" on opening night because "those mysterious girls might have pulled a fast one on me." He needn't have worried: there wasn't a fan of Frankie's within listening distance.
>
> In a concert-stage stance, Tibbett wallops out three of the week's hit tunes but the rafters don't ring the way they used to. He seems magnificently out of step with the rest of the show, but he's optimistic. He says "It's a sweet and charming show. I'm getting a kick out of it. I would love to build a kid following. There's no reason why a well-trained classic voice shouldn't be popular."

> Cynics of Radio Row say there is nothing to indicate that Tibbett's sponsors want him to have a kid audience or to compete with Sinatra's popularity record. The guess is that Tibbett was hired . . . not to sell the product but as a terrific publicity stunt. After all, who else ever imported an opera star in a razzmatazz show?[17]

The American Tobacco Company, makers of Lucky Strikes, moved immediately to stand behind its new singer. In a fancy brochure dated 8 January 1945, Vincent Riggio, vice president, addressed "the entire sales organization":

> Last Saturday night, Lawrence Tibbett, world-famous star of opera, radio, screen and the concert stage, began his new role of singing America's favorite songs on "Your Hit Parade."
>
> Mr. Tibbett is noted for his magnificent resonant and expressive voice—his rare gift of simplicity *and* versatility. Just as his singing makes them stand up and cheer at the Metropolitan—so did his renditions of "Don't Fence Me In" and "I Got Plenty O' Nuttin" last Saturday night on "Your Hit Parade" win for him a tremendous ovation. We are proud to have Mr. Tibbett on "Your Hit Parade" and, of course, associated with our product—Lucky Strike Cigarettes.[18]

The brochure goes on, even invoking Caruso, and announces a new pitch to be used by the sales staff beginning 22 January.

Larry persevered. He saw this as a chance to prove that an opera singer who did not patronize the music could tell a story with his singing voice and could put over popular music as effectively, as mesmerizingly as he did the classical repertoire. During the first two weeks, his most popular song on *Your Hit Parade* was Cole Porter's atypical "Don't Fence Me In." Two other crowd pleasers—"Jonah and the Whale" and "Sentimental Journey"—were "Lucky Strike Extras," not the Top Ten of the day. One New York columnist commented sympathetically:

> For all his perennially adolescent features and his relaxed, easy-going charm, Tibbett has always had plenty of what it takes—what his long-haired fans called "intestinal fortitude." He had been born to be a star. Maybe not on "Your Hit Parade"—as still loudly maintained by both Sinatra's followers and die-hard admirers of "pure music"—but, once on the show, he continued to make headlines—a little habit which Tibbett always had as natural as breathing—and almost as valuable to a singer's career.[19]

This was not the first time that Larry had competed against a popular balladeer. In 1934, the "Questioning Reporter" for the *Chicago Daily News* pitted him against Bing Crosby by putting the following question to six passers-by on the street: "If Bing Crosby and Lawrence Tibbett were on radio programs at the same time, which program would you listen to?" Five of the six queried had chosen Larry.

Signing Larry for *Your Hit Parade* had been a bold risk for Lucky Strike and it was equally bold for Larry to have accepted it, but in the end both the company and the singer enjoyed even greater success then they had experienced before. What was first perceived as a joke became a brilliant stroke of commercial and personal marketing.

After singing Iago in Chicago, Larry made appearances at the Metropolitan during the 1944–45 season as Amonasro, the elder Germont, Rigoletto, and Golaud. The air check of the 13 January 1945 performance of *Pelléas et Mélisande* reveals his Golaud as deeply human, never roughly sadistic as the role is sometimes played. Larry is touchingly honest and noble. Pure voice is not of paramount importance in this role, and the internalized mortal love and suffering projected through his vocal instrument make this one of Tibbett's greatest portrayals. He was not yet lost to the lyric stage.

The cast from the January 1944 Met performances of the French opera was intact for this 1945 broadcast: Bidú Sayão as Mélisande; Martial Singher as Pelléas; and Alexander Kipnis as Arkel, with Emil Cooper conducting. Contacted in 1993, Sayão reacted warmly to Larry's name: "Larry Tibbett! Always his face is in front of me." Sayão continued,

> What a great singer he was, and as an actor, so perfect! His Golaud was something extraordinary. He changed his makeup in every scene. His suffering was so real. He inspired me. The words are very important, and he sang beautiful French. "La verité"—that scene was terrific. He took my arm and threw me as if I were a ball.
>
> No one will take the place of Tibbett. I admired him immensely. He was a wonderful person, kind, elegant, pleasant. To sing *The Barber* with him! He was so elegant, so great—in any performance. *Traviata*. His artistry! Not one person will forget Tibbett. He was unique. He left a mark.[20]

The stage and radio successes of 1945 not only gave renewed life to Larry's faltering career but also offered a new perspective on the home-front. That same year he and Jane purchased three acres of land in Naples, Florida, just two miles north of the Naples pier. In this land of cabbage palms and palmettos, their new acreage consisted of three sand dunes with a fair-sized pond in the middle, home to alligators and wild ducks. It was accessible only by four-wheel-drive jeep or by swamp buggy.

Although this property was a long-desired acquisition, the Tibbetts had not yet quite decided how they would divide their time between it, Honey Hill Farm, and their New York pied-à-terre at the Savoy. Larry's professional engagements would of course be a factor.

Shortly before, the Tibbetts had become acquainted socially with John Volk, a Palm Beach architect, and his wife, who was also named Jane. They eventually hired Volk and his colleague Robert Hays for the project, telling the men they were interested in building only a small beach house. But by the time the Tibbetts and the architects finished the plans, the simple house they had envisioned had blossomed into a flat-roofed, single-story cottage à la Frank Lloyd Wright of over 4000 square feet, dominating the pond. The scheme even provided for a caretaker's cottage on the property, plus an eventual 40-acre farm to be worked by Larry.

The foundation of the new house, which came to be called Bali Ha'i after the song from *South Pacific*, was constructed on pilings 20 feet high, driven into bedrock and bound together by slabs of reinforced concrete. Over this a concrete floor was poured, later to be covered by coquina tile. The walls were paneled in red cypress boards 10 inches wide, and the doors too were of cypress, 10 feet high and with jalousied inlays. Picture windows gave views of the landscape. A separate bar-room was set off from the guest rooms, and Larry and Jane located their sleeping quarters in a private wing. All the rooms had 12-foot ceilings.

Larry himself planned the landscaping of the property with palm, avocado, banana, and sea-grape trees. He also worked hard in the actual building of Bali Ha'i, helping to carry bricks and lumber to the work-men and even hammering a nail or two. As it turned out, he worked the land in Naples for a total of eight years and managed over that time to harvest several crops.[21]

In the mid-1940s, Naples had a population of approximately 4000 in-habitants, some of whom, including Larry, formed an elite band of drinkers to whom drying out in the private sanitariums nearby was a matter of routine. Though the flurry of activity associated with his latest property might seem to indicate that the great baritone had turned around his drinking problem, the truth was otherwise. According to Michael Tibbett, by 1945 his father had become a confirmed alcoholic, struggling against an addiction that held him in an iron grip.

In the summer of 1945, Larry performed in the Cincinnati Summer Opera's season, singing two Iagos (the first of which was praised for both acting and singing), a Rigoletto (hailed as *his* show), and a single "perfect" Scarpia.[22] Soon afterward, he entered a sanitarium to dry out, and upon his release, he continued a busy schedule of appearances. Thus the cycle continued.

The baritone made his debut with the Philadelphia touring La Scala Opera Company that autumn, singing three Rigolettos. In Washington, on 22 November 1945, he had his photograph taken with young Margaret Truman, the president's daughter, to whom he had given several voice lessons.

By November 1945, America was once more at peace. Larry Jr., discharged from duty the previous June, had returned from Guam. He came to New York and was staying with his father. He had married Edith Ernestine ("Tina") Witte, a godchild of the contralto Ernestine Schumann-Heink, in 1942, but had received a "Dear John" letter while still on Guam; they quickly divorced, a wartime romance. Richard was still overseas, at Clark Field in the Philippines; he would be discharged as a captain on 13 June 1946.

Jane's oldest son, Clark, had risen to squadron commander in the U.S. Air Force and earned a Silver Star. He then entered into business in Bangkok. He was at home, in bed with his wife, when an intruder broke in and shot him. The crime was never solved. His body was cremated and returned to Larry and Jane in a matchbox. They were devastated by the loss. Jan Kiepura came home after an evening with Larry at that time and told his wife, Marta Eggerth, that Larry was extremely depressed, that Clark's death had been a "terrible shock."[23]

During the Metropolitan season of 1945–46, Larry appeared only eight times in three roles during three months. He sang five Scarpias and drew praise from critics who felt that Larry had mastered the subtleties of the role. Some expressed the optimistic belief that Tibbett's vocal decline might have reversed itself. On 5 January 1946, he sang another new role, that of the vengeful husband Michele in Puccini's one-act melodrama *Il Tabarro*, with Licia Albanese and Frederick Jagel. Critics commented that Tibbett tired easily.[24] But in the air check of that performance, which was broadcast, he is overpowering. He commands a flow of dramatic vocal sound that seems unending.[25]

Larry sang often with Albanese, in several operas. In 1993 she recalled that they would discuss their roles, especially Violetta and the elder Germont in *La Traviata*, at great length. Albanese continued:

> [He] was a kind, pleasant, courteous man, always willing to learn more about acting. He understood all the characters he was to portray and always made the audience aware of the importance of the words and the music. He possessed a magnificent baritone voice with the ability to sing *forte* and *piano* with great ease. I found him to be a top performer and an inspiring human being.[26]

This is the man whom drink was destroying. Albanese pointedly refused to comment on anything but Larry's artistry and charm, saying with a bit of mystery, "Who am I to judge?"[27]

A month after the *Tabarro* broadcast, Larry undertook another Scarpia. Fortunately the 9 February 1946 *Tosca* air check, despite its occasional lapses, is available for study. His first act is close to disaster; his voice often wanders without control. The listener is thus totally unprepared for Act Two, where the baritone is the ringing Scarpia of legend, capable of taking vocal chances, all successful. His line readings—the way he shapes and molds Scarpia's words—are his alone, and one is forced into the special world Larry peoples with his characterizations.

As Tosca in this performance, Grace Moore reacts with Larry and is in fine form on her own, with admirable high notes. Jan Peerce is a young, free, and Italianate Cavaradossi. A bonus of this performance is the casting of Salvatore Baccaloni as the Sacristan, and Alessio De Paolis and Cehanovsky as Scarpia's men, roles they seemingly sang forever and always definitively.

The baritone Robert Merrill, who himself enjoyed a long, respected career at the Metropolitan, was befriended by Larry soon after his debut in this 1945–46 season. Merrill was appearing in his first Sunday evening concert, waiting to part the curtain and begin the *Pagliacci* Prologue, when he looked offstage and saw Larry and John Charles Thomas standing together in the wings, waiting to hear the new kid on the block. Merrill recalled:

> I was scared, but I sang the hell out of it. I thought then that if I can do that, with those two watching, I can do anything. Tibbett and I became friends, not good friends but friends. He sang my

> praises. I used to sit with him in his dressing room before a show. He would be shaking with nerves but smoking and drinking.
>
> I was invited to some of his and Jane's parties. They were society parties—you know, well-dressed people drinking champagne. Tibbett would get up and sing tenor arias. It broke my heart. He was a great artist, a noble artist.[28]

Larry's appreciation of Merrill's talent was sincere and forthright. He once told the impresario Robert Gewald that Merrill had the most naturally beautiful voice he had ever heard.[29] But then Larry was always helpful to younger artists and obviously never afraid of competition, clear evidence of a healthy self-confidence and a real love for the art form. Kurt Weinhold, who in 1945 succeeded Lawrence Evans as his manager, had his problems with Larry, but he nonetheless appreciated this undeniably admirable facet of the singer's character:

> Larry loved to tell young artists what they should do, things he never did himself. Whether in New York or on tour, young artists would come to him as King of the Road and seek out his advice. Walter Cassel was an example of this. He came to New York because Tibbett had heard him and recommended him to La Forge.
>
> Again, Tibbett would extend himself for a fellow artist—even a student singer. Many people in these music clubs who scheduled Tibbett would ask him to listen to a local singer, and again, unlike other artists, Tibbett would always try to oblige, and he would give him or her advice. If he felt the singer had no future, he would say so. Cassel came from Council Bluffs, Iowa, and when Tibbett gave a concert in Omaha, Cassel sang for him. Cassel later said that Tibbett told him he had a beautiful voice and gave him some advice about going to New York, as he had received many years ago in California. Walter did just that and made a career for himself.[30]

After fulfilling his professional commitments, it might have been salutary for Larry to take the summer of 1946 off to rest, but he did nothing of the sort. He embarked instead on another European tour, singing for American troops stationed in Germany.

One evening in Berlin, Larry dined out in the company of Jane, Kurt Weinhold, and his accompanist Stewart Wille. The liquor flowed freely among the group, and secure in the belief they were speaking a language that would not be understood by others in the restaurant, their conversation turned into an avalanche of off-color jokes and stories; the baritone's repertoire in this field was as extensive as that of his operatic roles. Suddenly three young American girls approached and asked

Larry for his autograph. Obviously, to his mortification, they hadn't missed a thing.

"You heard it all?" he asked lamely.

"We certainly did," they responded mischievously.

Larry dropped the subject and quickly signed his name for them. Never again did he engage in raunchy jokes in public.[31]

He and Jane traveled on to Italy, where he sang concerts in a long list of places, including American army camps. A concert in Rome included music from *Porgy and Bess*. He also sang *Rigoletto* in Rome, and Jane reported that the Italians (she uses another word, indicating her upper-class superiority to foreigners) "adored him and are a bit disconcerted over his bel canto, which was learned outside of Italy." Adding to their list of social coups, the Tibbetts also had an audience with the pope and dined with a Chinese diplomat in Mussolini's former villa.[32] As it happened, Doris Wyckoff was also in Rome at the time, and Larry, continuing his courtly behavior toward her, took her for a ride through the city in a horse-drawn carriage.[33]

Back in the States and under Erich Leinsdorf's baton, Larry brought *Emperor Jones* to Chicago on 4 October 1946. The opera was offered on the same evening as Menotti's *Amelia Goes to the Ball*, and Claudia Cassidy noted that in a dull season, "the Chicago Opera Company had the right idea last night when it ventured out on a limb of an unusual double bill."[34] He also sang the elder Germont in November. These were his last operatic appearances in that city.

Back at the Metropolitan for the 1946–47 season, Larry sang five performances: two Rigolettos, one Amonasro, one Germont, and one Iago. Occasionally he would surprise with flashes of his old vigor and vocal ease, but in the main his voice was forced and under poor control. His high notes were strained and too often on the verge of cracking. The decline of this once great artist became more and more heartbreaking, all the more so because Larry would not acknowledge his paralyzing fear, or the alcoholic abuse he used to numb it.

One of the pernicious effects of liquor is that it clouds one's ability to make reasoned judgments. The affected drinker can gradually become more and more confused when confronted with choices or can hold strongly to increasingly irrational opinions. On 28 March 1947, Larry, as president of AGMA, called an unusual meeting of the 45-member board of governors and expressed just such a startling opinion. He proceeded to exhort the board to draft an ill-natured resolution directed at one of their own members, the peerless soprano Kirsten Flagstad, whose career as one of the greatest Wagnerian singers of all time had honored the United States and whose Norwegian patriotism was not questioned by even her countrymen themselves.

The story is well known. In 1941 Flagstad had returned home voluntarily to German-occupied Norway. She believed that her place was with her husband, Henry Johansen, a wealthy lumber merchant. To all intents and purposes, she retired from the stage and never appeared professionally before the occupying Germans. After the war, Johansen was arrested by the free Norwegian government and accused of being a member of the traitor Vidkun Quisling's National Samling Party. He was also charged with profiteering by selling lumber to the invaders.

In Norway, Flagstad herself was never charged with being an active or even passive Nazi sympathizer. But since most of her repertoire, including the Wagner operas, was sung in German, and since she had returned to Norway without a passport (this was denied her by the Norwegian government-in-exile), more than enough material was available to those who wanted to cause her harm when she sought to renew her career in America in March 1947.

The anti-Flagstad campaign was fueled by most of the best-known but reactionary columnists of the day: Walter Winchell, Ed Sullivan, Leonard Lyons, George Sokolsky, and Danton Walker—none noted for acute political expertise. Even the music critic Irving Kolodin joined this group, which was led by Winchell. Winchell most effectively persuaded the American Legion and the Veterans of Foreign Wars to picket the concert halls where Flagstad was scheduled to sing.

The soprano made her re-entry into America's musical life at Philadelphia's Academy of Music. The loyal audience, anxious to hear her lustrous, effortlessly produced voice once again, had to force its way through bands of jeering, sign-carrying pickets. The recital began with a welcoming ovation overlaid with her opponents' catcalls and hisses. Jeers and boos interrupted Flagstad's first song, and police stationed in the aisles ejected the offenders. The singer continued, apparently unperturbed.

A series of disturbances, worked out in advance, continued. Police again ejected hecklers. As a climax a stink bomb was set off, a "patriotic" reaction from self-proclaimed protectors of America. The soprano calmly finished her concert and later sang at Carnegie Hall, where New York provided its own pickets and catcalls.

Tibbett had been known all his life for his compassionate sympathy for the underdog. During his concert tours overseas, Larry had seen the devastation wrought on the cities of Europe by the German war machine. He had also visited concentration camps soon after their liberation. Nevertheless, only the toll taken by alcohol on his mental and emotional faculties can sufficiently account for his harsh position with respect to Kirsten Flagstad. Using his full weight as president and founding father of AGMA, he insisted on pushing through this resolution:

> Be it resolved that in the view of the serious statements made in the press concerning Mme. Kirsten Flagstad, the Board of Governors does not feel warranted in restoring to Mme. Flagstad the privileges of full membership in AGMA. Nevertheless, since such charges have not as yet been substantiated by any official body of our government, of Mme. Flagstad's native land or any government, the Board will grant to Mme. Flagstad a working permit, subject to revocation with respect to her engagements in this country.[35]

Flagstad's supporters quickly rose to her defense. Eminent conductor Walter Damrosch offered to be her recital pianist, and the columnist Daniel Poling wrote that Flagstad was guilty of nothing more serious than taking her marriage vows seriously enough to return to Norway when she believed her husband needed her. Other artists stood up for Flagstad, including those from the Metropolitan, among them Geraldine Farrar, Gladys Swarthout (a member of AGMA's board of governors, who uncharacteristically broke with Larry here), Julius Huehn, Karin Branzell, and Paul Althouse. Also prominent in Flagstad's defense was critic and composer Virgil Thomson, who summed up the whole matter with his usual Midwestern terseness: "Flagstad was away for six years on private business of a legitimate nature."[36]

Larry made no like attempt to understand the pressures of the soprano's personal life. When asked about his intransigence in this matter, Regina Resnik just shrugged and said, "It was a thing with him."[37]

With the help of other artists and an ultimately fair American public, Flagstad was able to continue her American concert career and eventually to resume her rightful position as a treasured artist at the Metropolitan. Although Johnson did not invite her back during his tenure, her imminent return to the Met in his initial season, 1950–51, was one of Rudolf Bing's first announcements upon being appointed general manager.[38]

In early summer of 1947 Larry went to London for a brief stay, singing on 9 June at Albert Hall, with Sir Adrian Boult conducting. From there he went on to South Africa, for a surprisingly successful month-long round of performances. The local press welcomed him as "the greatest singer-actor ever to appear in the Union."[39]

But by the autumn of 1947 Larry's operatic career had reached its nadir. He made four appearances at the San Francisco Opera to mixed reviews. At the Met he was scheduled for three Scarpias, but illness prevented his singing two of them. That season of 1947–48, he would give but a single, forced performance in the house he loved so well. He was 51 years old.

Even more pitiful was the announcement from Columbia Artists Management that Larry's scheduled tour of the Caribbean had been canceled because of illness. What was not made public was that Columbia Artists had terminated the baritone's contract when Kurt Weinhold, Larry's personal manager, had found him hopelessly drunk in his hotel suite an hour or so before his ship was to sail. The longtime business partnership was over.[40]

"Columbia Artists terminated with Tibbett," Kurt Weinhold explained,

> because we just couldn't get him any more engagements. He understood that. He was here [at CAMI's offices] several times afterward to see us. He was intelligent enough to realize what a mess he had made of his life. He had had constant fights with Jane over his drinking problem.[41]

Indeed, this was also the beginning of the end of his second marriage. Weinhold recalled Jane's state of mind at the time of this fiasco:

> She finally became aware of Tibbett's unfortunate position and tried to get him to shake the habit, but it was too late. One cannot put all the blame on Jane, but she had a lot to do with it by emphasizing social activities above his profession. But Tibbett had such an outgoing personality. He loved to go to parties, big and small . . .[42]

Chapter 10

NOT FAREWELL BUT GOODBYE

"Leb' wohl! Leb' wohl!" With these words, with infinite sadness, Wotan bids farewell to his daughter Brünnhilde as he puts her to sleep on a rock encircled by Loge's magic fire in Wagner's *Die Walküre*. Too soon in his career, Larry's own years of poignant farewells were beginning for him, made necessary not by age, but by his apparently hopeless addiction to drink.

Over the years, Honey Hill Farm had begun to lose its charm for Larry and Jane. Their older children had grown and gone, leaving behind a profusion of empty rooms, and the gregarious couple soon filled the place with so many houseguests that they had little privacy left for themselves. When they went to the country for the weekend, Larry and Jane would routinely invite 20 or so people to go along. A frequent guest and one of Larry's great friends was Metropolitan Opera and radio tenor James Melton, a neighbor who was fond of elegant food and wine. Melton, too, was an alcoholic, though he was careful to hide it. He and Larry would often get drunk together.[1]

Late in 1948 Larry and Jane sold part of the farm, including the main house, to actor Raymond Massey and moved into the gardener's cottage. They now had a large living and dining room and a couple of bedrooms. This proved to be an ideal arrangement for a time, and weekends became periods of blissful relaxation. Soon, however, they both came to feel that it was unbearable to live so close to the main house yet no longer own it. They decided to move their primary residence to Florida, while holding on to their suite at the Savoy. Wherever they were, there would be beds for their two youngest, Michael and Peter, as long as they needed them.

As for Larry's twins, Richard's already distant relationship with his father had gone through a particularly troubled period of late: during his army stint, Richard had begun to date a young dancer of whom his father, without offering any valid reason, disapproved. When Richard demanded an explanation, it proved to be a shocker: Larry admitted he had slept with the girl. A year's breach between father and son followed this confrontation, but a reconciliation took place before Richard married his first wife, Barbara McInnes, in 1948, and Larry even sang at their wedding. Larry Jr. was in Hollywood, where, in 1949, he would appear in two B films, *El Paso* and *Captain China*. That same year he would marry for the second time. His new wife was Norma Fletcher Sheppard, the heiress of the Fletcher's Castoria (laxative) fortune. This second marriage was about as brief as his first, and also childless, lasting approximately two years.

During the Metropolitan season of 1948–49, Larry sang six performances: three Rigolettos and, characteristically for him, three performances in a new role, Captain Balstrode in Benjamin Britten's *Peter Grimes*, premiered on 21 January 1949. He won critical acclaim as Balstrode for his natural presence, his dignity, and—as with all the operas where he sang in English—his exemplary diction. In the next day's *New York Times*, Olin Downes remarked upon Larry's respect for the English language, which Downes regarded as unique among all stage artists. With Larry, the character was made "a living person"; one heard the text, enunciated and colored by "the art of a great singing actor."[2]

At the final curtain opening night, Larry—to his utter astonishment and with the stage still set with the huts and drying nets of a Suffolk fishing village—was surrounded by a host of friends as well as opera house personnel who poured onstage from the wings for a testimonial party in his honor. The occasion celebrated Larry's silver anniversary, 25 years performing with the Metropolitan. A short speech was made by the bass Louis D'Angelo, who in November 1923 had sung "A Soldier" on the evening that Larry made his unnoticed debut as Lovitsky in Mussorgsky's *Boris Godunov*.

Mrs. August Belmont, founder of the Metropolitan Opera Guild, also spoke a few words, as did Larry's former colleague Lucrezia Bori and general manager Edward Johnson. It remained for Charles Spofford, the guild's president, to present the baritone with a commemorative scroll, which read:

> The Metropolitan Opera Association desires to record its appreciation of a quarter of a century of service on the part of the distinguished American baritone, Lawrence Tibbett—who from his debut rose steadily in artistic stature to leadership on the operatic stage, which was the richer for his noble voice and vital personality.[3]

In addition to the scroll, Larry received from his colleagues a Steuben glass bowl, a pair of bookends, a gold chain, a set of gold cufflinks, and a gold watch inscribed "To Larry." His fellow artists obviously knew that Larry was an inveterate collector of gold trinkets and trifles. (At the time of his death, more than 100 gold items were listed in his estate.) Hundreds more who could not attend in person sent congratulatory wires, letters, and notes. A huge scrapbook to commemorate the event was literally crammed with expressions of best wishes from all over the world.[4]

With tears in his eyes, Larry addressed the group: "An expression of love from one's associates is the dearest and most stimulating thing in the world. Now look what you've done! Tonight you've started me off on another 25 years!"[5] His friends laughed and applauded. In fact, he had but one more season at the Metropolitan before his protector, Edward Johnson, retired and Larry would have to bid farewell to his beloved stage.

Among those who had quietly planned the affair were the Australian baritone John Brownlee, Deems Taylor, and Basil Rathbone. Additional help came from Birch Mayo, an oil producer from Oklahoma, and Nelson Rockefeller, both of whom got together to play canasta with Larry several nights a week when the singer was in New York.

This extravagant expression of love and appreciation was given in spite of the fact that the baritone's drinking problem was by now common knowledge. On the nights when Larry was scheduled to sing at the Met, the atmosphere backstage was thick with apprehension and worry as the principals, choristers, and stagehands all wondered whether he would be able to make it through the performance.

In the summer of 1949 Larry was forced to cancel what would have been his first Gérard in *Andrea Chénier* in Cincinnati, a role he would have been fabulous in during his prime. His last appearances with the San Francisco Opera, with which company he had performed since 1927, were that autumn. He sang Scarpia and two of the *Hoffmann* villains, Dapertutto and Dr. Miracle.[6] He did assume a new role in New Orleans that November, an untypical one for him. This was Jokanaan in Strauss's *Salome*, the only time he sang in a Strauss opera. The press resorted to safe, respectful adjectives such as "stalwart" and "worthy."[7] It is tantalizing to consider how Larry would have sounded in this role in his prime.

It was the end of an era. There has been much speculation as to the manner in which Larry left the Metropolitan. Some observers claim that he asked to go, finally realizing that his voice was gone for good and no longer of Metropolitan stature. Henry Jaffe, Tibbett's lawyer, confirmed that Larry himself decided to leave. "When Larry heard that Rudolf Bing had been appointed general manager of the Metropolitan, and that Edward Johnson would no longer stand protectively in the wings, he knew he was finished."[8]

In any case, it seems that Bing, whose term of office was to begin in the 1950–51 season, was not actively instrumental in Larry's departure. He had issued orders to his assistants that no pressure was to be put on the legendary baritone, that the new management would wait and see what move Tibbett himself would make. He made none. It was over.[9] An irony is that Larry himself had been strongly considered as Johnson's successor.

Under the extreme conditions imposed by a singing career, a period of 27 consecutive seasons performing leading roles in one of the world's great opera houses is highly creditable. And yet when the curtain rose on the new Metropolitan season of 1949–50, Larry's last, on 21 November, he was just a few days past his 53rd birthday. When he managed to stay away from the bottle, he was full of energy and otherwise in good health. He could have sung a 28th season and beyond.[10]

True, hard living and hard drinking had altered his appearance. His face had become flushed and somewhat bloated. He no longer worked out regularly on his rowing machine and had consequently put on weight and developed something of a paunch. But though the passage of time inevitably diminishes the freshness of any voice, he most certainly would have continued for many years in the opera house, using his extraordinary dramatic talents to distract from vocal weaknesses, had it not been for the lifestyle he had adopted for himself.

In his final season at the Met, while ascendant baritones such as Leonard Warren, Robert Merrill, Frank Guarrera, John Brownlee, Alexander Sved, and Enzo Mascherini appeared in what had been Larry's roles—Valentin, Amonasro, the elder Germont—the played-out baritone managed to substitute twice as Scarpia in *Tosca*. His second performance, on 28 February 1950, was called "a gallant gesture" by Kolodin.[11] The magnificently volatile Ljuba Welitsch was Tosca, and Larry countered her dramatic antics as professionally as he had Maria Jeritza's in the past. Ferruccio Tagliavini, the Cavaradossi and quite a bit shorter than the fiery soprano, had a bit more trouble with Welitsch. When she exited after their first-act duet, his obvious relief sent the audience into gales of laughter.[12] The opera was a prologue to a gala testimonial costume parade and ceremony in honor of retiring general manager Edward Johnson, and Larry certainly belonged on the stage that night.

True to his established form at the Met, Larry tackled his final new role on 16 February 1950, Prince Ivan Khovansky in the Metropolitan's belated first performance of *Khovanchina* by Mussorgsky, the composer of one of Larry's first concert successes, "Song of the Flea." It was sung in English, not Russian. Larry's presence onstage was still imposing, and in the next day's *New York Times*, critic Olin Downes proclaimed that of all American artists advanced by the Metropolitan in the last 25 years, Larry was "the greatest male singer."[13]

There is an air check of the second performance of *Khovanchina*, 25 February 1950. The large cast, the one from opening night, includes Risë Stevens, Polyna Stoska, Brian Sullivan, Charles Kullman, Robert Weede, and Jerome Hines. The conductor is Emil Cooper, who had led the opera for Diaghilev's Paris season with Chaliapin three decades before. Stevens's Marfa steals the show with the creamy smoothness of her Slavic-sounding voice, but Larry is no disgrace. As written, Khovansky's role is more conversational and declamatory than lyric, and Larry's superb diction covers a certain stiffness in his sound. His final notes ring out fully and superbly—the last notes heard by the Metropolitan radio audience who had known and loved him for so long.

Risë Stevens confirmed the characteristic "ring" of those final notes. Speaking with undiminished enthusiasm in 1988, she continued:

> This man was so sensational. I had a crush on him. *Everybody* had a crush on him! He was an overpowering personality on the stage; he gave the impression of being even taller than he was. He was fascinating. He had tremendous charisma.
>
> Before I went to Europe, when I was still a student at Juilliard, I used to sing ditties on the radio. This was in the same studio building where Larry had his radio show, and I used to run down the hall just to look at him. This was the period of his success,

> when everything was Tibbett, Tibbett, Tibbett. He had a special way of singing, of emphasizing a phrase. I heard a recording of his recently: the record doesn't show the overtones in his voice.
>
> When I came to the Met [1938], we didn't share the same repertoire. He didn't sing in *Mignon* or my other operas and he no longer did Escamillo in *Carmen*. In *Khovanchina*, we didn't have a scene together. But I still hear those overtones.[14]

The fourth performance of *Khovanchina*, 24 March 1950, was the last time that the great baritone would appear on the stage of the Metropolitan Opera as a member of the company.

From the very beginning of his professional career, Larry had kept up his odd, tender relationship with Doris Wyckoff, the young girl from Charleston, West Virginia. She had married in 1937 and had her first child in 1940. In 1942, on a visit to her parents, who lived just outside of New York City, she spent an evening with her famous friend, by then an internationally renowned baritone. Later she would comment, "I don't know why, but I had the uneasy feeling that that was the beginning of the end."[15]

Doris had seen Larry briefly in Rome in 1946. Then, in 1947, she and her family moved to New Jersey, and she sent Larry her new address. Strangely, she heard nothing from him until 1950. Soon after his last performance with the Metropolitan, her telephone rang, and there on the other end of the line was Lawrence Tibbett's richly resonant voice saying that he had been cleaning out his desk at the Lotus Club and had found her number, which he thought he had lost. Doris continued:

> We arranged to meet for lunch in New York. He was waiting for me when I arrived at the restaurant. He looked absolutely fabulous—handsome and well dressed. He certainly didn't look like a man whose career was on the skids, or down and out.
>
> I remember being very conscious of the rumors. I carefully avoided asking him any questions that might be in a fuzzy area; I did not want to embarrass him or intrude on his privacy. I remember being so careful about it that I didn't ask what he was doing now, although it would have been a natural question. He offered the information, though. He was coaching and teaching, he said, giving voice lessons, and it kept him busy. I remember thinking, "I'm so glad he has something to fill his life," because I had the impression his career was finished.

> We had a wonderful day. He could not have been more charming. He was just as I had remembered him.
>
> I've known a lot of alcoholics, and they can turn on the charm—they can present a normal front much of the time, but they have a disease, which like any sickness can lay them low. They can also be "up" again for a while, but I recall feeling that my dear friend Lawrence had gotten himself together.
>
> We left the restaurant and walked back to his apartment. "Do you really have to go?" he asked. I sensed his loneliness, but I had left three children at home. But we were finding so much to catch up on from the past 10 years and philosophizing about life and its joys and sorrows, so we continued the conversation at his apartment for another couple of hours. I didn't get home until nine o'clock that night. And I didn't realize until later that possibly the reason for my husband's lack of enthusiasm about the trip was that it had been my wedding anniversary![16]

In truth, at the beginning of 1950, shortly before this meeting, Larry had gone on an intense alcoholic binge, so Doris's impression that he had overcome his addiction was more hopeful than accurate. This was the last time she saw the glamorous figure who had dropped into her life so many years before.

After his departure from the Met, Larry was determined to keep busy. He had worked and played tirelessly for the first half-century of his life, and his energy remained high.

During the decade prior to his last performance at the Metropolitan, despite his increasingly frequent bouts of heavy drinking, Larry's range of activities was astonishingly broad. He took part in various Metropolitan Opera fund drives and helped arrange the Metropolitan Opera Guild's gala concerts. At the request of Secretary of the Navy James Forrestal, he was named one of the musical advisors for a project to interpret American culture to the world. He was a leader in the movement for government support of the arts, testifying at congressional committee hearings. He instigated a petition to Congress to reduce taxes on opera and concert tickets, and assisted in drawing up new AGMA agreements with various artists' managements. In addition to his union work and commitment to the Sister Elizabeth Kenny Foundation, he had done everything from address the New York Singing Teachers' Association to assist in a plan to send gifts to composer Jean Sibelius, who was cut off in Finland by World War II. Even the Fairfield, Connecticut, Community Chest Drive benefited from his participation.

Ever on the move, he sang with the New York Philharmonic, at a dinner for the Antoinette Perry Awards, at the opening of the New York City Center for Music and Dance, and at President Truman's inauguration. He sang to benefit the Thrift Shops' Children's Charity Fund in Washington, D.C., and flew to Toronto to sing and act as master of ceremonies for a special benefit show for the Easter Seal Fund for Crippled Children. He made numerous appearances for the benefit of the Red Cross and sang at the organization's annual convention in Atlantic City. He became one of the backers of the Israeli Music Foundation and sang the Israeli national anthem at Madison Square Garden on the first anniversary of that new republic in 1949. In these late appearances he was often helped by Sholom Secunda and other savvy conductors, who could bring up the orchestra's volume to cover a wandering Tibbett high note.

Small wonder that once, when asked how his billing should read, the baritone quipped "Lawrence Tibbett—charity singer." With a rueful expression, he added, "Also available for funerals and weddings."[17]

Larry was a pioneer in trying to bring opera, acted naturally and in English, to the new medium of television. He was a founder of CBS's *Opera Television Theatre*, and on New Year's Day 1950 he introduced, live on camera, a 75-minute version of Bizet's *Carmen* featuring Gladys Swarthout, Robert Roundsville, and Robert Merrill. The opera was sung in French, not English, and was conducted and staged by Boris Goldovsky. A second production, a 95-minute version of *La Traviata*, was sung in English on 12 March 1950. Larry himself portrayed the elder Germont but with tragic results, as his voice shattered in the aria "Di provenza." The long morning rehearsal followed by the live telecast had been too much for him. Because no commercial sponsors could be found for the program series, it met its untimely end with the *Traviata*.

Milton Goldman was now his manager for theater and on 11 November 1950, Larry starred in a full-scale performance for the first time since leaving the Met. After previews in Baltimore, he opened at the Broadhurst Theater on Broadway in *The Barrier*, music by Jan Meyerowitz and lyrics by Langston Hughes. Also in the cast were Muriel Rahn and Reri Grist. The show was not a success and ran only four performances, although it did have a small local tour on the Brandt circuit to theaters in Brooklyn and the Bronx, at that time legitimate playhouses.

The Barrier was adapted by Hughes from his play *The Mulatto*, which in turn had been expanded from his short story *Father and Son*. Larry played Lt. Col. Thomas Norwood, a plantation owner who has had three children by his black housekeeper.

Years later, composer Jan Meyerowitz was still in pain but philosophical about this production of *The Barrier*. He blamed the producer, who insisted on a Broadway run, rather than his aging baritone. All the same, he had only faint praise for Larry's performance:

> *The Barrier* was an opera and was later done as an opera in Naples and Palermo. It was never meant for Broadway and did not fit there. Tibbett was hired for his name; he loved the work and wanted to do it. He missed rehearsals—drunk—but when he did perform, he tried instinctively to live up to his name. He wanted to give value for the money. His was a secondary role, but he forced it to be the lead. He squeezed the role out, gave it Wagnerian phrasing.
>
> I wanted to close the show on opening night. It was incredibly bad. Tibbett sang badly. It was a sad chapter in my life.[18]

Reri Grist took a more admiring view of her fellow performer. In a 1988 letter from her Berlin home, she wrote:

> Lawrence Tibbett—one of the figures from my past who remains alive for me. I was a young girl when I met him in *The Barrier*, but I recall a very troubled, sensitive, extremely kind-to-me man; thinning, dirty-blond/grayish hair; ruddy complexion; simple dress; soft, sometimes turned-off-from-the-environment eyes.
>
> He seemed to want to be alone yet needed people to talk to. I cannot remember if he was close to his colleagues or not. He sometimes did not show up at rehearsals. I remember being asked once to go to Tibbett's dressing room and coax him into coming onstage for a rehearsal for which he was late. The feeling of him holding my hand and the two of us walking onstage is a tender moment. I cannot tell you what I said to him, but he did get up from his chair in his bare, cold dressing room to take my hand and attend the rehearsal.
>
> He seemed to need alcohol—red wine, often with a raw egg dropped into the wine—fairly often. One sometimes spoke of his inability to attend rehearsals because of intoxication. I don't recall having seen him drunk.
>
> Onstage: hard worker, very concentrated, considerate of his colleagues, an intense actor, constantly reaching for further definition of his character.

> His voice: powerful, warm, free, even though somewhat abused by time or his lifestyle (whatever that was), technically well developed and exciting, a little strained at the top.
>
> He remains for me one of the unconscious (at that time) inspirations of my life, a gentleman, a great singer/performer whom I would like to have heard in his prime.[19]

On 2 July 1951, Larry opened a nine-week tour on the summer stock circuit as the priggish and then fallen Reverend Davidson, a non-singing role, in Somerset Maugham's *Rain*, with Elsbeth Hofman as Sadie Thompson. According to Milton Goldman, Larry took the designation "non-singing" literally, and since they were not in the script, categorically refused Goldman's suggestion that he sing one or two hymns, even though that was what the audience would most want to hear. Larry considered himself an actor; he had acted without music before, and he would do so again. The fact that he did not sing hurt attendance, and the tour was not a financial success.[20]

Still eager to perform, Larry next took on the part of Captain Hook in a musical version of *Peter Pan*. Veronica Lake, famed on film in the late 1930s and early 40s for her smoldering sexuality and peek-a-boo hairdo, played a close-cropped Peter. This ill-starred venture opened on 10 October 1951 and closed in Chicago two months later. Larry was not faulted; Lake seemed to have been the problem, and she too ended her career as an alcoholic.

During 1951 Larry also appeared on various radio and television programs out of New York City. Here he met with a measure of success, for his rich, expressive speaking voice was still particularly effective when heard on the air. On one New York Philharmonic television broadcast, he and Gladys Swarthout discussed opera during the intermission. On another, he and Jane discussed music in general. On 21 November 1951, he served as host of the Metropolitan Opera Auditions of the Air, recalling his own audition experiences at the Met.

One of the many young vocalists Larry befriended was Emile Renan, one of the original artists of the New York City Opera. Renan remembers an occasion when he shared a taxi with Larry, soon after his return to New York following the failure of *Peter Pan*:

> Larry started to tell me about his problems—how he seemed to catch so many "colds" lately, and usually just before an opening.
>
> Within me I was crying out, "You're such a smart man, a bright man; you know why you're catching so many colds. You mean

you're looking for one excuse after another." Of course I couldn't say this aloud, so I introduced the topic of a new book that had just come out, *My Six Convicts*, because I wanted to lead to the subject of personal awareness, which played a big part in the book. Larry was interested. He said he wanted very much to read the book.

Now during all this time with Larry, the cabdriver had paid no attention. But when I left Larry off, the cabby looked at me through his rearview mirror and said, "Hey, who was that guy who just got off?"

"Oh, that was Lawrence Tibbett."

"Lawrence Tibbett! After I let you off I gotta go home and tell my wife."

"Aren't you always picking up celebrities?"

"Oh, sure. I've had Joe DiMaggio, Jack Dempsey, Marilyn Monroe. But that's Lawrence Tibbett!"

I found that the cabby had never heard Larry in the opera, on records, or on the radio and had never even seen him in the movies, so I asked him what the big deal was.

The driver looked very pityingly at me, as though talking to an idiot. "Look, Mister, I never seen him, I never heard him—but *that was Lawrence Tibbett*." As though that explained everything. And to him it did.

Later I dropped Tibbett a note telling him about the incident. I thought he would be pleased.[21]

And so Larry struggled to carry on despite the alcoholism that was destroying him. Equally steadfastly he refused to acknowledge that he had a drinking problem. He turned increasingly to appearances on radio and television, on talk shows or as a classical disk jockey. Although he had put on weight, and his hair had receded and was turning white, he was always careful of his appearance. If he spent the day at home he dressed informally, in slacks and sport shirts; when Jane and he went out in the evening, he put on a finely tailored suit, white shirt, and a tie. His vanity was intact, as was his sometimes crude sense of humor. He had an obsession with neckties, ordering them by the box; he particularly liked what he called his "party tie," which when he took a deep singer's breath, popped out to display a nude woman with oversized breasts.

Richard had divorced his first wife and married Patricia Jameson Barnes on 3 November 1951 in Palm Desert, California. Larry did not attend, much less sing at, this wedding. Richard's first marriage had produced a son, Richard Lawrence, and his second brought forth Robin Mackay and Brian Jameson. Larry Jr. had given up on his acting career, and now both Tibbett twins had settled down and were working for the Hughes Aircraft Company.

On 31 December 1952 Larry wrote Richard and his wife Pat from a sanitarium, where he was undergoing yet another "cure." The letter is addressed to "You two dearest people!"; in it he continues his habit of homilies and warns the couple that "after all, loss of money, position, etc., is nothing compared to loss of time. Time however is only lost when the lesson is not learned and we continue to lose it."[22] The irony and self-delusion of the sentiment are self-evident.

Nor had he lost his roving eye for women. During this period of his life, Larry, with the combined deviousness of the alcoholic and the roué, maintained two sets of appointment books—or rather his secretary, Doris Wittschen, kept one set while Larry used the other. Doris's books were meticulously typed records of Larry's broadcasts and other professional engagements; his were little blue books, stamped with his initials and the year in gold and studded with mysterious names—mostly female—and telephone numbers, with only here and there an entry about a television or radio show. Beside many of the women's names in Larry's books were memory-jogging penciled notations about their work or skills: "writer," "nurse," "actress," "sales clerk." These little books spanned the years 1951 through 1957.

After their father's death, Richard and Larry Jr. found the little books and realized they were looking at a chronicle of their father's one-night stands. In these declining years, alcoholic or not, there was apparently no diminution of the singer's sexual appetite.

In March 1953 Larry went on another dismaying alcoholic binge; this one landed him in the White Plains Recovery Center outside New York City, where he was kept busy with "two hours of carpentry, three hours of gym and/or baseball, golf, volleyball, badminton, or just walking."[23] The following month he wrote to his son Michael, who was about to graduate from Fountain Valley School in Colorado. Michael was trying to decide which school, the University of Florida or Wesleyan College in Connecticut, would provide him with a better pre-med education; his plan was to enroll in medical school eventually.

After years of being an absentee father, primarily involved with his own music, career, or social affairs, Larry reached out to his youngest son, now 19 years old, demonstrating the great tenderness of which he was capable. The long letter begins thus:

> April 20, 1953
> My dearest Michael,
> Your sweet letter was most welcome if somewhat unexpected. Unexpected because you and I are both rather remiss as correspondents. In fact it has been three weeks since you wrote me, and despite thinking about you constantly and wanting to write—somehow I've procrastinated until now. Actually I've been very busy here, and time rushes by with frightening speed. Despite two nasty and disagreeable bouts with virus infections, I'm feeling superbly well—haven't felt as well in 10 years . . . I'm more than pleased with the results of the therapy here and feel more hopeful that I'm through with the lovely stuff.

The letter continued with a thoughtful discussion of Michael's college alternatives, followed by an offer born of true fatherly affection:

> Since I am in very good voice now, how would you like the idea of my singing at your graduation exercises? Ask Mr. Poole or whoever is in charge of arrangements whether or not I would fit into the ceremony. It might easily be that an outside element (me) would discombobulate matters—if so, forget it. Anyway, let me know as soon as possible. Also, if the answer is yes, get suggestions for the song or songs from your music instructor and send them to me.
>
> My time here is up on June 7th—but they are letting me out a few days early so I can make your graduation comfortably.

Then Larry offered joyous news of his own. Within days of the 1935 Broadway premiere of the folk musical *Porgy and Bess*, he and Helen Jepson had recorded excerpts from it at composer George Gershwin's express request. And what a set of records this was! Jepson is flawless, singing the women's music, and Larry, portraying three different characters in the opera, gave each one a distinctive characterization. The set enjoyed immense popularity internationally. Now a New York revival of *Porgy and Bess* followed by a tour of Europe and the Soviet Union was planned. Although the terms of the Gershwin estate (the composer died in 1937) stated that the opera staged by an American company must be performed by an all-black cast of singers, as it had been at the premiere, Larry had been offered the singular honor of appearing as the crippled Porgy on the tour of this production. It was not a matter of whites cashing in on its popularity; it had always been Gershwin's wish that Larry sing Porgy. Gershwin thought very highly of Larry and was thrilled with the way he sang the *Porgy* music; he wanted the Metropolitan Opera to produce *Porgy*, and if they had, it would certainly have been Larry who sung the role.

Larry finished the letter to his youngest son:

> I may take it—I have not made up my mind as yet. But it's good to get offers anyway, particularly after being out of harness for so long.
>
> Warmest love for you always, my dearest son,
>
> Dad[24]

After three months of alcohol withdrawal therapy, Larry was released from the sanitarium, healthy and optimistic. In June 1953 he drove out to Michael's graduation; there he gave a healthy and amusing rendition of Sportin' Life's "It ain't necessarily so" from *Porgy*. Jane had traveled to Colorado for the commencement ceremonies separately, by train. As close friends noted, a certain independent distance seemed to be the keynote of their marriage by this time, but it was not yet a total parting of the ways. Michael, Jane, and Larry then drove back to New York together.

Larry was in good voice[25] and decided to sign the contract to sing Porgy on the European/Russian tour. Now he faced some hard work, for *Porgy and Bess* is not easy music. It has a complicated score with many complex ensembles. Seemingly revivified by his recent treatments, Larry worked at Porgy with all the intensity and ardor that had made him such a great artist. His assistant in this learning process, feeding him lines and cues and drawing closer to his father than ever before, was Michael.

Tragically, Larry's best efforts were undone by his wife's high-flying lifestyle. Where her husband's self-esteem was gained by his giving unparalleled performances on the world's stages, Jane derived hers from the adulation of guests at her endless round of parties, the feeling of being the absolute center of attention in her own small, stylish world. She would not cooperate in Larry's attempted recovery.

As Larry worked in one part of their suite at the Savoy to learn the demanding role of Porgy, the parties continued in the adjacent rooms. Temptation was but a few steps away—the peals of false laughter, the music, the familiar ring of ice in whiskey glasses—and an alcoholic is appallingly vulnerable to temptation.

In the end Larry succumbed. His contract for *Porgy and Bess* was canceled, and Jane Tibbett pronounced her husband a drunken failure. She bought her own apartment at the Savoy and moved into it, taking Michael.[26] She afterward spent most of her time at Bali Ha'i in Naples, Florida and came back to New York only occasionally. Larry went off on another drunken episode, this one lasting eight weeks.

Mrs. Charles Gleaves, daughter of the longtime assistant general manager of the Metropolitan Edward Ziegler, summed up the final break between Larry and Jane:

> Jane left Larry because of his excessive drinking, not that she was incapable of taking a good belt herself now and then. Apparently it was a wild and spangled love affair, which lasted for many years, and when he began to slip as an artist, it must have distressed her terribly. I think this is one of the most tragic stories ever to come out of the old Met, and everyone's to blame.[27]

For the first time in his life Larry was without the love of a woman who cherished him as a person and believed in him as an artist. His mother, Frances Ellen Tibbet, had set the standard. Even Grace, his first wife, with all her ambitious possessiveness, had unswerving faith in his voice and artistry at a time when few others believed in Larry's future. In Jane, he had found this same devoted loyalty combined with enticing beauty, the equal of the powerful looks that had drawn him into the embraces of such leading film stars as Grace Moore and Lupe Velez.

Jane, in her turn, had basked in the light of Larry's stardom and in the attention invariably drawn by his larger-than-life physique and personality. But now that light had dimmed. Sadly, the great singer had become a seedy, often incoherent shell of his former self, a man who could no longer keep up with the fast-paced, hard-drinking society that nurtured her. She saw no reason to stand by him. By the spring of 1954, their marriage had become a sham; they separated, although they legally remained man and wife.

Enter now, provocatively, a vivacious red-haired, green-eyed beauty named Betty Fox, just turned 39. She was married to a physician, Charles Fox. No children had resulted from this union, which was just as well since soon after his marriage, the doctor discovered that his wife was prone to chronic depression. In the first three years of their marriage, Betty Fox had left her husband once and attempted suicide on another occasion. They would have divorced, but Charles did not want to face the legal difficulties associated with those proceedings at the time.

Betty, an excellent pianist and knowledgeable in her field, was employed by a music publisher for many years. Composers would drop by with their newly composed music, and she would play through the compositions on the fine Steinway her husband had given her. She would then make recommendations to her superiors at the publishing house, who would act on them.

At the time the Foxes first met Larry, at an AGMA fund-raising event, they were living at opposite ends of their apartment on Central Park West. The Foxes had problems of their own, and thus they responded compassionately to the famous alcoholic singer with a wreck of a voice, living out, as they were, a loveless marriage. The highly emotional and empathetic Betty was immediately and particularly taken with Larry, and the lonely, disturbed people gravitated toward each other, soon forming a threesome.

Nearly every evening Larry would wind up at the Foxes' apartment singing to Betty's accompaniment, bickering with Charles, or playing Scrabble. Drink had made Larry increasingly nettlesome, even over a word game, and Scrabble had become a passion for him; he was a first-rate player and few could beat him at it. Larry had always been fascinated by the English language and derived as much pleasure from his unabridged Webster's as others might obtain from a good novel. Pursuing words with the same zeal with which he pored through music scores, he searched out their etymology and meaning, a habit that may help to account for his early focus on vocal nuance in singing.

During this period the companionship of the Foxes proved an absolute godsend for Larry, whose world was coming apart around him.

In February 1954 Larry was forced to make another heart-rending, heartwarming farewell. Long ago he had been the prime mover in the founding of AGMA and from its inception in 1936 to 1952 he had served as its president; for the past two years, he had been its honorary president. Now it was time to step down. Others were waiting in the wings to continue his and Jascha Heifetz's pioneering work. Larry, whose love for the union was boundless, realized this.

Plans were made for a lavish ceremonial dinner for Larry on the occasion of his retirement. Frank Chapman, the public relations expert and husband of beloved Met contralto Gladys Swarthout, had with

Larry helped to found the musicians' union 18 years before. It was he who set the wheels in motion for the grand occasion. The letter he sent to Francis Robinson of the Met read as follows:

> December 11, 1953
> Dear Francis,
> Since you are one of the sponsors of the dinner for Lawrence Tibbett, I want to let you know that the event has been set for the 25th of February, and will take place at the Hotel Astor in the Grand Ballroom at 7 p.m. This is not, in any sense, a testimonial dinner to Larry but it is rather a tribute to one who happens to be an outstanding artist and who has, over the years, contributed much more than his artistry, not only to the entertainment world, but to a variety of important causes.
> Yours,
> Frank Chapman[28]

Formal invitations to the event were also signed by Chapman. Dinner was to be $15 per plate and tables were to seat 10. Twelve hundred people accepted the invitation with pleasure. All Larry's devoted colleagues, friends, and admirers were determined to make the evening unforgettable.

Larry had sung for presidents at the White House and in command performances before royalty. But on the evening of 25 February 1954, as he entered the grand ballroom of the Hotel Astor in the company of composer Deems Taylor (who would serve as toastmaster), Chapman, and General David Sarnoff (the head of RCA and NBC), Larry seemed more nervous and jumpy than ever before in his long career. Behind him came his estranged wife Jane, their son Michael, and Jane's two brothers Edgar and Hunter. Once safely seated at the table of honor, Larry found plenty of alcohol available to steady his nerves.

Taylor, known as a felicitous speaker, began the night with an opening address. He read from a review of Larry's first performance in *Faust* at the Metropolitan on 30 November 1923, a critique that Taylor, who also worked as a music critic, conceded was rather "snippy." He then traced the progress of the young baritone through a career that included more than a thousand concerts, six Hollywood films, radio and recording engagements without end, and season after season of brilliant performances at the Met. Continued Taylor:

> This is a humble man. Humility is a characteristic of most great artists. Tibbett has it; Heifetz has it; John McCormack had it; and many more. They are people who have achieved such mastery of

> their art that they know better than anyone else that mastery can never be complete.
>
> This is a generous man. I've no need to remind you that AGMA owes its existence to him, its first president. If ever two men had no possible need for a guild to protect their interests, it was Lawrence Tibbett and Jascha Heifetz, its first vice president. But the less well-known artists—singers, dancers, instrumentalists—were badly in need of such protection.[29]

A quartet of other speakers, all beloved colleagues, followed: Gladys Swarthout, Helen Traubel, Jussi Björling, and Jerome Hines. All gave eloquent, personal tributes; it was an emotionally charged evening for Larry.

Next came the musical portion of the evening. First up were four of the younger singers at the Metropolitan of the day: Heidi Krall, Margaret Roggero, Charles Anthony, and Frank Guarrera. Next, the inimitable and cherished Thelma Votipka, known to all as "Tippy," accompanied herself at the piano in a set of Czech folk songs.

On the dais sat such notables of the music and business worlds as Mrs. August Belmont, Rudolf Bing, Lucrezia Bori, Swarthout and Chapman, Newbold Morris of the New York City Opera, John Brownlee, who had succeeded Larry as president of AGMA, Harvey Firestone Jr., IBM's Thomas Watson, and of course Jane Tibbett, reveling once more in husband's glory.

The evening stretched on to the accompaniment of abundant drink. When Larry finally rose to give his words of thanks, he stumbled over them and could hardly get them out. As a conclusion, all in the room stood and joined in a chorus of one of Larry's (and every baritone's) most famous concert and radio songs, "On the Road to Mandalay." The baritone also stood and attempted to sing, but it was all too much. Signaling his chum and drinking companion Birch Mayo to follow, he sneaked away.[30]

Much later that night, Michael and a friend were talking near the door to Larry's suite at the Savoy when the elevator door opened. Out crept Tibbett and Mayo, on their hands and knees, howling like coyotes. Open-mouthed and incredulous, Michael watched while the two drunks unlocked the apartment door with trembling, groping hands and crawled inside.[31]

So ended Lawrence Tibbett's final evening of triumph in the company of his peers—a sodden conclusion, the legendary singer howling on his hands and knees.

Larry had long cherished his swift, beautifully designed Armstrong Siddeley motor car. A fast but safe driver, he had spent many happy hours on the road with tenor James Melton, who collected antique cars as a hobby. By 1954, with his professional schedule severely truncated, Larry began to spend much more time in his Siddeley, visiting friends in California, New Mexico, Oklahoma, Colorado, and Wyoming. Heading eastward, he would stop off for visits in Ohio and Maryland before returning to New York. Soon he would start off again, this time northward, to spots in Connecticut, upstate New York, and Maine, which attracted him with the unspoiled beauty of their woods and lakes. Since many of his friends were fishermen, he always carried appropriate gear and tackle (as in the opening scene of his 1935 film *Metropolitan*). His companions derided his angling efforts; strategies were lost on him, as whether he was told to appear at a certain fishing spot at dawn or dusk, he invariably showed up at midday.

Just as his compulsive drinking had decimated his professional career, it now began to strangle his personal life as well. In the autumn of 1954, Larry decided to drive out to California, to visit Larry Jr., who had married his third wife, Dorothy ("Dotie") Nilson Beal, in February 1953.

Many years later, Lori, one of Larry Jr.'s two daughters with Dorothy, told the story of her grandfather's visit, which had taken its place beside the other legends in the family's history:

> Granddad had driven clear across the country by himself, visiting friends on the way, and finally arrived at our house in Pacific Palisades. After remaining with us for about three weeks, he took off on a sentimental journey to Bakersfield, where he wanted to visit the old house where he was born. He was stopped by the police in Van Nuys after he drove through a red light and collided with a small pickup truck. No one was hurt, although his car was totally destroyed.
>
> The *Van Nuys Daily* reported that police at the scene of the accident claimed they had smelled alcohol and that when Granddad got out of his car, he swayed and fell back against a signpost to maintain his balance. Then he became sarcastic and so uncooperative that they had to handcuff him and take him to the stationhouse under arrest.
>
> A photographer from one of the local papers happened to be in the stationhouse and caught Granddad just as they were finger-

> printing him. Well, that lousy shot went all over the country—and probably the world![32]

Lori was right. The damning photograph of Larry being fingerprinted was picked up by the International News Service and reprinted around the globe.

So ended Larry's driving days, and one more route by which he escaped himself was closed. Once a celebrated public figure, Tibbett was now known to the world as a drunk. As a drunk, there was only one response to his feelings of shame and humiliation—and that was to drink more.

Chapter 11

THE THIRD GLASS

In 1955, on a visit to the West Coast, Jane called Richard and Larry Jr. to a meeting with her at the Beverly Hills Hotel. She told them they would have to take over their father's affairs and somehow straighten them out. His financial worth, she claimed, was down to $100,000 and continued to drop. He had been in and out of hospitals, "drying out," but nothing had helped, and there seemed no end to his medical expenses.

The twins suspected that Jane was manipulating both them and the figures and told her, truthfully, that they could not assume this responsibility as they had young children of their own to care for and were themselves struggling to stay afloat. Reminding Jane that she was still married to their father, they countered that since she had lived with him and shared his good years, she should now help him in his time of need. Larry had once confided to Michael that the only expense his mother had to bear was her clothes, that he was happy to provide for all her other needs. The twins knew that Jane was wealthy enough in her own right to provide easily the help their father needed.

Jane resented the brothers' attitude but had to accept it, at least for the moment. There was, of course, another way out: she could divorce her derelict husband. But on the advice of her lawyer, she decided to stay the course.

It is hard to believe that around this time, Larry made, and obviously approved for release, a series of recordings that can only be called unfortunate. May no one come across them without previous knowledge of the singer's voice and think that *this* was Lawrence Tibbett.

By 1956 Larry showed all the symptoms of advanced alcoholism. He had put on more weight and was now petulant and irritable. Though his addiction to drink seemed uncontrollable, the fact was that he could still check himself—if there were a strong enough reason.

Two such reasons presented themselves in 1956. Frank Loesser, the composer and lyricist of the Broadway musical *Guys and Dolls*, had turned to a new project, a musical adaption of Sidney Howard's play *They Knew What They Wanted*, about a rowdy, Italian California winegrower and his mail-order bride. Loesser wrote what was virtually an opera, through-composed with only some spoken dialogue. This new Broadway musical, *The Most Happy Fella*, called for a mature actor with a true operatic baritone voice—a natural for Lawrence Tibbett.

Serious and cold sober, Larry auditioned for the part of Tony and was told he could definitely have it; he was still a box office draw. Contracts would be signed as soon as details were in order.

For some reason—perhaps he was afraid that the role would be given to him, or perhaps he never really believed that it would be his—he decided to take the next plane to California and so informed Loesser and the musical director of the show, Herb Green. The two, aware of the baritone's reputation as an alcoholic, had him followed, and at some point on the trip Larry was observed steadying himself with a drink. That was enough for them. When *Most Happy Fella* opened on 3 May 1956, the role of Tony, which Larry could have portrayed with such truth and strength, was played instead by his former colleague at the Met, baritone Robert Weede, who with this beginning embarked upon a successful second career on Broadway.

Larry sank into despair. Yet once more he rallied. Two years previously, the musical *Fanny* had opened on Broadway. It costarred Ezio Pinza, the quintessential middle-aged sex symbol, who followed up a long Metropolitan career with his great success in *South Pacific*. Larry had seen the show twice, the second time with his friends Charles and Betty Fox and had pointed out to them what a perfect role César, the bar owner, would be for him to portray. *Fanny* was still enjoying a healthy run when the news came in 1956 that Pinza, stricken by a stroke, had left the show.

Upon hearing the news about Pinza, Larry began to bombard composer Harold Rome with telephone calls, holding the handset close to his mouth and insisting, "I feel fine, Harold, fine. And the voice is just great."[1]

Larry managed to allay Rome's doubts, together with those of producer Nat Behrens and director Joshua Logan. He could still be tremendously persuasive, and adding to the dramatic conviction of his tone was the classic self-delusion of the alcoholic: *I'll never take another drink*. So it was agreed that Larry would have two weeks to prepare for the role of César, during which time the cast of *Fanny* would take a break. The show was to reopen in early June.

By this time Larry and Betty Fox had become open lovers; but her estranged husband remained the baritone's friend, and his doubts about Larry's drinking had not diminished. He felt compelled to remind Larry that the role required him to play a bartender, which could make it impossible for him to refrain from alcohol. Knowing that Larry was no longer the master of his behavior, Fox gave him four weeks as César—tops. Larry disagreed; he had been able to control his drinking through many operas with drinking scenes. He could do it again, especially with Betty to help him.

For her part, Betty was overjoyed at this chance for him to resume his career and remake his life. Rapturously, she accompanied him at the piano as he rehearsed his songs from *Fanny*. By going before the public again night after night and following the strict routine that a performer's life imposed, she believed he might be able to stop drinking. But then, of course, she was deeply in love with him and willing to believe anything. Ravaged by alcohol though he might be, Larry's magnetism had not failed him.

On 6 June 1956, the marquee of the Majestic Theater on West Forty-fourth Street lit up the night sky with "Lawrence Tibbett in Fanny." Alas, within the auditorium the old Tibbett magic failed to light up the audience. Larry had lost his old power to excite. His friend Emile Renan, who attended a performance during the fourth week of Tibbett's run with the show, recalled:

> This was not the old Tibbett. His performance was stilted, there was little acting as such—only careful elocution, as though he was watching himself closely. There was only one long moment that suddenly came alive, when he sang "Welcome Home." All of a sudden you understood, even if you had never known the old magic.[2]

But for a brief time, Larry was once more home—on the stage. Betty Fox went with him to the theater for every show, watching closely as he performed. Afterward they would return to his apartment and take turns making supper. They reviewed that night's performance in general and Larry's work in particular. Betty carefully refrained from passing judgment on Larry's singing. Usually they would be in bed by four a.m.

Although Betty realized how dependent Larry had become on her, she was genuinely happy. He had become so much a part of *Fanny* that he hadn't touched a drop of liquor in weeks—he was reformed! A ruddy color even suffused his cheeks. And they rarely missed a day of passionate lovemaking. Betty, who called Larry "something else," relished every moment of his excitement: here was a man and a lover—even though he let the name Jane slip from his lips several times.

Betty knew, however, that the happy interlude was soon to end. As with many who suffer from mental disorders, she could recognize when a depressive attack was about to hit her. More than once, she worried that she might become pregnant, even though she was certain she had passed her menopause. And she realized, in those pre-lithium days, that she would sooner or later have to commit herself once again to the sanitarium in Holbrook, Massachusetts. Until then she would revel in the joy of Larry's passion, which, by his own report, was undiminished.[3]

On the night he saw *Fanny*, Emile Renan went backstage to greet the man who had encouraged him when he was a beginner.

> Tibbett was acting with the kind of controlled nonchalance that someone puts on when he feels insecure, when he cannot face the reality of failure.
>
> There was a baseball game on TV, there were visitors in the room and a lot of fussing around. When Larry saw me, there was a big embrace: his handshake told me he was drinking. In the course of all this activity a woman asked, "Larry, when did you start this show?" Larry turned to the woman and repeated, haltingly, "Start? When did I start?"
>
> Since I had already figured out the date during the performance, I did not hesitate to respond. "June 6th," I said. There was an instant's hush.
>
> "You remembered that?" Larry asked, taking my hand in his. Someone he respected had cared enough about him to remember. This seemed very important to Tibbett.[4]

Actor Walter Slezak, the ebullient co-star of *Fanny*, remembered how exactly one month after the baritone assumed the role of César,

Larry came backstage dressed to kill. Then, with the unpredictable behavior of the alcoholic, he casually announced that he was quitting the show. "As the cast stood by in astonishment, he said his goodbye, blew a kiss, and disappeared. Fortunately, there was a standby."[5]

He had used up his last chance. After *Fanny*, Larry never again appeared on the stage. Every door was now closed to him, and he realized at last that his performing days were over. Even Betty's devotion and love could help him only intermittently, for she was now in and out of the sanitarium, sharing his apartment only occasionally.

"Drink not the third glasse, which thou canst not tame, when once it is within thee." This was the counsel of English poet George Herbert, first printed in 1633.[6] By now the third glass had become Larry's way of life. If he made an engagement for lunch, he might cancel at the last moment because of a "cold" or because he "had to go out of town." A good friend would know the real reason for the broken appointment, and Larry would know the friend knew. Once a bon vivant with a huge circle of friends, Larry now led a tightly circumscribed life, but despite the picture Jane had painted for the twins, he was not financially strapped.

Larry Jr. described, as he knew it, his father's diminished existence during his final years.

> After Dad broke up with Jane, my wife, Dotie, and I visited him when we could, which was not too often since we lived in California and he lived in New York City. But when we did visit and stay with him, he always liked to cook for us. Dad was a good cook. I particularly liked to have him fry my bacon. By this time he looked old and paunchy. I wasn't used to his white hair. In spite of his big collection of books and records, I knew he was a lonely man.
>
> There was this woman, a pianist, who stayed with him occasionally: that's the way it was. Of course, he pulled down a job now and then—guest shots on TV and radio shows, like Ed Sullivan's, for example. Financially he was well off. Fortunately, most of his money was in A-plus stocks. He just lived off the interest; he never touched the principal. This was the money he had earned as a singer.[7]

He had quit the Savoy and now lived in an apartment on Manhattan's East Fifty-sixth Street, where he did all his own cooking, for all intents and purposes alone when Betty was away. When he was fit, he would sally forth to the supermarket dressed in an old sweater and slacks, make his frugal purchases, and return with a bag of groceries.

Alcoholics are prone to accidents. Once, before drifting off to sleep sprawled on his couch, Larry left a hamburger frying on the stove. The meat began to burn. Neighbors smelled the smoke and quickly guessed what was happening. They called Timothy, the doorman, who grabbed a key, quietly let himself into the singer's apartment, and turned off the gas.

The neighbors also knew Larry was well off. He had an expensive apartment in the same building where Carol Burnett, the TV star, lived. He paid in cash for everything he bought, including liquor. People of the neighborhood, noting his sleepwalker's shuffle, also knew that he drank. But since he kept to himself and exchanged few words with them, they left him alone.

The younger tenants of the building would not have recognized the name of Lawrence Tibbett; his heyday had been 25 years before. But longtime public relations representative, Richard H. Roffman, known as "the mayor of Times Square," remembered Larry kindly:

> I was public relations and publicity aide, confidante, and friend for the last few years of his life to Mr. Lawrence Tibbett. We went out a few nights a week to receptions, meetings, shows, affairs of all kinds. He was very low-key, very subdued for a great, great singer, not seeking recognition from others in the crowd, but happy to be out on the town enjoying as much as he could what was happening "around town."
>
> I wish to add this fact for the record: Lawrence Tibbett in this period was with no temperament, no ego, not throwing his fame and accomplishments around but delighted to be a member of the elite crowd attending such functions.
>
> I am proud to be able to state that, in my experience of almost 60 years in communications talent representation, Mr. Lawrence Tibbett was one of the most illustrious lights of my career.[8]

During Larry's last years in New York City, Roosevelt Hospital (now St. Luke's Roosevelt) on West Fifty-ninth Street, across Manhattan from his East Side apartment, came to be his refuge in time of crisis. With the conflicting instincts of the alcoholic, he fought to survive even as he destroyed himself. When he became so drunk that he could no longer function, he would manage to call the hospital and summon help. The green ambulance would arrive, and the attendants would load him into it. If Larry thought he recognized a familiar face, he would grin and wave feebly as the vehicle moved off.

The first day in the hospital, while Larry detoxified, going "cold turkey," the doctors left him strictly alone. During this initial period, his symptoms of withdrawal ran the gamut from headaches to vomiting to diarrhea, and his peripheral nervous system remained semi-paralyzed. The next day, it took three medical attendants to lift him to his feet and walk him, shakily, to the examining room, where he would undergo tests of his blood, urine, and stool, and finally, a brain scan. Results showed that alcohol had damaged Larry's brain and that his liver had lost most of its normal functioning.

Betty Fox, despite her own struggles with depression, was still in love with Larry and remained loyal to him. She begged him repeatedly to join Alcoholics Anonymous, an organization that has helped countless alcoholics. The first step to joining AA, however, is to admit frankly and honestly that one *is* an alcoholic. Perseverance was one of the strongest elements in Larry's character, but perseverance can be the blood brother of ordinary obstinacy. Despite the hospitals and sanitariums, the "drying-out tanks" and the many therapeutic programs he had endured, Larry simply would not face the fact of his disease, and he was therefore doomed to a death that would not be easy.

By the spring of 1959, he was the neighborhood's invisible man, and the public that once adored him had all but forgotten that he existed. Music critic Bill Zakariasen, at the time a young singer, passed Larry on the street at this time and has never forgotten the shock of seeing the depths to which his idol had apparently sunk.[9]

The next time Larry set out to visit family in California, some five years after his 1954 arrest for drunken driving, it was necessary to go by air. This time he stayed with Richard, who had always been somewhat closer to his mother, Grace, than to the father he could only worship from afar. This was Larry's second visit to Richard and Pat. Pat Tibbett recalled this November 1959 stay:

> Richard and I were looking forward to this visit as Dad had apparently been on the wagon for some time. I had never had the opportunity to talk to my father-in-law while he was in a sober

state during Richard's and my eight years of marriage. Unfortunately, he arrived at our home with a supply of champagne and so it began—*again*!

Richard had to rise early, so retired early, but Dad was determined to make a night of it. I kept him company and had the opportunity to have many hours of sober conversation with him. It was then that he told me of his deep pride in his son, Richard. He boasted of Rich's accomplishments and how much he loved him. Too bad he had *never* said these things to Richard himself. Of course, he spoke fondly of his other sons as well, but I knew how much my husband longed to hear his father's praise.

The liquor had been removed from the house prior to his arrival, but he arranged to have a supply delivered. He would arise in the morning after Richard had left for the office, eat enough to pacify me, and then start to drink. The children were, in the beginning, sent to play in their rooms but had to be removed to a neighbor's home as his behavior worsened. This went on for a week, and on the weekend Richard experienced the horror for himself. The children and I had been through enough. He had to go!

What a terrible position he put his son in. Richard told his father he was no longer welcome in his home and that he must leave. He insisted that he wanted to go to a motel, and a cab was called.

When the taxi arrived to get him, Richard had to grab his father by belt and collar, drag him like a sack of potatoes to the cab, and dump him in. Then he burst into tears as the cab and his father pulled away. I tried to console him. The driver took Dad to a nearby motel where he stayed for another week in a constant drunken state. Larry Jr. and Dorothy watched over him there and finally, after another of our many family conferences, we called on Marion Davies for help. Larry Jr. and Dorothy took him to Marion's where he was sobered up enough to board the plane for home. Larry Jr. drove his father to the airport where Richard was waiting to see their father off. Larry threw his arms around Richard and, clinging to him, said, "I don't think I'll be seeing you again, son. Please take my tie clip. It's the only thing of value I have on me."

It was indeed a sad goodbye, particularly as Richard and Larry Jr. were never to see him alive again. At least I was able to ease Richard's pain somewhat by relating to him his father's words of praise.[10]

Both twins, trying to mask their grief, watched their dad board the plane, his shoulders slumped in weariness and shame, his feet shuffling from lack of coordination—the man who as a new father had washed their diapers in a little California ranch house. From a dizzying height of fame and riches he had come to this ruin, a sick old drunk. His sons tried to pick up their own lives again.

By the end of 1959, Betty's depressions recurred with increasing frequency, possibly in reaction to Larry's attitude of denial and worsening condition. As the New Year approached, instead of returning to a sanitarium as usual, she made a decision born of desperation. The two of them, both condemned souls, would have one last fling on New Year's Eve.

On 2 January 1960, the headline of a New York tabloid cried out, "Overdose Kills Tibbett's Date":

> A gay pre–New Year's party for two ended tragically yesterday in the apartment of Lawrence Tibbett, famed former baritone of the Metropolitan Opera.
>
> Redhaired Betty Fox, 44, "a very old friend" of the singer's, was found dead in bed, apparently from an overdose of barbiturates, while Tibbett was in Roosevelt Hospital under treatment for arthritis.
>
> They were celebrating together in his sixth-floor suite at 150 E. 56th St., when Tibbett was stricken with severe pains early Thursday. Betty phoned for an ambulance and he was admitted to the hospital at 5 a.m.
>
> That was the last time Tibbett saw Betty. A doorman saw her later in the day. She was to have called Tibbett at the hospital but there was no word from her, and it was Tibbett's inquiries that led to the discovery of the body yesterday.
>
> Betty was in a negligee. In a waste basket at the bedside were two empty bottles that had contained barbiturates, one of them a prescription filled only last Wednesday. That was when she and Tibbett began their early New Year's celebration.
>
> There were other empty bottles in the apartment—four that had contained Scotch whiskey.
>
> Betty and Tibbett became friends years ago because of her interest in music, which she had studied at Hunter College after her graduation from high school at Norwalk, Connecticut.
>
> In the hospital Tibbett said Betty had been depressed lately

> and had recently been discharged from a sanitarium at Hollybrook, Mass. She had not occupied her apartment on Central Park West for six months but sometimes stayed with her sister in Westport.
>
> Tibbett returned from California two weeks ago. He was a patient at Roosevelt Hospital from December 21 to Christmas Eve, then reentered in the midst of toasting the approaching New Year.[11]

Shaken to the core by his companion's death, Larry now rarely left his apartment, venturing out mostly to shop for food and whiskey. Without Betty's warm, comforting presence, neither his books nor music brought him any joy. Betty had moved her Steinway into the apartment, and Larry, unable to concentrate, found himself staring at piano. Poor Betty! She had taken the weakling's way out and killed herself. And Larry, mired in weakness himself, despised weaklings.

Paradox remained central to this deeply divided human being. Who was he? A rough-hewn Californian, at home on the open spaces, or a New Yorker, a citizen of the world, smooth and suave in white tie and tails? An exhibitionist, happiest in the public eye, or the scrawny, unsure boy of his youth? A hale and hearty outdoorsman? Or an artist of infinite subtlety, capable of expressing an almost feminine tenderness? A crude lecher? A family man? Champion of the underdog? A man always generous in praise of others? A humbug? Perhaps one personality could not contain so many divergent elements without eventually coming apart. And so he lifted more and more glasses of whiskey to his lips, deliberately drinking himself into oblivion.

On 2 March 1960, Larry ventured forth to his beloved Metropolitan Opera House to lead the applause for Leonard Warren, then in his magnificent prime, as Simon Boccanegra in a revival of the Verdi opera. Larry's own Simon was remembered in the reviews. Two days later Warren died onstage in *La forza del destino*.

One month later calamity befell the older baritone as well. On the afternoon of 3 April, Larry slipped and struck his head against the sharp corner of his television set. His cries of pain were heard by neighbors, and he was rushed once again to Roosevelt Hospital, this time to be treated for a severe concussion.

Discharged—perhaps too soon, but he insisted that he wanted to watch a boxing match on TV—he returned to his apartment in a confused mental state that was intensified by more drinking. More routine detox visits to the hospital followed. The medical evaluations concluded as they had for some time, with a terse word: *terminal*.[12] On 27 June he suffered a painfully similar accident. While reaching to change the channel on the television his foot again got tangled in a small, unbacked persian runner, one he knew was dangerous but had always loved. He struck his head at exactly the same spot as he had three months before. This time his skull was fractured, and he was unable to call for help. He lay helpless on the floor in a widening pool of blood until discovered by the doorman, who had come to deliver a package.

At the hospital, surgeons unsuccessfully attempted to remove particles of bone from his brain. His chances for a full recovery were virtually nil, and he spent the next two weeks in a coma, his head swollen to twice its normal size. He had no visitors except his 27-year-old son Michael, who last saw him eight hours before his death.

Michael Tibbett was staying with Jane at the Savoy Plaza at this time. He tried to persuade his mother to visit his father, her husband, but she refused. All the visits, all the final consultations with hospital personnel were left to Michael. Just before his father's death, Michael asked the attending physician, Larry's own Dr. Santey, for a prognosis. He answered that it was difficult to say in such a case: "Your father could die any minute, or he could continue in a coma indefinitely. Or he could regain consciousness at any time, but if he does, he'll never be more than a vegetable."[13]

When Michael reported this to Jane, she burst into tears and muttered softly to herself, "Poor Lawrence. Why must God let him suffer so?"[14] Very early the next morning Dr. Santey called Jane with the news that her husband had died. The date was 15 July 1960.

When Jane told Michael of his father's death, he stared at her then bitterly turned away. Later, she said she could not face handling the details of the funeral. Peter Burgard was in Japan, and both Larry Jr. and Richard were in California, leaving Michael little choice. Once again, he would have to do it all.

Roosevelt Hospital had no place to hold Larry's body pending an autopsy and the issuance of a death certificate, so it was removed to the city's Bellevue Hospital, where there was a morgue. When Michael arrived at Bellevue to identify his father's body, he noticed that a tracheotomy had been performed to help Larry breathe. The death certificate was made out and given to Jane as Tibbett's widow. The cause of death was the second head injury, listed as accidental.

As it had Larry's breakthrough performance as Ford back in 1925, the *New York Times* ranked the passing of "the great singing actor" as front-page news, with a headline that proclaimed: "Lawrence Tibbett Dies at 63: Baritone Starred at the Met, Singer-Actor Achieved Wide Success in Films and Radio—In Opera 25 Years." In the piece that follows, there is no reference to Larry's tragic decline nor to the addiction that had caused it, only a celebration of his once remarkable voice and artistry. He had simply undergone surgery at Roosevelt Hospital "for an old head wound" on 29 June and "never regained consciousness."[15]

Jascha Heifetz gave a concert at the Hollywood Bowl just after hearing of his colleague's death. He dedicated an encore, a movement from a Bach partita, to Larry and to their friendship. John Pfeiffer, record producer for RCA Victor, remembers the emotion caused by the event and "the sound of that solo violin, singing over 20,000 people in the dark."[16]

On 18 July 1960, a memorial service was held for Larry at Riverside Church in New York City. Along with Michael and Jane, hundreds of the late singer's friends and colleagues attended. Among them were Lauder Greenway, chairman of the board of the Metropolitan Opera; Langdon Van Norden, president of the Metropolitan Opera Guild; Frank Paola, the Metropolitan's company manager; John Brownlee, president of AGMA; Howard Laramy and DeLloyd Tibbs, assistant executive secretaries of AGMA; and Newbold Morris, then city parks commissioner. Karin Branzell, Charles Kullman, Jan Peerce, and Robert Merrill were in the forefront of the singers from the Metropolitan, and May Savage led a delegation from the chorus.[17]

Five days after the service at Riverside, on 23 July 1960, a second memorial was held at Forest Lawn in Glendale, California, where Larry would be interred next to his mother, Frances Ellen. Jane and Michael flew from New York with Larry's ashes and attended the ceremony.

Larry Jr. and Richard escorted their mother, Grace, to the service at Forest Lawn. When their stepmother, Jane, arrived, she called the twins to an anteroom and asked them to sit with her and Michael. Larry Jr. agreed but Richard refused, choosing instead to return to his mother and her longtime companion, *Ben Hur*'s Ramon Novarro, in the rear of the hall. A recording of Tibbett singing "Goin' Home" sent his voice echoing poignantly through the halls of the chapel.

Present at this ceremony were Jascha Heifetz, cofounder of AGMA with Larry; the tenor Richard Crooks; Lee Harris, AGMA's top man in Los Angeles; and representatives of other unions, including Angus

Duncan of Actors' Equity, Clayton Collyer of AFTRA, and Kenneth Thompson of SAG.

Letters of tribute poured into AGMA, from Gladys Swarthout and Frank Chapman, from Efrem Zimbalist, Mischa Elman, Elizabeth Hoeppel, Mrs. August Belmont, Larry Evans, Lanny Ross, Rosa Ponselle, Richard Bonelli, James Melton, and Deems Taylor among many others.

A final homage to Larry took place six months later, on 23 January 1961, but this time, instead of celebrating Larry's past, the ceremony was directed toward assuring his place in the future of American music. The Research Library of the Performing Arts at Lincoln Center in New York City established the Lawrence Tibbett Collection of American Music. A check for $7000 was presented by AGMA's John Brownlee to Philip Miller, chief of the music division of the library, as an initial book purchasing fund.[18]

Francis Robinson of the Met then affectionately recalled highlights in Tibbett's life, interspersing his remarks with four recordings that illustrated both the character and the art of the man: his virile manliness in Valentin's aria from *Faust*; his bold lasciviousness in the Te Deum from *Tosca*; the tenderness of his Song to the Evening Star from *Tannhäuser*; and his dignified authority in the legato measure of Handel's "Where E'er You Walk." The magnificent voice soared and filled the auditorium, stirring the heart of every listener. In closing, Robinson's words rang out: "Art is an affirmation of love. That's why we love Lawrence Tibbett and honor him and will never forget him."[19]

Larry's will had been signed on 15 April 1955 in Naples, Florida. In spite of Jane's predictions of penury to the twins, he left a net estate of close to $400,000, and its division was in most respects uncomplicated. Bequests in varying amounts were made to his brothers and sister Betty Lee, none of whom he had been in touch with for years; his secretary Doris Wittschen; his last piano accompanist Edward Harris; and Tom Clancy, who had been Jane's chauffeur since before she and Larry had married and who upon his retirement became caretaker of Honey Hill Farm, staying on after the Tibbetts moved away. Larry's three sons received the bulk of his estate in the following shares: Richard and Larry Jr., three-eighths each, and Michael, one fourth. Peter Burgard, who had more or less grown up with Michael, received a share of the personal property equal to Michael's.

Obviously Larry had assumed that Jane would, in her turn, provide substantially for Michael and Peter, her two remaining children. Like Clark Burgard, who was murdered mysteriously in Thailand, her son Marston too died young, in a diving accident in Hawaii. He had gone over a waterfall into a deep pool, but he neglected to cover his nose; the resulting hemorrhage of the palatine bone and nasal septum allowed water to seep into his brain, killing him instantly. Jane was omitted from the will altogether, which turned out to be most unfortunate.

For all its good intentions, Item 4 of the will proved to be the sticking point. It read as follows:

> I desire it to be known that I have the deepest love and affection for all my sons: Richard, Larry Jr., Michael and Peter, my stepson. I have been motivated solely by the expectation that Peter and Michael will be adequately provided for otherwise than through this Last Will and Testament.[20]

In July 1960, just after the internment ceremony at Forest Lawn, Jane met with Richard, Larry Jr., and Michael at the Beverly Hills Hotel. At the meeting she was all sweetness. After she read them Larry's will, she told them, "I want no part of this estate. It's yours." Months later, however, the three Tibbett sons received identical letters dated 30 December 1960 from Jack London, the lawyer for the estate, informing them that Jane had applied for a one-third share of the net estate under Section 18 of the New York State Decedent Estates Law.

Jane had not known she had any legal option to Larry's estate until her lawyer advised her of her "dower rights" under New York law. She qualified as a New York resident because even though she spent most of her time in Florida, she owned her apartment at the Savoy Plaza Hotel and lived there at least six weeks each year, which was legally sufficient. And although Larry and she had separated in 1954, they never divorced and had not legally waived their rights to each other's property. She could therefore claim the portion of the estate to which she would have been entitled had her husband died without a will.

The reactions of the three legatees were predictable. Michael was very upset with his extremely wealthy mother for taking advantage of her dower rights, and he angrily told her so, spitting out "It's a monstrous inequity to all three sons!" Then he walked out on her.[21]

Richard, true to his nature, wrote Jane a more temperate letter dated 10 April 1961:

When Dad visited us in November, 1959, he stated to me that his three sons would inherit his estate and that because of the size of your own estate he had provided for Michael (who would someday share in your estate) to a lesser degree than Larry and myself. He further indicated that because of your wealth he wanted to leave his possessions to his sons.

He always spoke to us of his love for you, and certainly his marriage of many years to you proved this. Therefore it is hard for me to understand why you are contesting the will. You have great wealth, certainly much more than Dad, and you enjoy the assets of good health and friendships. I can't see any grounds for vindictiveness because he never gave anyone cause for that, that I know of. At best the last few years he was perplexed, upset, and a man without a drive or purpose, but never consciously seeking to hurt or offend. . . .

Please do me the kindness of letting me know why you felt this step was necessary.[22]

Jane answered that by claiming her share, she was reducing the inheritance tax on Larry's estate, which the boys would have to pay. This was true enough, but her action also greatly reduced the inheritance. She also charged the estate with all the expenses related to Tibbett's two funerals, plus all the costs of her California trip, including her hotel bills. Her claim even hit Walter Winchell's gossip column; Michael wrote to Richard, "It indicates to me that she has been doing some loose-talking about town. Publicity always did appeal to her."[23]

In the end, Jane was granted nearly $150,000 from Larry's net estate. In addition, the estate continued to pay Grace $300 a month until her death.

As to what possessed Jane, worth millions on her own, to deprive Larry's children of a third of their birthright, one can only guess, but it seems that her meanness and disloyalty extended even to those closest to her.

Rupert Pole, the son of Larry's friend Reginald, pulled no punches about Jane:

Larry should never have married Jane, although he did love her as he had never loved Grace. He also was too big a man to pursue society as he did. Jane was a bitch. She was a bitch in a different way than Grace. She was as hard as nails. At least Grace was human, Jane was not human. She was a social climber and a hard drinker. In her selfishness, I believe that Jane was the main cause of Larry's illness and eventual death.[24]

Jane later married a photographer named Bingham, but this union soon ended in a divorce, prompted by Michael. Michael, who considered Bingham something of a leech, visited his mother often, acting as watchdog and advisor.[25] She lived on into old age at Bali Ha'i in Naples, Florida. Her son Peter, the last of the Burgard children, saw her only occasionally; the twins had no contact.

Peter died of an overdose of Valium in 1978 at the age of 48, a probable suicide. He had been unable to fight off a depression brought about by an unhappy marriage. Plagued by strokes and afflicted with Alzheimer's disease, Jane herself died in the summer of 1985, shortly after her son Michael's death in August, at the age of 85. All four of her sons preceded her in death.

As to Larry's first wife, Grace, her final years make no prettier a story than do those of Larry. Heavy drinking made her more irritable and ultimately, toward the end of her life, impaired her mental faculties.

By 1965, her income was reduced to the $300 a month from Larry's estate. She supplemented this by renting out the upper portion of her house in Laurel Canyon, but she reached a state where she could no longer manage her own affairs and the court appointed Richard as her guardian. Because she had been involved in several accidents, her car had to be taken from her. When it became necessary to sell the Laurel Canyon house, she lived in a series of apartments until Richard and Larry Jr., driven to desperation, committed her to an institution. Only Richard and his family visited her now. Totally irrational and often failing to recognize him when he visited, Grace accused Richard of trying to steal her money.

In 1972 Grace Mackay Smith Tibbett, to whom destiny had not meted out much happiness, underwent surgery for a perforated ulcer, a condition common in alcoholics. She died of pneumonia on 24 June and was buried at the Forest Lawn Cemetery in Hollywood Hills, California, approximately eight miles from the Forest Lawn where her first husband was buried.

Of Larry's progeny, Larry Jr. worked for Hughes Aircraft until his retirement. No children came from either of his first two unions, but he had two daughters, Teri Kay and Lori Christine, with his third wife, Dotie. They were together until her death in the early 1980s, and he continued to live peacefully in Canoga Park, California, within driving distance of his daughters, grandchildren, brother, and sister-in-law until his death of cancer on 10 October 1992.

Richard, the more conservative of the twins, lives happily with his second wife, Pat, near the California-Nevada border, but not too far from their children, one of whom, like his great-grandfather, is a deputy sheriff.

Michael married his first wife, Marion Elizabeth Goddard, in 1957. They had two children, Joan and Mark, and divorced in the early 1960s. He married Virginia Ann Graves and had two more children, Laura Jane and Michelle. He lived in Vero Beach, Florida, until his death of cancer in August 1985.

The reputation of Lawrence Tibbett, who cut such a regal swath in the music and entertainment worlds during his glory days, quickly faded. Only a few LP records were issued from the original 78 rpms, as historical collections. Now Larry's recordings—commercial, "private," and "pirate"—are being released in the CD format, with British and Italian companies taking the lead. He is once again recognized as the titan he was, "in all probability the finest actor-baritone of this century," to quote the booklet for Pearl's two-CD collection, *The Emperor Tibbett*.

American-trained, Larry made his career in America. He sang American music at the Metropolitan Opera, on the concert stage, and on the radio. He campaigned for American music and for the English language. Yet he was the quintessential Italian baritone and was also unsurpassed in his French and Wagner roles. Irving Kolodin thought of Larry as a "jewel beyond price" for his accomplishments in the Italian, French, and German repertoire.[26] As Henry Pleasants put it in *The Great Singers*, "No other baritone has ever sounded like Tibbett. And, short of improbable duplication, none ever will."[27]

He lived a full life and he shared his vitality widely. He is an integral component of America's heritage, and of the world's. But let us leave the last word on Lawrence Tibbett to a neighbor of his at the Savoy, the beloved soprano Marta Eggerth:

> You could only adore him in every way. He was a colleague, a friend, everything. They don't make people like Larry any more.[28]

Amen.

Appendix A

THE LAST BIG GUN BATTLE OF THE OLD WEST

The following excerpt, from the book Shotguns on Sunday *by Joseph E. Doctor (Westernlore Press, 1958), is reprinted with permission.*

Early Sunday morning, April 19, Sheriff Kelly of Kern County and Marshal Packard of Bakersfield, with their posse, left the jail in separate horse-drawn wagons—in order to avoid attracting undue attention to themselves—and took different routes toward their meeting place at the rear of the Durval boarding house, across L Street, west of the Chinese joss house. Will Tibbet rode in Packard's wagon, while his brother Bert rode with the rest of the deputies aboard a horse-drawn bus, which was part of the sheriff's equipment.

Then, as Jeff and Will slipped quietly down the stairway to the basement of the joss house and disappeared, Sheriff Kelly staked out his deputies at strategic points all around the temple, their pistols at the ready.

Jeff and Will first moved carefully through the opium den in the cellar, checking the bunks. Then they went to the first floor by way of the rear stairs and began checking the rooms on each side of the hall. In most of the rooms they found only Chinese who, under questioning, feigned ignorance of English or denied having seen any white person in the place. The door to the room at the rear of the joss house, on the south side of the hall, was locked, and there was no response to their knock. Determined to have a look inside the room, Packard went in search of a Chinese who might have a key to the door, but he could find no one to help him.

Packard came back to the door where Tibbet was waiting, and the two decided to try a skeleton key Tibbet carried on his key ring. In order to work at the lock with both hands, Tibbet set the butt of his shotgun on the floor and leaned the weapon up against the wall. Packard held his rifle across his body to cover the door when it opened. No trained police officer today would so approach a door behind which a deadly gunman might be lurking, but raw courage, rather than a knowledge of police methods, was the chief asset of the frontier lawman.

Inside the room, according to Jenny Fox, the occupants heard Packard and Tibbet talking outside and immediately tensed. They heard a voice demand to know who was in the room, and they heard a Chinese accent reply that he did not know. There was a pause of a minute or two, and then they heard a key turning in the lock.

"We're in for it," McKinney quietly told his companions.

"Let's go," said Hulse.

With that, they picked up weapons, one a rifle and the other a shotgun—it was never quite determined who had which—and aimed at the door. The third man in the room did not arm himself, according to Jenny, but remained on the bed. McKinney took a stance squarely in front of the door. Hulse remained behind and to one side of McKinney.

As the door was thrown open from the outside, Jenny watched only the firing of the first shots before jumping between the bed and the wall and flinging herself to the floor.

There was a deafening discharge of guns reverberating in the little room. In pauses in the uproar, Jenny heard the excited, high-pitched voice of Jim McKinney.

"There goes old Four Eyes!" he exulted, obviously referring to Packard, who always wore glasses, as the marshal tumbled backward from the onslaught of shot and bullets.

"And there goes old Overall!" shouted McKinney mistaking Tibbet for his old enemy, the former sheriff of Tulare County whom he knew to be active in the hunt for him.

"Let's go for Gus," Jenny heard McKinney say to Hulse as the two men stepped through the doorway into the hall. Jenny fled from the room and could offer no more eye-witness testimony. She entered a closet to hide and someone locked the door behind her.

Packard's account of the fight as told to Dr. Shafer before the marshal died indicated that Jeff and Will were taken quite by surprise. As the door swung open after Will succeeded in unlocking it, Packard saw McKinney standing squarely in the center of the room, his shotgun to his shoulder and trained on Tibbet.

"Look out, Will, he has got you," Packard cried out, at the same time throwing his rifle to his shoulder and pulling the trigger. Simultaneously with the crash of the gun's discharge, Packard felt his right arm and hand grow numb and drop uncontrollably to his side. As he tried to bring the arm back into use and cock his rifle, the roar of gunfire at pointblank range almost burst his eardrums and he felt his left arm become useless. The rifle clattered to the floor. "Then," he told Dr. Shafer, "I was blown clear out of the house."

Packard was literally overwhelmed with rifle and shotgun fire. The plucky peace officer, as the evidence of bullet marks on the opposite wall was to show, managed to fire his heavy rifle twice, but his aim was spoiled by counterfire. It was brought out in the investigation that the bullet from a rifle in the hands of someone in the room had struck the end of Packard's rifle, knocking off the sight. A portion of the bullet actually entered the barrel of Packard's gun, so that when he discharged it the recoil was strong enough to force the wounded man backward and he fell out the rear door.

Poor Will Tibbet never fired a shot.

With a gaping wound from a rifle bullet in his right side and buckshot wounds in his hands and face, Will staggered through the rear door and collapsed at the foot of the steps.

But the fight was not over, and McKinney was not destined to enjoy for long the fruits of his temporary victory. Outside were many courageous man, among them Will's brother Bert, who was not afraid of a gun fight.

Bert, from his position in the alley beside Mrs. Durval's boarding house, heard the shooting start and immediately ran down the alley, crossing L Street. As fast as he could run he headed for the rear of the joss house, where the shots seemed to be concentrated. As he passed the rear window of the building he saw Deputy Etter firing his revolver through the window.

Bert ran around the fenced rear yard to the gate on the south side. "Come on in, you fellows! Come on in," he heard Packard call.

Bert jumped through the gate to see Packard standing, weaponless, in the doorway of the urinal side of the outhouse, his arms dangling uselessly at his side and blood running down his fingers.

The door to the other compartment of the outhouse was closed, and Bert leveled his shotgun at it.

"No, no," shouted Packard, motioning with his head toward the rear door of the joss house.

"Look out! He's in the door!"

Bert whirled and looked at the rear door of the joss house in time to see the barrel of McKinney's shotgun poke the crack of the partly opened door. The outlaw stuck his head part way out to get a cautious look.

At almost pointblank range, not more than a dozen feet separating them, the two men stared down the murderous barrels of their shotguns for a vital instant.

Tibbet was first to recover from the momentary surprise both men felt. He fired and McKinney reeled back, falling to the floor and dropping his gun.

"I advanced toward the door and I heard McKinney get up and walk away to the window of the kitchen," Bert said at the inquest.

"He came back again and I saw the barrel of his gun come out the door, then his whole body. He throwed his gun out at me and at that moment I shot him and turned around and saw my brother lying there. Etter came in and led Packard out and Tower came to where McKinney's body was."

Bert Tibbet's second shot had been fired at a range of less than six feet.

Will Tibbet was lying on his side a foot or two from the backdoor. Bert leaned over and removed his brave brother's gun belt.

"Will, are you shot?" Bert asked.

"Yes," groaned Will. "Let me turn over."

"Who shot you?" Bert queried.

"Hulse shot me," was the reply, according to Bert's sworn testimony.

Bert stated at the inquest that as he talked with his brother he could hear footsteps receding down the hall of the joss house. He was convinced that these were the footsteps of Al Hulse.

McKinney had died instantly from the second shot. The first had torn a gaping hole in the side of his neck. The second blasted away most of the left side of his face and several shots entered his brain near the side of the left ear.

The more urgent business after the shooting was to get the sorely wounded peace officers out of the area of danger and to places where they might receive medical attention. Will Tibbet's brother and fellow officers moved him in Packard's buggy to Baer's Drug Store at Nineteenth and Chester, three blocks away, and there a crowd gathered to get a glimpse of him as he lay on the floor, writhing with pain. Packard, apparently less critically wounded, was taken in Sheriff Kelly's buggy several blocks to the Packard home on 18th Street.

Will, suffering greatly, was later removed to the Southern Hotel for surgery, as Bakersfield, for all its wealth, had no hospital! Before he was removed from the drug store, his aged mother visited him and a tender deathbed scene ensued between mother and son, for Will told her he knew he was not to survive. [Will's aged mother and Lawrence

Tibbett's grandmother was Rebecca Tibbet, widow of Edward Tibbet, one of the earliest settlers in Bakersfield.] Ed Tibbet, another brother, arrived in time to perform the last meaningful rite common to men of the Old West: at Will's request, Ed removed his brother's shoes, that he might not die with them on.

Dr. C. W. Kellogg, Dr. S. F. Smith, and Dr. J. L. Carson were summoned to attend Tibbet. The wound in his right side was made by a steel-jacketed rifle bullet, which had virtually destroyed the right kidney. Will's right hand bore a severe wound made by shotgun pellets, and he also had two shotgun pellets in his face.

The doctors could do nothing for him. He died at 12:10 o'clock, less than two hours after he was shot and before surgery could be started. Marshal Packard died two hours later.

As a result of the indictment growing out of Coroner Mullin's inquest, Al Hulse was arraigned and charged with murder in the first degree on May 9.

At his trial, September 1903, Hulse's request for a change of venue was denied. Paradoxically, the jury later deadlocked for Hulse's acquittal seven to five.

However, after a second trial, May 24, 1904, Hulse was found guilty of murder in the second degree and sentenced to life imprisonment at Folsom, but he remained in the Kern County jail as the long appellate process was taking place. Then, one day, after screaming that the Tibbets were out to get him, he slashed his throat with a razor and died, October 14, 1906.

Herewith follows an ironic footnote to the whole bloody episode. Writer E. Guy Hughes, whose book Battle of Joss House *also covers in detail "The Last Big Gun Battle of the Old West," suggests that Marshal Packard fell victim to his own ambition, and used poor judgment in personally attempting to flush out McKinney the way he did. To quote Hughes:*

Jim Quinn [another deputy in the posse that surrounded the joss house that fateful Sunday] emphatically insisted that Packard was making a mistake and endangering his own life and that of Will Tibbet's by entering the joss house and trying to get McKinney to surrender.

Marshal Packard had argued with Quinn. "Well, he knows I am his friend. Didn't I get him out of the Tom Sears trouble? If he will surrender to me no one will get hurt. There is no question that he will do so when he finds out it is I, Jeff Packard, his proven friend, who is asking him to lay down his arms and trust himself to my care!"

Quinn certainly didn't agree and said so in no uncertain terms. "This is not the man you know. Too much water has run under the bridge since those other days. This Jim McKinney will kill anyone who gets in his way. Why give him that chance?"

But City Marshal Packard was so thoroughly convinced that the cornered killer was just his old friend, McKinney (perhaps not really guilty of all those crimes ascribed to him). Also, what a political boost it would give him, Packard, for the ultimate Sheriffship a few years hence. He just knew his usual good judgment, gained by many years as a peace officer in a town that was not entirely populated by citizens of exemplary and Christian-like character, could not be so far wrong.

Bakersfield, at this time, was an oil town in the height of a very vigorous boom, with every attendant evil. These officers were proficient in the exercise of their duty. They had to be to survive.

Jeff Packard was at the zenith of his career. He thought he could cope with any situation that could possibly arrive. He had tried and tested aides. One attribute they all had that I've never heard questioned, that was their courage. A more determined group of men to try to bluff or bamboozle in any way couldn't have been gathered together.

Sheriff Lovin said in Calexico, California, that there was no reason for anyone to have been killed that fateful Sunday morning. That the joss house was completely surrounded. Impossible for anyone to get out. All the posse had to do was wait. McKinney would be starved out eventually. Anyone else with McKinney would starve also.

I've written before that Jeff Packard was a quick-thinking, alert, quick-moving product of his pioneer ancestry. He was most sure of himself. He knew what he wanted to do and did it. The thought that he might be endangering anyone's life, especially his good friend Will Tibbet's never entered his mind. He was going to the aid of another old-time friend, McKinney. If he could derive some favorable publicity thereby, what was wrong with that?

I'm convinced that City Marshal Packard had not the faintest idea that McKinney would do anything but surrender to him peacefully, if he was just able to make this outlaw know that it was his old friend, Jeff Packard, who was demanding this action on his part.

Appendix B

WAR-RELATED BENEFIT APPEARANCES

6 February 1941—New York City
Benefit, Friends of the Soldiers and Sailors, Plaza Hotel

23 November 1941—New York City
Keep Them Rolling, WOR radio broadcast

11 May 1942—New York City
Benefit, USO inauguration, Hotel Astor

14 June 1942—Boston, Massachusetts
Benefit, Flag Day rally for Allied nations, Boston Garden

30 September 1942—New York City
Seaman's Service Club

5 October 1942—Indianapolis, Indiana
USO rally

9 October 1942—Philadelphia, Pennsylvania
Benefit, United China Relief, Academy of Music

9 November 1942—Rockford, Illinois
Camp Grant

10 November 1942—Waukegan, Illinois
Great Lakes Naval Training

20 November 1942—New York City
All-star benefit, United China Relief, Radio City Music Hall

22 February 1943—New York City
Treasury Department recording

12 March 1943—New York City
Memorial service, Theatre People's Dedication, Winter Garden

30 April 1943—Pawling, New York
USO, U.S. Army Air Force Technical Training Command

16 May 1943—New York City
"I Am an American Day," Central Park

20 May 1943—Fort Monmouth, New Jersey
USO, Fort Monmouth

30 May 1943—Quantico, Virginia
Memorial Day program, U.S. Marine Corps Base

10 June 1943—Amherst, Massachusetts
USO, 58th College Training Detachment (Aircrew), Massachusetts State College

13 June 1943—Long Island, New York
USO, Camp Upton

1 November 1943—Ottawa, Canada
War bond rally, Ottawa Auditorium

3 November 1943—New York City
"Report to our Fighting Forces" luncheon program, New York committee of the National War Fund, Commodore Hotel

7 December 1943—New York City
Pearl Harbor Day ceremonies, Sub-Treasury Building

7 January 1944—New York City
Stage Door Canteen, CBS radio broadcast (500 Marines in audience), Maxine Elliot Theatre

29 February 1944—New York City
Kick-off rally, 1944 Red Cross Drive in Greater New York, Madison Square Garden

26 June 1944—New York City
War bond rally, New York Exchange

17 July 1944—Garden City, New York
U.S. Army Air Force program sponsored by the USAAF entertainment section for wounded soldiers, Mitchel Field

7 August 1944—Galesburg, Illinois
Red Cross–sponsored appearance for wounded soldiers, Mayo General Hospital

15 November 1944—New York City
Mail Call, transcription for shortwave radio broadcast by 428 overseas U.S. Army Expeditionary Force Stations

7 December 1944—New York City
Freedom in Their Eyes, CBS radio broadcast in connection with Sixth War Loan Drive

28 December 1944—Orangeburg, New York
Camp Shanks

28 February 1945—Washington, D.C.
Kick-off rally, Navy Red Cross Drive

1 March 1945—Garden City, New York
U.S. Army Air Force program sponsored by the USAAF entertainment section for wounded soldiers, Mitchel Field

24 March 1945—New York City
Red Cross appeal, NBC radio intermission broadcast, Metropolitan Opera House

4 April 1945—New York City
WAVES Training Station for USC, Hunter College

9 April 1945—Garden City, New York
U.S. Army Air Force program sponsored by the USAAF entertainment section for wounded soldiers, Mitchel Field

13 April 1945—New York City
Benefit for the orphans of Stalingrad, Carnegie Hall

23 April 1945—Montreal, Canada
Information Please, radio broadcast in connection with Canada's Eighth War Loan Drive

7 May 1945—Treasure Island, California
U.S. Naval Base

17 May 1945—Santa Ana, California
U.S. Army Base

24 May 1945—Santa Barbara, California
U.S. Army Redistribution Station

17 June 1945—New York City
Organized labor's salute to the Seventh War Loan Drive, Central Park

19 June 1945—New York City
Dinner for General Eisenhower, Waldorf Astoria

16 July 1945—Garden City, New York
U.S. Army Air Force program sponsored by the USAAF entertainment section for wounded soldiers, Mitchel Field

17 July 1945—New York City
"Wings for Tomorrow," U.S. Army Air Force program

29 July 1945—New York City
Stage Door Canteen, CBS radio broadcast, Maxine Elliot Theatre

8 August 1945—Norwalk, Connecticut
"Christmas in Connecticut," party for servicemen and -women given by the City of Norwalk

27 October 1945—New York City
Navy Day program, Port of New York Authority

12 January 1946—New York City
Dinner, 82nd Airborne Division, U.S. Army, Waldorf Astoria

14 January 1946—Garden City, New York
U.S. Army Air Force, final program sponsored by the USAAF entertainment section for wounded soldiers, Mitchel Field

NOTES

Chapter 1

1. Notes from William R. Moran to HW; *A Brief History of Kern County*, an anonymous account published in 1903 by Wallace and Co.
2. George Wear, *Pioneer Days, Keho Club Nights*.
3. In adult life, Larry was never close to his family and seldom mentioned them. His son Richard M. Tibbett recalls that he was never much around his aunt, uncles, or even his father, for that matter. He does add that uncle Jesse Tibbet died in May 1943 and had possibly been a miner. Richard Tibbett says that once, when he was eight or nine years old, he met his Uncle Jesse. Aunt Lena ("Betty Lee") Tibbet married George Conner and then Lawrence G. Sherman. She died 30 November 1976 at the age of 90. Uncle Ernest Ivan Tibbet was a bus driver and owned a butcher shop before retiring to Phoenix, Arizona. He had a tenor voice that was said to be the equal of Tibbett's, but he never wanted to appear before audiences. His wife died in 1966 and he died "of grief" a year later. Richard Tibbett says that Uncle Ernest was very kind and loved his twin nephews, Richard and Larry Jr., very much. Letters from Richard M. Tibbett to HW, 27 February 1993, and to BW, 23 April 1993.
4. From a genealogy developed by Richard M. Tibbett dated 3 March 1994.
5. Although the Irish never practiced Methodism in great numbers, many of them followed the example of Philip Emburry, an Irishman who began to preach as a Methodist in New York after 1766.
6. Robert Rushmore, *The Singing Voice*, pp. 207–208.
7. *The Glory Road* first appeared in *American Magazine*, serialized August 1933 through November 1933, and was subsequently published privately in hardcover. It was reprinted by Arno Press in 1977. In 1989, Amadeus Press, Portland, Oregon, reprinted Tibbett's sketches as Part II of *Law-*

rence Tibbett: Singing Actor, edited by Andrew Farkas. Page citations in this book refer to the 1989 Amadeus Press edition.

8. Lawrence Tibbett, *The Glory Road*, p. 50.
9. The complete account of Will Tibbet's death appears in Appendix A.
10. Tibbett, *The Glory Road*, pp. 58–59.
11. The original coroner's inquest certificate on the death of Will Tibbet is in the possession of Richard M. Tibbett. Reports on the inquest, arraignment and preliminary hearing, and the two trials of co-defendant Jim Hulse were sent to HW by Christopher D. Brewer, museum technician of the Kern County Museum, 2 September 1980.
12. Will Tibbet belonged to the Workmen of the World, the Native Sons, and the Fraternal Order of Eagles.
13. This piece of American history surfaced again on 10 June 1939 in the *New York Herald Tribune*. In reporting the death of Bert Tibbet, Lawrence Tibbett's uncle, the article reprised the fight at the joss house and the death of Will Tibbet.
14. Tibbett, *The Glory Road*, pp. 63–64.
15. *Manual Arts Weekly*, 14 March 1914.
16. Tibbett, *The Glory Road*, p. 53.
17. *Manual Arts Weekly*, 9 December 1914.
18. From the *Packard Radio Hour*, 10 March 1936.
19. Three of Ynez Love's letters to Larry, from 1915, are in the possession of Richard M. Tibbett. In one, she says that she "could moralize about the sex, but I will spare you." She felt hurt by him.
20. Her successful maternal great-grandfather, Duncan Mackay, had endowed Park College in Parkville, Missouri. Letter from Richard M. Tibbett to BW, 16 October 1988.
21. Grace was four years older than Larry. "Mother hid her true age for most of her life." Letter from Richard M. Tibbett to BW, 21 June 1994.
22. Conversation between Larry Tibbett Jr. and HW, May 1989.
23. Letters from Tibbett to his family through the ensuing years prove this conclusively. They are full of such lines as "I wish I could be with you in this crisis, but I am singing."
24. "I see his smile before me now. It's 33 years since he died, and I still see his smile." Conversation between Regina Resnik and BW, 29 November 1993.
25. Fragments of Grace's daily journal, her unpublished, handwritten memoir, and 27 undated letters exchanged by Larry and Grace are in the possession of Richard M. Tibbett. Internal evidence establishes the general period in which the letters were written.
26. Grace's mother died 16 December 1917 in Salt Lake City.
27. From Grace's journal.
28. The telegram, date illegible, is in the possession of Richard M. Tibbett.
29. From Grace's memoir.
30. Ibid.

Chapter 2

1. This marriage certificate is in the possession of Richard M. Tibbett.
2. Arthur Millier, *Los Angeles Times*, 2 August 1931, sec. 3, p. 1. This story is suspect as the article was written after the divorce to pander to Grace and to make money.
3. From Grace's journal.
4. Tibbett, *The Glory Road*, p. 65.
5. From Grace's journal, 24 May 1919.
6. Tibbett, *The Glory Road*, p. 47.
7. Ibid., p. 48.
8. Ibid., p. 75.
9. Ibid., p. 49.
10. Rupert Hughes was also the uncle of Howard Hughes. Both Richard and Larry Jr. eventually worked for Hughes Aircraft Company, a coincidence.
11. Tibbett, *The Glory Road*, pp. 73–74.
12. According to Regina Resnik, the chance to assure that young artists had these essentials was one of the motivations for Larry's later involvement in the founding of the American Guild of Musical Artists. Conversation between Regina Resnik and BW, 29 November 1993.
13. This letter was given to Grace Tibbett by La Forge. It is in the possession of Richard M. Tibbett.
14. Letter from James G. Warren to Grace Tibbett, dated 9 May 1925, in the possession of Richard M. Tibbett. Larry credits Warren, but with different details, for his help in *The Glory Road*, p. 74.
15. From Grace's memoir.
16. "He looked like a god," Wood nonetheless recalled. Conversation between Beatrice Wood and HW, 1982.
17. Frank La Forge was born on 22 October 1879 in Rockford, Illinois. He studied piano with Theodore Leschetizky in Vienna. He settled in New York in 1920. Other voice students besides Tibbett included Marian Anderson, Lucrezia Bori, and Richard Crooks. Lily Pons recorded his song "Cupid Captive" in 1940, with La Forge at the piano, and Lauritz Melchior his "Into the Light" in 1937. He died at the piano on 5 May 1953, during a dinner of the Musicians' Club. Nicolas Slonimsky, *Baker's Biographical Dictionary of Musicians*, 8th ed., p. 996.
18. Conversations between Helen Moss and HW, June 1982.
19. Ibid.
20. This series of letters from 1922 is in the possession of Richard M. Tibbett.
21. Conversations between Helen Moss and HW, June 1982.
22. This series of letters from 1922 is in the possession of Richard M. Tibbett.
23. Conversation between Beatrice Wood and HW, 1982.

Chapter 3

1. Unpaginated clipping from one of Larry's many scrapbooks. These and all scrapbook items cited hereafter are in the possession of Richard M. Tibbett.

2. Conversations between Helen Moss and HW, June 1982. Michael Tibbett believes there was romance between the two.
3. Ibid.
4. Tibbett, *The Glory Road*, p. 75.
5. Thomas R. Bullard, "Lawrence Tibbett," *The Record Collector* 23, nos. 11–12, p. 246.
6. From Grace's memoir.
7. "The brilliant career of Lawrence Tibbett began about as inconspicuously as possible." Irving Kolodin, *The Metropolitan Opera*, pp. 318–319.
8. Larry had not even seen much opera, though he had worked as an usher in Los Angeles when the Chicago Opera came to town, which company included Mary Garden and Claudia Muzio. "I envied them, of course, as a street urchin envies a king." Tibbett, *The Glory Road*, p. 72.
9. Kolodin, *The Metropolitan Opera*, p. 319.
10. Much of the information about Larry's first Valentin comes from conversations between Francis Robinson and HW in 1980. Robinson also devoted a Metropolitan Opera broadcast intermission feature to this story on 20 January 1962, rebroadcast 16 April 1994. In *The Glory Road* (pp. 81–82), Larry surprisingly devotes only one paragraph to the event, adding that every time he sings Valentin, his knees still shake.
11. Olin Downes, *New York Times*, 1 December 1923, p. 17.
12. Telephone conversation between Rose Bampton (who became Wilfred Pelletier's wife) and BW, 18 April 1993. Likewise, in a conversation with BW, 26 January 1992, Helen Jepson stressed that Larry "was wonderful with young singers, helping them with the staging." In a conversation with BW, 29 November 1993, Regina Resnik recalled her first Tosca, which she sang unexpectedly and unrehearsed, with Larry as the Scarpia. Before the second act he said "Baby, it's your show. Do what you want and I'll follow." (Jussi Björling, the tenor in this same production, was also extremely helpful, according to Ms. Resnik.) In a conversation with BW, 24 January 1993, Patrice Munsel exclaimed upon hearing Tibbett's name: "What a joy to work with that man! He was so helpful—I was just starting out." She was 17 years old when she first sang with Tibbett.
13. Operatic legend but pure hearsay.
14. La Forge remained loyal to both the Tibbetts, often writing warm letters to them. He set at least one of Grace's poems to music. A 1927 postcard to Larry from La Forge, who was fishing in Nova Scotia, confirms the completion of "Grace's song." This postcard is in the possession of Richard M. Tibbett. Two sheets of yellowing typewritten pages, undated, appear among Larry's papers. It is an appreciation of La Forge, apparently written by Grace, detailing some of La Forge's generosities toward the young couple. It ends: "I shall never forget his understanding and kindness in those years. Of course his happiness, his belief in Lawrence's great talent have come true. He has that added satisfaction, but I am sure that at that time he believed and wanted to help him whether anything came of it or not." The document is in the possession of Richard M. Tibbett.
15. The letter is in the possession of Richard M. Tibbett.

16. Frances Alda, *Men, Women and Tenors*, p. 256.
17. Michael Tibbett insisted this was true in a conversation with HW, 9 April 1982.
18. Ibid.
19. Oscar Thompson, *The American Singer*, pp. 365–366.
20. Tibbett, *The Glory Road*, p. 77.
21. Quoted by William H. Seltsam, *Metropolitan Opera Annals*, pp. 431–432.
22. Tibbett, *The Glory Road*, p. 77.
23. Thompson, *The American Singer*, pp. 365–366. Rupert Hughes also describes the ovation in a laudatory article about Larry in *American Magazine* for August 1930, p. 90. Larry's ovation might also be compared, in more modern times, to the ovations at the Metropolitan debuts of Ljuba Welitsch and Renata Tebaldi. No one knew of Welitsch before her explosive *Salome*; Tebaldi already had her rabid fans who had come that evening to cheer.
24. Ponselle had first heard Larry in California, in an audition requested by Frank La Forge. "I auditioned Tibbett, and I thought he was very talented. You couldn't help but be impressed by his voice—it had a color all its own, and he had fine technique. But Tibbett was at that stage where a young singer is either going to make it, or he isn't. Knowing the odds involved in making an operatic career, I wouldn't have been surprised at his success or at his failure. If he hadn't been totally dedicated—if he hadn't really wanted to make it, I mean—and if he hadn't gotten the right breaks at the right time, we might never have heard of Lawrence Tibbett. But lucky for us, we did." From James A. Drake's upcoming biography of Rosa Ponselle, to be published by Amadeus Press, Portland, Oregon. Used with permission.
25. Tibbett, *The Glory Road*, p. 77
26. *New York Times*, 3 January 1925, p. 1.
27. Alda, *Men, Women and Tenors*, p. 258.
28. Kolodin, *The Metropolitan Opera*, p. 324.
29. Telephone conversation between Bidú Sayão and BW, 21 March 1993.
30. The note is in the possession of Richard M. Tibbett.
31. There is an accounting from Charles L. Wagner to Lawrence Tibbett, dated 10 November 1924, for nine concerts at $250 and one concert at $150, minus 10 percent commission, so Wagner had represented Larry before the *Falstaff* success, at least for these concerts. Documents are in the possession of Richard M. Tibbett.
32. Letters from Lawrence Evans to Tibbett, on business letterheads, in the possession of Richard M. Tibbett.
33. Conversation between Kurt Weinhold (former president of Columbia Artists) and HW, 30 August 1980. Weinhold had been brought from Germany to America by Elisabeth Rethberg as her personal representative and served in this capacity at the time she was managed by Evans and Salter.
34. Rosalyn M. Story, *And So I Sing*, p. 79.
35. Conversation between Michael Tibbett and HW, 4 April 1982.
36. "Larry Evans was in love with his profession. While not a musician, he had

a very good ear and a love for music. He managed to project his own enthusiasm on to Tibbett and other artists he handled. He gained their respect and confidence by his enthusiasm. The relationship between artist and manager is a very human one. Larry Evans was that way with all his artists: very personal and very friendly." Conversation between Kurt Weinhold and HW, 30 August 1980.

37. Unpaginated clipping on a loose scrapbook page. Grace also had poems published in an April 1924 issue of the *Salt Lake City Tribune* and a magazine, *The West Wind*, February 1925, published in Hollywood; clippings of both are also found in a Tibbett scrapbook.

Chapter 4

1. *The Californian* (Bakersfield) June 1925.
2. Ibid.
3. Tibbett, *The Glory Road*, p. 82.
4. Conversations between Helen Moss and HW, June 1982.
5. A copy of *Word Etchings* is in the possession of Richard M. Tibbett.
6. The letter and list are in the possession of Richard M. Tibbett.
7. Quoted by Kolodin, *The Metropolitan Opera*, p. 329.
8. Conversation between George Cehanovsky and HW, 13 February 1985.
9. Conversation between Kurt Weinhold and HW, 6 September 1980.
10. From an undated press book distributed by Evans and Salter. A further, alliterative sampling from its 15 pages of hype: "There's a tang to Tibbett testimonials."
11. Tibbett's agendas are in the possession of Richard M. Tibbett.
12. Indeed, 75 percent of *all* concertgoers at the time were female. It was the day of women's clubs; the ladies subscribed for tickets and their husbands traditionally had to be dragged to concerts. Conversation between Kurt Weinhold and HW, 6 September 1993.
13. One of the photographs is reproduced in this volume, courtesy of Doris Wyckoff.
14. Doris Wyckoff, conversation and correspondence with HW, November-December 1979, and conversation with HW and BW, 28 March 1993.
15. Herman Klein, writing in the English publication *The Gramophone*, was astounded by the recording: "Tibbett may not strike you as a very formidable name in an opera bill, but be assured that his voice, once you hear it, will impress you mightily alike by its size, its quality, and its carrying power." Klein complained about Larry's Italian enunciation and hoped that time would remedy it. "Meanwhile you can enjoy Mr. Tibbett's dark Italian tone and that sense of reserve power which you recognise when he lets go *fortissimo* in the final passage." Herman Klein, *Herman Klein and The Gramophone*, edited by William R. Moran, p. 217.
16. Queena Mario and Giovanni Martinelli were the other two leads; Vincenzo Bellezza conducted.
17. The role of the friar is not too far from Kothner and is usually sung by a

basso-buffo. Giuseppe Danise was the Don Carlos, a role one would consider more congenial to Tibbett and one which he would sing in a later season, too late in his career.

18. Bori and Edward Johnson were the lovers, Hasselmans, the conductor.
19. Others in the cast were Ponselle, Gigli, and Adamo Didur. Ezio Pinza later took on Archibaldo. Serafin conducted.
20. Florence Easton sang Aelfrida, and Edward Johnson, Aethelwold; Tullio Serafin conducted.
21. A couple of recordings of excerpts from *The King's Henchman* prove Downes was right about the opera's quality. On 5 April 1928, the Victor Talking Machine Company (later to become RCA Victor, now BMG/RCA) recorded two baritone excerpts from *The King's Henchman* with Larry, Giulio Setti conducting. These have been re-released in successive recording formats and have seldom been out of print. Another recording, marked 15 January 1942, was taken from a radio broadcast, not from the Metropolitan; Deems Taylor narrated (and perhaps conducted), and tenor Jan Peerce, as shown by this performance, is Tibbett's match in both diction and passion. Richard M. Tibbett inherited this recording from his father. It is unidentified except for Tibbett, Peerce, and Taylor. The female voice is identified on the box as that of Rïse Stevens who, after hearing it in April 1993, said that it was not she. Just who sings soprano and who conducts what orchestra on this recording remain a mystery.
22. Olin Downes, *New York Times*, 18 February 1927, pp. 1, 24.
23. Lawrence Evans told Rose Bampton that Tibbett could receive the score for a new role and know it the next day. Conversation between Rose Bampton and BW, 18 April 1993.
24. Conversation between Regina Resnik and BW, 29 November 1993.
25. Unpaginated item on a loose scrapbook page.
26. Tibbett, *The Glory Road*, p. 85.
27. In a telephone conversation on 21 March 1993 with BW, soprano Bidú Sayão recalled Jane's beauty and "those green eyes." Richard M. Tibbett, however, in a letter to BW dated 15 September 1993, insists that Jane's eyes were blue.
28. Quoted by Arthur Bloomfield, *The San Francisco Opera*, p. 40. *Aida* had a cast of Elisabeth Rethberg, Marion Telva, Edward Johnson, and Ezio Pinza, a grand array for the young Tibbett to match. The conductor was Gaetano Merola, who also had conducted *Falstaff*.
29. Lawrence Tibbett's Evans and Salter tour itinerary for October 1927 is in the possession of Richard M. Tibbett.
30. Kolodin, *The Metropolitan Opera*, p. 343.
31. Olin Downes, *New York Times*, 28 January 1928, p. 9.

Chapter 5

1. The letter continued: "It is our desire that you sense this sincere regard, and this thank-you note is to personalize the appreciation which we have

already requested our advertising agency and the National Broadcasting Company to extend you." The letter is in the possession of Richard M. Tibbett.

2. The letter from Lawrence Evans to Tibbett dated 26 May 1928 is in the possession of Richard M. Tibbett. Evans writes that the *Elijah* performance was "set."
3. Tibbett, *The Glory Road*, p. 52.
4. Ibid.
5. Marion Bauer, *Twentieth-Century Music*, p. 261.
6. Susan C. Cook, *Opera for a New Republic*, p. 108.
7. Lionel Barrymore, *We Barrymores*, pp. 237–238.
8. Frances Marion, *Off With Their Heads*, pp. 212–214.
9. Ibid.
10. Undated clipping from one of Larry's scrapbooks. This might only have been part of the studio's publicity for the film.
11. Barrymore, *We Barrymores*, p. 238.
12. Richard M. Tibbett's description in a letter to BW, 21 June 1994.
13. Documents in the possession of Richard M. Tibbett.
14. Letter from Richard M. Tibbett to HW, May 1990. His twin confirms this: "We could have all the free food and everything else." Larry Jr. also intimated a relationship between his father and Catherine Dale Owen, Larry's leading lady. Conversation between Larry Tibbett Jr. and HW, 9 April 1982.
15. Conversation between Richard Tibbett and HW, 4 January 1982.
16. Conversation between Vera Gebbert and HW, 4 July 1983.
17. Frederick Lewis Allen, *Only Yesterday*, p. 337.
18. Tibbett, *The Glory Road*, pp. 59–60.
19. Quoted by Bullard, "Lawrence Tibbett," p. 250.
20. On 14 January 1930, while *en route*, Grace wired Jane Burgard that, in spite of the twins' health problems, she was rushing to Hollywood for the premiere. "Hope to write soon," she added, giving Jane the Rexford Drive address. The relationship between Grace and Jane is vague. Was Jane's fortune a factor in Grace's mind, as she did later approach her for money? Was she merely deluding herself as to Larry and Jane's relationship? One does not know. The Western Union forms are in the possession of Richard M. Tibbett.
21. Undated clipping from one of Larry's scrapbooks.
22. Ibid.
23. Enclosed with this letter was Larry's concert schedule from 2 April to 12 May 1930, including 13 concerts that would take him to Fort Wayne, Indiana, back to the East Coast, then to Green Bay, Wisconsin. He sang in high school auditoriums in Bridgeport, Connecticut, and Poughkeepsie, New York. A Victor broadcast was scheduled for New York on 17 April. Letter and enclosure are in the possession of Richard M. Tibbett.
24. Perhaps it was Larry's success with "Lover Come Back to Me" and "Wanting You" from *New Moon* (both with piano) that made the powerful artist and orchestra manager Arthur Judson convince Nelson Eddy to give up his burgeoning career as an operatic baritone to become—well, Nelson Eddy.

25. A loose page from a Tibbett scrapbook.
26. Charles O'Connell, *The Other Side of the Record*. This judgment of Moore was supported by her manager Fred Schang but was bitterly disputed by others. It is seriously called into question by her friend Jean Dalrymple (conversation with BW, 9 April 1992), by Moore's commercial recordings, and by the air checks of her live performances. She had a sense of humor that was legendary at the Metropolitan Opera House.
27. Pelican Records later released a recording of excerpts (12 numbers and some dialogue scenes) from the sound track of *New Moon*.
28. A typewritten copy of a letter dated 19 June 1929 from Metropolitan assistant general manager Edward Ziegler to William M. Sullivan, who evidently was taking care of Larry's affairs, refers to a cable from Gatti accepting the proposition that Larry's salary for the 1930–31 season be $550 a week, and for 1931–32, $600. Another letter signed by Gatti to Larry, 13 February 1931, informs him that he is engaged for a period of three weeks on tour and that he will receive $550 a week. Both documents are in the possession of Richard M. Tibbett.
29. Conversation between Richard M. Tibbett and HW, 8 August 1979.
30. Conversation between Larry Tibbett Jr. and HW, 9 April 1982.
31. Conversations between Rupert Pole and HW, 17 June 1989.
32. Conversation between Kurt Weinhold and HW, 6 September 1980.
33. His grandmother's death certificate is in the possession of Richard M. Tibbett.
34. Conversation between Richard M. Tibbett and HW, 12 January 1985.
35. Letter in the possession of Richard M. Tibbett.
36. A telegram from Jane to Grace, dated 11 February 1931, reads: "Poverty seems to have over-powered the whole community. Terribly sorry not to be able to do more for the Quartet . . . Love and again my thanks." Again a seeming friendship—or at least civility—between the wife and the "other woman," but was Grace asking Jane for money? It appears that Jane was turning down such a request. Telegram is in the possession of Richard M. Tibbett.
37. Conversation between Larry Tibbett Jr. and HW, 9 April 1982.
38. Conversation between Doris Wittschen and HW, September 1983.
39. Letter in the possession of Richard M. Tibbett.
40. Conversation between Doris Wittschen and HW, September 1983.
41. Conversation between Larry Tibbett Jr. and HW, 9 April 1982.
42. Letter from Richard M. Tibbett to BW, 15 September 1993.
43. Conversation between Francis Robinson and HW, February 1985.
44. Quoted by Seltsam, *Metropolitan Opera Annals*, p. 534.
45. Kolodin, *The Metropolitan Opera*, p. 358.
46. Pirating began in the cylinder era, at the dawn of recording. "Pirate" is still a generic name for recordings that find their way to the market but that were not commercially made by established record companies. Most of them, including in their sound the audience's coughs and squeals of delight, are taken off the air, recorded surreptitiously in the auditorium during a performance, or taken off the opera house's internal loudspeaker sys-

tem by whatever means the technology of the era permits. They are often issued without the participants' authorization. The Metropolitan Opera, for example, has never given permission to release its performances except to its own organization, and that only for fund-raising. "Private" recordings can come from the performers' own collections, whether they were commissioned by the performers or pirated for them, and are issued with the performers' permission. Larry had an extensive collection of private recordings of his work. Though this may change, "privates," too, as they are not commercial recordings, are still generically called "pirates" by the lay collector.

47. Letters in the possession of Richard M. Tibbett.
48. Elsa Schallert, *Motion Picture Magazine*, November 1931, p. 54.
49. Arthur Millier, *Los Angeles Times*, 2 August 1931, sec. 3, p. 1.
50. Conversation between Larry Tibbett Jr. and HW, January 1985.

Chapter 6

1. *Variety*, 6 December 1931.
2. Tibbett, *The Glory Road*, pp. 67, 68.
3. Quoted by Seltsam, *Metropolitan Opera Annals*, p. 551.
4. Lawrence Gilman, *New York Herald Tribune*, 29 January 1932, p. 1.
5. Quoted by Seltsam, *Metropolitan Opera Annals*, p. 563.
6. Olin Downes, *Olin Downes on Music*, p. 177.
7. Bauer, *Twentieth-Century Music*, p. 268.
8. Lawrence Gilman, *New York Herald Tribune*, 8 January 1933, pp. 1, 19.
9. Conversation between Rose Bampton and BW, 18 April 1993. Bampton further recalled Larry as a wonderful colleague and a fascinating person, with great appeal and charisma. "He was a real gentleman."
10. Conversation between George London and BW, 1959.
11. Rushmore, *The Singing Voice*, pp. 302–303.
12. Conversations between Richard M. Tibbett and HW, 1985–93.
13. Conversation between Larry Tibbett Jr. and HW, 9 April 1982.
14. Letter from Margo Melton Nutt to BW, 27 December 1993.
15. Conversations between Larry Tibbett Jr. and HW, May 1989.
16. Conversations between Larry Tibbett Jr. and HW, 1984.
17. Conversation between Larry Tibbett Jr. and HW, 9 April 1982.
18. Conversation between Henry Jaffe and HW, 16 April 1984.
19. Citation, medal, and text of acceptance speech are in the possession of Lori Tibbett.
20. John Dizikes, *Opera in America*, p. 452.
21. Quoted by Bloomfield, *The San Francisco Opera*, pp. 41, 56, 57.
22. Description from a July 1948 sales brochure in the possession of Richard M. Tibbett.
23. Letter from Richard M. Tibbett to HW, 26 May 1990.
24. Ibid.
25. Conversation between Larry Tibbett Jr. and HW, 9 April 1982.
26. Ibid.

27. Quoted by Seltsam, *Metropolitan Opera Annals*, p. 576.
28. Gatti had cast *Merry Mount* from strength. With Tibbett, the cast included Göta Ljungberg, Edward Johnson, Gladys Swarthout, and Irra Petina; Serafin conducted.
29. Conversation between Helen Jepson and BW, 14 February 1992. She recalled that Larry was always "wrapped up" in the roles he played onstage.
30. "What a splendid introduction to Tibbett's Italian manner his singing of the Prologue provides. . . . [It] shows the baritone in the fullest command of his powers." Paul Jackson, *Saturday Afternoons at the Old Met*, p. 62.
31. Archives of New York University.
32. Ibid.
33. Ibid., and undated, unidentified newspaper clippings on Larry's scrapbook pages.
34. Letter from Richard M. Tibbett to HW, 14 January 1990.
35. Conversation between Larry Tibbett Jr. and HW, 9 April 1982.
36. William Shaman, William J. Collins, and Calvin M. Goodwin, *EJS: Discography of the Edward J. Smith Recordings*, p. 19.
37. Evidently Larry more than once had this effect on his stage partners, as noted in his performance recordings. The American soprano Dusolina Giannini described a 1936 *Aida* she sang with Larry where, in the third-act duet "something absolutely magical took place," as though an electric shock had passed through the audience. Quoted by William R. Moran, *Lawrence Tibbett: Singing Actor*, p. 12.
38. "He ends the aria with the gentlest of head tones, the F taken *mezzo piano* with a crescendo not only of volume but of feeling." Jackson, *Saturday Afternoons at the Old Met*, p. 69.
39. Dizikes, *Opera in America*, p. 443. Dizikes also called Larry an erratic performer, a criticism unnoted by other commentators.
40. Conversation between Larry Tibbett Jr. and HW, 1979.
41. Conversation between Helen Jepson and BW, January 1992.
42. Kolodin, *The Metropolitan Opera*, p. 383.
43. Quoted by Bullard, "Lawrence Tibbett," p. 254.
44. Helen Noble, *Life with the Met*, p. 70.
45. Walter Damrosch, as well as Larry, was an ardent crusader for opera in English.
46. Perhaps Edward Johnson (then general manager at the Met, following the brief stint of Gatti's successor, Herbert Witherspoon) just did not "need" another Wagnerian baritone. Similarly, he never allowed Melchior to sing Italian opera at the Met, saying that he had enough Italian tenors but not enough Wagnerian ones.
47. Stokowski also experimented with music from Act One of *Siegfried* with baritone Martial Singher as the young hero, rehearsing it extensively. The baritone finally refused to sing it in public or to record it with the conductor. As Singher said in a 1959 conversation with BW, "I felt it just was not right for my voice."
48. Conversation between Doris Wyckoff and HW and BW, 28 March 1993. Doris did not know of Larry's womanizing and, at this 1993 meeting, won-

dered with bemusement if something had been wrong with her since Larry had never made a pass!

Chapter 7

1. *Los Angeles Times*, 18 October 1935.
2. On 27 February 1944, Grace would marry again; Larry Jr. attended the service at the Palm Springs Community Church. Grace's third husband was Horace G. Brown Jr., a radio engineer and a third mate in the merchant marines. The marriage lasted two years, during which time Brown went to school and then rejoined the merchant marines with the rank of captain. He borrowed money from Grace, and after their divorce she successfully sued him for it. Brown evidently had something to offer, for he next married Marion Davies, the once glamorous and still very wealthy movie star and one-time intimate of newspaper mogul William Randolph Hearst.
3. Conversation between Larry Tibbett Jr. and HW, 9 April 1982.
4. Letter from Richard M. Tibbett to HW, 17 May 1990.
5. Letter to Richard and Larry Tibbett Jr. from Larry Sr., 2 March 1935. In other letters Larry supported the boys' various pursuits, and their marks did improve.
6. *Metropolitan* was shown in a well-attended and well-received Bel Canto Society public screening in 1992 and turns up occasionally on television. It is a good candidate for revival.
7. Otto Preminger, *Autobiography*, p. 15.
8. "To hear Tibbett sing Wagner is to discover another facet of his art, a simplicity of utterance, a directness of manner entirely right for Wolfram. . . . This Wolfram is no shadowy, hopeless languisher after Elisabeth but a man of strength and intensity of feeling." Jackson, *Saturday Afternoons at the Old Met*, p. 104.
9. Shaman, Collins, and Goodwin, *EJS: Discography of the Edward J. Smith Recordings*, p. 17.
10. Conversation between Hy Faine (executive secretary of AGMA for 25 years) and HW, June 1981. Much of the information on the founding of AGMA comes from conversations between Hy Faine and HW in June 1981, supplemented in a telephone conversation between Faine and BW, 8 July 1993, and a conversation between Regina Resnik and BW, 29 November 1993.
11. Eugene Ormandy continued to pay Arthur Judson a commission until the end of his tenure with the Philadelphia Orchestra. Conversation between Arthur Judson and BW, 1967.
12. Bass Herbert Witherspoon was appointed general manager of the Metropolitan following Gatti's departure but died shortly after he assumed the position. Assistant manager Edward Johnson replaced him.
13. Conversation between Regina Resnik and BW, 29 November 1993. Resnik was thrilled that, at the time of this 1993 meeting, she was occupying Tibbett's chair as president of AGMA.

14. Conversation between Kurt Weinhold and HW, 6 September 1980.
15. Conversation between Hy Faine and HW, June 1981.
16. Ibid.
17. This document is on file at the offices of the American Guild of Musical Artists in New York City.
18. Conversation between Elizabeth Hoeppel and HW, 14 August 1985.
19. *New York Times*, 28 January 1937, p. 9, col. 4.
20. This description of the choristers' attitudes derives from a conversation between former Metropolitan Opera choristers Stella Gentile and Lilias d'Elia and HW and BW, 20 September 1989.
21. Letter from Marie Klein to HW, 15 November 1979.
22. Kolodin, *The Metropolitan Opera*, p. 402.
23. Ibid., p. 398.
24. Jackson (in *Saturday Afternoons at the Old Met*, p. 128) praises Larry's high G but faults his French diction, especially when compared to Bovy and Maison.
25. This family story was related by Michael Tibbett to HW, 17 February 1980.
26. Quoted by Bullard, "Lawrence Tibbett," p. 256.
27. Quoted by J. B. Steane, *Voices: Singers and Critics*, p. 262.
28. Ibid., p. 250.
29. Bullard, "Lawrence Tibbett," pp. 256–257.
30. Claire Whitcomb, "A passage to romance," *Victoria Magazine* (July 1994).
31. The photograph was shown to HW by Michael Tibbett, June 1986.
32. Conversation between Michael Tibbett and HW, 9 April 1982.

Chapter 8

1. Conversation between Larry Tibbett Jr. and HW, 9 April 1982.
2. The music critic "R. M." and film critic "A. B." in *Aftenposten*, 22 November 1937, p. 2.
3. M. P., *Svenska Dagbladet*, 25 September 1937, p. 6.
4. C. B-g, *Dagens Nyheter*, 25 September 1937, p. 9.
5. Letter from Frank Hedman to BW, 1 September 1988.
6. *Dagens Nyheter*, 25 September 1937, p. 19.
7. H. M-g, *Svenska Dagbladet*, 2 October 1937, p. 11.
8. *Svenska Dagbladet*, 2 October 1937, p. 11, no author.
9. As related by Larry Tibbett Jr. in conversation with HW, 9 April 1982.
10. Paris newspaper reports quoted by Bullard, "Lawrence Tibbett," p. 257.
11. Ibid.
12. Ibid.
13. Conversation between George Jellinek and BW, October 1988.
14. All quoted by Bullard, "Lawrence Tibbett," p. 257.
15. Ibid.
16. Ibid., p. 258.
17. Ibid.
18. Undated, unsigned clipping from a Tibbett scrapbook.
19. *Opera News* 2, no. 6 (20 December 1937).

20. Ibid.
21. Quoted by Seltsam, *Metropolitan Opera Annals*, p. 625. All but the last sentence also quoted by Bullard, "Lawrence Tibbett," p. 258.
22. "Tibbett's Schicchi was grossly overdone and his efforts to articulate rather distorted the musical line." Kolodin, *The Metropolitan Opera*, p. 395. The posed photographs of Larry as Schicchi in San Francisco are just grim, not at all funny.
23. Marjorie Lawrence, *Interrupted Melody*, pp. 50–51.
24. Claude Kingston, *It Don't Seem a Day Too Much*, p. 85.
25. Bullard, "Lawrence Tibbett," p. 258.
26. Letter from Lawrence Tibbett to Richard M. Tibbett, 31 May 1938.
27. Kingston, *It Don't Seem a Day Too Much*, p. 96.
28. Ibid., pp. 150–162.
29. *New York Times*, 1 October 1938.
30. It has been suggested that Larry's friendship with Australian soprano Marjorie Lawrence, who had contracted polio, led him to Sister Kenny. But in her autobiography, *Interrupted Melody*, Lawrence herself, although she thanks Larry several times for his support of her comeback attempts, never mentions such a connection. Both singers represented the Metropolitan Opera in January 1943 at functions celebrating the birthday of President Franklin D. Roosevelt, proceeds accruing to the National Foundation for Infantile Paralysis.
31. This and much of the following information comes from a conversation between Michael Tibbett and HW, 9 April 1982.
32. *New York Times*, 5 November 1945, p. 10.
33. Telephone conversation between Richard Tibbett and BW, 30 March 1994. Richard did not know where the Burgard boys were at this time; with no real "home base," communication among Larry's boys was nonexistent. Richard would get a notice that his father wanted to see him on a particular Christmas, but once arrived, between parties and performances, he would never see anyone. Richard believed that his father had been seduced by Jane's way of life.
34. Conversation between Larry Tibbett Jr. and HW, May 1989.
35. "Mezza voce and bel canto line are the prominent features of the baritone's Rigoletto on this afternoon." Jackson, *Saturday Afternoons at the Old Met*, p. 114.
36. Conversation between Jarmila Novotná and BW, 8 March 1993.
37. Conversation between Marta Eggerth and BW, 24 April 1994.
38. Conversation between Patrice Munsel and BW, 24 January 1993.
39. *Opera News* 10, no. 11 (15 January 1945).
40. Bullard, "Lawrence Tibbett," p. 258.
41. Francis D. Perkins, *New York Herald Tribune*, 17 December 1938, entertainment section.
42. Kolodin, *The Metropolitan Opera*, p. 412.
43. Story, *And So I Sing*, p. 50.
44. *Chicago American*, 22 August 1939, sec. 2, p. 1.
45. *Musical America*, July 1939.

46. Ted Barsky, "Your radio reporter says," *New Castle* (Delaware) *Gazette*, 2 June 1939.
47. Danton Walker, "Broadway," *New York Daily News*, 28 June 1939 and nationally syndicated. Larry might have had the opportunity to sing Boris if he had sung in opera houses in post–World War II Germany. There, baritones often undertook the title role in the Rimsky-Korsakov version. Given the parallels between the characters of Simon Boccanegra and Boris Godunov, it is natural to wonder what Larry might have done with the role.
48. Bridgeport (Connecticut) *Sunday Herald*, 9 July 1939.
49. Irving Hoffman, "Tales of Hoffman," *Hollywood Reporter*, 21 July 1939.
50. *Motion Picture Daily*, August 1939. All items in this paragraph come from clippings, some otherwise unidentified, pasted in Larry's scrapbook for part of 1939. He subscribed to the Original Romeike Press Clipping Bureau, which was obviously kept very busy. The *New York Times* for 4 August 1939 had a note that Lawrence Tibbett Jr., as "William Tibbett," was appearing at the summer theater in Peterborough, New Hampshire, in a production of *Little Women*. This clipping is in Larry's scrapbook too—because of his son or because his son's patrimony is mentioned?
51. Conversation between Marta Eggerth and BW, 24 April 1994.
52. In the final copy of the agenda, Larry is listed as an alumnus of the school. In fact, he had not attended the school but received an honorary degree from USC in 1928. The agenda and a letter inviting Richard to sit on the dais in his father's stead are in the possession of Richard M. Tibbett.
53. The American Federation of Radio Artists (AFRA) became the American Federation of Television and Radio Artists (AFTRA) in 1952. When queried on 19 November 1993 about Larry's activities with the union, AFTRA responded through its public relations representative that it had no knowledge of or interest in Lawrence Tibbett.
54. Note from William R. Moran to BW, 24 October 1994.
55. Conversation between Jerome Hines and BW, 15 March 1988.
56. *Newsweek*, 24 January 1949, p. 68.
57. Conversation between Rupert Pole and HW, 19 July 1983.
58. Conversation between Helen Jepson and BW, 14 February 1992.
59. Conversation between George Cehanovsky and HW, 13 February 1985.
60. Conversation between Hy Faine and HW, June 1981.
61. Letter from Richard M. Tibbett to BW, 22 June 1989.
62. Lawrence, *Interrupted Melody*, p. 163.
63. Conversation between Risë Stevens and BW, 25 April 1988.
64. Conversation between Robert Merrill and BW, 12 December 1989.
65. Olin Downes, *New York Times*, 4 January 1941, p. 14.
66. Noel Straus, *New York Times*, 10 January 1941.

Chapter 9

1. Robert Berkow, *The Merck Manual of Diagnosis and Therapy*, 16th ed., p. 1552. Copyright 1992 by Merck & Co., Inc. Used with permission.
2. Conversation between Jerome Hines and HW, 14 June 1985.

3. Ibid.
4. See Appendix B.
5. Conversation between Doris Wittschen and HW, 6 November 1983.
6. Conversation between Larry Tibbett Jr. and HW, May 1989.
7. Quoted by Hy Faine in conversation with HW, June 1981.
8. *New York Times*, 29 July 1942, saved on a page in Tibbett's personal scrapbook.
9. A photocopy of the tax return is in the possession of Richard M. Tibbett.
10. Oscar Thompson, *New York Sun*, 10 January 1943.
11. Conversation between Elizabeth Cooper and HW, 17 March 1981.
12. Tibbett, *The Glory Road*, p. 49.
13. Conversation between Larry Tibbett Jr. and HW, 9 April 1982.
14. Quoted by Bullard, "Lawrence Tibbett," p. 261.
15. Eleanor Steber, *Eleanor Steber: An Autobiography*, p. 63. Strangely, when interviewed by BW for this book, Steber denied knowing Larry or ever singing with him. A photograph of the two of them together appears in her book.
16. *New York Times*, 7 January 1945.
17. Undated clipping from a Tibbett scrapbook.
18. The brochure is in the possession of Richard M. Tibbett.
19. Unsigned, undated clipping from a Tibbett scrapbook.
20. Telephone conversation between Bidú Sayão and BW, 21 March 1993. She and Larry first sang the opera together at the Met in January 1944 and repeated their roles in Chicago in November 1944 and October 1945, and in both Chicago and San Francisco in October 1947. With great energy, Sayão went on to describe the opera and the 1945 performances of it in detail: action, music, words. She had not heard a recording of the broadcast, and when sent one, wrote her thanks, underlining three times that to hear it "was very emotional." Letter from Bidú Sayão to BW, 14 April 1993.
21. Conversations between Michael Tibbett and HW, 1979 and 1986.
22. Quoted by Bullard, "Lawrence Tibbett," p. 262.
23. Conversation between Marta Eggerth and BW, 24 April 1994.
24. Quoted by Bullard, "Lawrence Tibbett," p. 262.
25. "His monologue is touched with the hollowness of age, concentrated in intent and capped by a secure top note." Jackson, *Saturday Afternoons at the Old Met*, p. 379.
26. Letter from Licia Albanese to BW, 27 May 1993.
27. Telephone conversation between Licia Albanese and BW, 5 May 1993.
28. Conversation between Robert Merrill and BW, 18 November 1988.
29. Conversation between Robert Gewald and BW, 14 September 1989.
30. Conversation between Kurt Weinhold and HW, 6 September 1980. Walter Cassel had a long and successful career singing a large variety of leading roles, actually a more varied repertoire than Larry had, in America and Europe. While never as popular or as well known as Tibbett, Cassel was very possibly a stronger Scarpia in *Tosca* than Tibbett was.
31. This anecdote was related by Kurt Weinhold to HW, 6 September 1980. For Larry, giving autographs had become automatic. At the end of a neatly

typed, newsy letter to his son Richard, written in 1944, there is a full-blown, inky "Lawrence Tibbett." Larry continued in a handwritten postscript: "You see I get so darn used to writing this signature that it slipped up on me." Then, simply, "Dad."

32. Letter from Jane Tibbett, 2 June 1946, evidently sent to her secretary to be copied for Peter Burgard, Michael, and Larry Jr. The original is in the possession of Richard M. Tibbett.
33. Conversation between Doris Wyckoff and HW and BW, 28 March 1993.
34. Quoted by Ronald Davis, *Opera in Chicago*, p. 225.
35. Document is in the archives of the American Guild of Musical Artists.
36. Quoted by Kirsten Flagstad, *The Flagstad Manuscript*, p. 273.
37. Conversation between Regina Resnik and BW, 29 November 1993.
38. When the curtain went up Flagstad's reappearance at the Met, in *Tristan und Isolde* on 22 January 1951, the audience rose as one and cheered her for some minutes. There was not one negative reaction. Every appearance of hers at the Met from then on was a special occasion until her retirement the next season.
39. Bullard, "Lawrence Tibbett," p. 263.
40. Conversation between Kurt Weinhold and HW, 6 September 1980. Larry had briefly left Evans and Salter, following an argument, to join the lecture firm of Colston-Leigh, which had turned to the guaranteed high fees of concert management; he returned to Evans and Salter in 1945.
41. Ibid.
42. Ibid.

Chapter 10

1. Letter from Margo Melton Nutt, James Melton's daughter, to BW, 15 January 1994.
2. Olin Downes, *New York Times*, 22 January 1949, p. 14. The premiere cast of *Peter Grimes* was led by Regina Resnik, Frederick Jagel, and Jerome Hines; Emil Cooper conducted.
3. The scroll is in the possession of Richard M. Tibbett.
4. This special scrapbook is in the possession of Richard M. Tibbett.
5. *Opera News*, February 1949.
6. Hearing Larry then, in his deteriorated vocal condition, Regina Resnik recalled, "I was in tears." Conversation between Regina Resnik and BW, 29 November 1993.
7. Quoted by Bullard, "Lawrence Tibbett," p. 263.
8. Conversation between Henry Jaffe and HW, 16 April 1984.
9. Conversation between Richard Boehm (the ghostwriter of Rudolf Bing's two volumes of memoirs) and BW, 24 April 1989.
10. Kurt Weinhold insisted that, if Larry had lived a singer's normal life, he could have had 10 more years of a wonderful career. Conversation between Weinhold and HW, 6 September 1980.
11. Kolodin, *The Metropolitan Opera*, p. 490.
12. Performance attended by BW.

13. Olin Downes, *New York Times*, 17 February 1950.
14. Conversation between Risë Stevens and BW, 25 April 1988.
15. Conversation between Doris Wyckoff and HW, 16 April 1982.
16. Ibid.
17. Conversation between Henry Jaffe and HW, 16 April 1984.
18. Conversation between Jan Meyerowitz and BW, 18 February 1988. Meyerowitz insisted that *The Barrier* was a good opera, recommending as proof the Cetra recording with Italo Tajo.
19. Letter from Reri Grist to BW, 24 January 1988. Grist concluded by asking whether Larry's sons might send her a photograph of the singer. Richard did.
20. Conversation between Milton Goldman and BW, 24 May 1988.
21. Conversation between Emile Renan and HW, 9 September 1985.
22. Handwritten letter in the possession of Richard M. Tibbett.
23. Letter from Lawrence Tibbett to Michael Tibbett, 20 April 1953. It is now with Michael Tibbett's widow, who will release none of the material in her possession.
24. Ibid.
25. "Your father looks marvelous and is singing beautifully, which I know you will be glad to hear." Letter from Doris Wittschen to Richard Tibbett, 19 June 1953. It sometimes fell to Larry's secretary to write the newsy, familial letters; this one was sent along with a clipping concerning Michael and the news that "he hopes to be accepted by the University of Florida, but we haven't heard yet. . . . Fondest greetings from us all." Letter in the possession of Richard M. Tibbett.
26. All described by Michael Tibbett in conversation with HW, 9 April 1982.
27. Conversation between Mrs. Charles Gleaves and HW, 17 March 1986.
28. Letter from Frank Chapman to Francis Robinson, shown by Robinson to HW, February 1985.
29. A copy of the speech was in the possession of Michael Tibbett.
30. This description of the dinner is a compilation of accounts from Michael Tibbett and Francis Robinson to HW.
31. Conversation between Michael Tibbett and HW, 9 April 1982.
32. Related by Lori Tibbett to HW, 10 April 1982.

Chapter 11

1. Conversation between Charles Fox and HW, 4 March 1986.
2. Conversation between Emile Renan and HW, 9 September 1985.
3. Conversation between Michael Tibbett and HW, 9 April 1982.
4. Conversation between Emile Renan and HW, 9 September 1985.
5. Conversation between Walter Slezak and HW, 17 November 1982.
6. George Herbert, *The Works of George Herbert*, p. 7.
7. Conversations between Larry Tibbett Jr. and HW, May 1985.
8. Letter from Richard H. Roffman to BW, 22 November 1991.
9. Conversation between Bill Zakariasen and BW, 24 April 1989.
10. This account was prepared for this book by Pat Tibbett, 22 October 1993.

11. *Daily Mirror*, 2 January 1960, pp. 1, 6.
12. Roosevelt Hospital reports on Lawrence Tibbett, 15 May 1960.
13. This and other information concerning Larry's final hospital stay comes from a conversation between Michael Tibbett and HW, 4 September 1982.
14. Ibid.
15. *New York Times*, 16 July 1960, pp. 1, 19.
16. Conversation between John Pfeiffer and BW, 14 February 1991.
17. *New York Times*, 19 July 1960, p. 29.
18. In 1965, Jane donated some Tibbett memorabilia, including his piano, to the library; a ceremony and an exhibit marked the acquisition. The piano is now in the recorded music room, but the rest of the material is integrated into the library's collections, without particular identification as to what was his.
19. Conversations between Francis Robinson and HW, 1980.
20. A copy of Lawrence Tibbett's will is in the possession of Richard M. Tibbett.
21. Conversation between Michael Tibbett and HW, 4 September 1982.
22. A copy of this letter is in the possession of Richard M. Tibbett.
23. Letter from Michael Tibbett to Richard M. Tibbett, 13 April 1961.
24. Conversation between Rupert Pole and HW, 17 June 1989.
25. Letter from Richard M. Tibbett to BW, 23 April 1994.
26. Kolodin, *The Metropolitan Opera*, p. 534.
27. Henry Pleasants, *The Great Singers*, p. 333.
28. Conversation between Marta Eggerth and BW, 24 April 1994.

BIBLIOGRAPHY

Alda, Frances. 1937. *Men, Women and Tenors*. Boston: Houghton Mifflin. Reprint 1970, Freeport, New York: Books for Libraries Press (page citations are to the reprint edition).

Allen, Frederick Lewis. 1931. *Only Yesterday*. New York: Harper Brothers.

Barrymore, Lionel. 1951. *We Barrymores*. New York: Appleton-Century-Crofts.

Bauer, Marion. 1933. *Twentieth-Century Music*. New York: G. P. Putnam's Sons.

Berkow, Robert, ed. 1992. *The Merck Manual of Diagnosis and Therapy*. 16th ed. Merck & Co., Inc.

Bloomfield, Arthur. 1978. *The San Francisco Opera*. Sausalito, California: Comstock Editions.

Bullard, Thomas R. 1977. "Lawrence Tibbett." *The Record Collector* 23, nos. 11–12: 243–272. Reprint 1989 in *Lawrence Tibbett: Singing Actor*, edited by Andrew Farkas, Portland, Oregon: Amadeus Press.

Cook, Susan C. 1988. *Opera for a New Republic: The Zeitopern of Krenek, Weill, and Hindemith*. Ann Arbor, Michigan: UMI Research Press.

Davis, Ronald. 1966. *Opera in Chicago: A Social and Cultural History 1850–1965*. New York: Appleton-Century-Crofts.

Dizikes, John. *Opera in America*. 1994. New Haven: Yale University Press.

Doctor, Joseph E. 1958. *Shotguns on Sunday*. Los Angeles: Westernlore Press.

Downes, Olin. 1937. *Olin Downes on Music*. Edited by Irene Downes. New York: Simon and Schuster.

Edwards, Harold M. 1988. *The Killing of Jim McKinney*. Privately printed (Edwards Book Publishers).

Flagstad, Kirsten. 1952. *The Flagstad Manuscript*. Narrated to Louis Biancolli. New York: G. P. Putnam's Sons.

Henrysson, Harald. 1993. *A Jussi Björling Phonography*. 2nd ed. Stockholm: Svensk Musikhostoriskt Arkiv.

Herbert, George. 1941. *The Works of George Herbert*. Edited by F. E. Hutchinson. Oxford: Clarendon Press. Reprint 1953 (page citation is to the reprint edition).

Jackson, Paul. 1992. *Saturday Afternoons at the Old Met*. Portland, Oregon: Amadeus Press.

Kingston, Claude. 1971. *It Don't Seem a Day Too Much*. Adelaide: Rigby.

Klein, Herman. 1990. *Herman Klein and The Gramophone*. Edited by William R. Moran. Portland, Oregon: Amadeus Press.

Kolodin, Irving. 1966. *The Metropolitan Opera: 1883–1966*. New York: Alfred A. Knopf, Inc.

Lawrence, Marjorie. 1949. *Interrupted Melody, The Story of My Life*. New York: Appleton-Century-Crofts.

Marco, Guy A., ed. 1993. *Encyclopedia of Recorded Sound in the United States*. New York: Garland Press.

Marion, Frances. 1972. *Off With Their Heads*. New York: Macmillan.

Mayer, Martin. 1983. *The Met*. New York: Simon and Schuster.

McArthur, Edwin. 1943. *Kirsten Flagstad: A Personal Memoir*. New York: Alfred A. Knopf, Inc.

Merrill, Robert, with Sandow Dody. 1965. *Once More From the Beginning*. New York: Macmillan.

Noble, Helen. 1954. *Life with the Met*. New York: G. P. Putnam's Sons.

O'Connell, Charles. 1947. *The Other Side of the Record*. New York: Alfred A. Knopf, Inc.

Peterson, Bernard L., Jr. 1993. *A Century of Musicals in Black and White*. Westport, Connecticut: Greenwood Press.

Pleasants, Henry. 1966. *The Great Singers*. New York: Simon and Schuster.

Preminger, Otto. 1977. *Autobiography*. Garden City, Long Island: Doubleday & Company, Inc.

Rasponi, Lanfranco. 1982. *The Last Prima Donnas*. New York: Alfred A. Knopf, Inc.

Rose, Brian G. 1986. *Television and the Performing Arts*. Westport, Connecticut: Greenwood Press.

Rushmore, Robert. 1971. *The Singing Voice*. New York: Drebner Books.

Schiøtz, Aksel. 1970. *The Singer and His Art*. New York: Harper & Row.

Seltsam, William H. 1947, 1957, 1968. *Metropolitan Opera Annals*. Original and two supplements. New York: The H. W. Wilson Company and The Metropolitan Opera Guild, Inc. (page citations are to the original volume).

Shallert, Elsa. 1931. "Did Hollywood wreck the Tibbett romance?" *Motion Picture Magazine* (November): 54.

Shaman, William, William J. Collins, and Calvin M. Goodwin. 1994. *EJS: Discography of the Edward J. Smith Recordings*. Westport, Connecticut: Greenwood Press.

Slezak, Walter. 1982. *What Time Is the Next Swan*. New York: Doubleday & Company, Inc.

Slonimsky, Nicolas. 1992. *Baker's Biographical Dictionary of Musicians*. 8th ed. New York: Schirmer Books.

Steber, Eleanor, with Marcia Sloat. 1992. *Eleanor Steber: An Autobiography*. Ridgewood, New Jersey: Wordsworth.

Steane, J. B. 1992. *Voices: Singers and Critics*. Portland, Oregon: Amadeus Press.

Story, Rosalyn M. 1993. *And So I Sing*. New York: Amistad.

Thompson, Oscar. 1937. *The American Singer*. New York: Dial Press.

Tibbett, Grace. 1925. *Word Etchings*. New York: Flying Stag Press.

Tibbett, Lawrence. 1933. *The Glory Road*. Originally appeared in *American Magazine* 116, no. 2; later privately bound and printed. Reprint 1977, New York: Arno Press. Reprint 1989 in *Lawrence Tibbett: Singing Actor*, edited by Andrew Farkas, Portland, Oregon: Amadeus Press (page citations are to this 1989 reprint edition).

Wayner, Robert J., ed. 1976. *What Did They Sing at the Met?* 2nd ed. New York: Wayner Publications.

Wear, George. 1932. *Pioneer Days, Keho Club Nights*. Publisher unknown.

Whitcomb, Claire. 1994. "A passage to romance." *Victoria Magazine* (July): 56–67.

COMPACT DISC DISCOGRAPHY

For information on copies of Lawrence Tibbett's films, contact the Bel Canto Society, 11 Riverside Drive, New York, New York 10023.

Complete Operas

Note: Metropolitan Opera performances not available in the United States.

Leoncavallo: *I Pagliacci*. With Norina Greco and Giovanni Martinelli; conducted by Ferruccio Calusio; Met 1941. Eklipse EKR-CD-1

Puccini: *Tosca*. With Grace Moore and Jan Peerce; conducted by Ettore Panizza; Met 1946. Myto 2 MCD 942.98

Verdi: *La forza del destino*. With Stella Roman, Frederick Jagel, Ezio Pinza, and Salvatore Baccaloni; Met 1943. The Fourties ENT FT 1503 [20]

Verdi: *La Traviata*. With Rosa Ponselle and Frederick Jagel; conducted by Ettore Panizza; Met 1935. Pearl GEMM CD 9317, The Fourties ENT FT 1513 [20]

Verdi: *La Traviata*. With Jarmila Novotná and Jan Peerce; conducted by Ettore Panizza; Met 1941. Myto 2 MCD 933.80

Verdi: *Otello*. With Elisabeth Rethberg and Giovanni Martinelli; conducted by Ettore Panizza; Met 1938. Music & Arts CD645

Verdi: *Otello*. With Stella Roman and Giovanni Martinelli; conducted by Ettore Panizza; Met 1941. Pearl GEMM CD 9267

Verdi: *Rigoletto*. With Jan Kiepura and Lily Pons; conducted by Gennaro Papi; Met 1939. Myto 2 MCD 921.56

Verdi: *Simon Boccanegra*. With Elisabeth Rethberg and Giovanni Martinelli; conducted by Ettore Panizza; Met 1939. Melodram CMD 27507

Opera Excerpts

Verdi: *Otello, Simon Boccanegro*. With Rose Bampton, Giovanni Martinelli, and Helen Jepson; conducted by Wilfred Pelletier; original 1939 RCA studio recording; includes the two RCA *Boccanegra* sides. Pearl GEMM CD 9914

Collections

The Best of Lawrence Tibbett. Pearl GEMM CD 9307

The Emperor Tibbett. 2 CDs; contains some live and previously unpublished material. Pearl CDS 9452

Lawrence Tibbett. BMG/RCA 7808-2-RG

Lawrence Tibbett from Broadway to Hollywood. Nimbus HRM 6005

Lawrence Tibbett at His Magnificent Best. Cantabile BIM-706-1

Lawrence Tibbett: His Rarities and Famous Performances on Radio, Films, and Records (1930–1943). The Radio Years RY 29.

Lawrence Tibbett: Portraits in Memory. Met 219

Lawrence Tibbett: The Song Is You. Memoir Classic CD MIOR 427

The Legendary Baritone Lawrence Tibbett. Legendary Recordings LR-CD 1021

Opera Arias 1935–1939; Concert Songs, Musicals, and Soundtracks 1928–1940. 2 CDs. Delos/Stanford Archive of Recorded Sound Series DE 5500

Tibbett in Opera. Nimbus Prima Voce NI 7825

INDEX